Corporate Banking Law

Corporate Banking Law

Anu Arora

The *ifs* is the official brand of The Chartered Institute of Bankers, a registered charity.

Institute of Financial Services
IFS House
4-9 Burgate Lane
Canterbury
Kent
CT1 2XJ
United Kingdom

T   01227 818649
F   01227 479641
E   editorial@ifslearning.com
W   www.ifslearning.com

Typeset by John Smith

Printed by Antony Rowe, Wilts.

© The Chartered Institute of Bankers 2004

ISBN 1-84516-065-7

Contents

Table of statutes

Contents

Table of statutory instruments

Table of cases

C

Contents

Contents

F

G

H

Contents

J

K

L

M

R

Contents

S

T

Contents

Y

Z

One

Sources of law, fundamental principles of the law of contract and competition law

1.1 Introductory principles

Sources of law

Compared to any other European country, the distinctive features of the English legal system are as follows.

Absence of a legal code

In most European countries, the law has been codified. This means that the whole of the law on a particular subject, for example Commercial Law, can be found in one document or code. In contrast, whilst an Act of Parliament in the UK will provide the main legal principles applicable to a particular case, the bulk of English law has been made and developed by judges in individual cases.

Occasionally, Parliament codifies an area of the law with a statute, eg the Bills of Exchange Act 1882. Such Acts aim to take all the relevant case law on a particular subject and codify it into one comprehensive statute. The Law Commission, an important Law Reform institution set up in 1965, has the codification of appropriate areas of law as one of its objectives. The majority of English law, however, remains uncodified.

The law making role of the judges

In most European countries, the judges interpret the legal code. They do not themselves deliberately set out to create law. The English courts are arranged in a hierarchical structure and the law courts must follow the previous decisions of the superior courts. Senior English judges therefore have a dual function:

♦ they interpret the existing law that is to be found in legislation and previous decisions of the higher courts;

♦ they create and develop the law by making legal principles, which the law courts are bound to follow.

Absence of Roman law

The Romans occupied England from 55BC to 430AD but English law has almost no Roman influence compared to other European countries, which have retained elements of Roman law. Scotland, although not conquered by the Romans, has more of a Roman law influence than English law. This influence was brought about by the traditional alliance of Spain and Scotland to Rome.

Importance of procedure in the Middle Ages

A legal right could only be enforced by means of a Writ (an Order signed by the King requiring a defendant to appear in court to answer the claim against him). There were few types of Writs and a claim could not be brought unless it fell within the confines of one of the Writs. Lawyers were therefore people who knew the procedure for obtaining an appropriate remedy. If the correct procedure was not rigidly adhered to then the claim would fail. To some extent, this is still true today but recent reforms of the judicial process have reduced the importance of procedure, which, nevertheless, still remains fundamental.

Adversarial system of law

Most European countries have an inquisitorial system of trial where the judge is the inquisitor who is determined to discover the truth. A French examining magistrate, for example, has enormous powers. He takes over the investigation of a criminal case from the police. He can interrogate and he can compel witnesses to give evidence and he can call surprise witnesses. In a civil case, a French judge will take a much more interventionist approach than an English judge and it is the judge, rather than the lawyer who manages the case. An important aspect of the adversarial system of trial is that it is the task of the lawyers to bring the relevant legal rules to the attention of the court, eg an English lawyer, who states that goods sold in the course of a business must be of satisfactory quality, must then provide legal authority for his statement.

The rules of English law therefore come from a mixture of the following.

1. Statutes

2. Case Law

3. European Community

The common law courts, therefore, draw on a variety of sources to give expression to the general standard of behaviour expected of banks, eg rules of common law and equity, statute and industry codes of practice. Important incentives for an industry to draw up codes of practice are public concerns and governmental pressure (backed by the threat of legislation). The Banking Codes are an obvious example but international codes of conduct and practice attempt to regulate trade and foreign exchange dealings. These Codes are used to help determine minimum standards of practice although such formulations are not conclusive.

Acts of Parliament

Acts of Parliament are called statutes. The theory of parliamentary sovereignty holds that Parliament has the power to enact, repeal or alter any law it pleases and that the courts cannot question the validity of such legislation. If there is a procedural defect in the course of the passage of a Bill through Parliament then Parliament must remedy that matter. The task of the courts is to interpret and apply Acts of Parliament and thereby give effect to the expressed will of Parliament. In *British Railways Board v Picken* [1974] AC 765 the House of Lords expressed the view:

> 'when an enactment is passed, there is finality unless and until it is amended or repealed by Parliament. In the courts there may be argument as to the correct interpretation of the enactment: there must be none as to whether it should be on the statute book at all.'

Parliament cannot pass an Act to bind its successors. It cannot say, for example, that any subsequent provision repealing the law in question shall be void. It is arguable, however, that membership of the European Union means that the United Kingdom Parliament is no longer truly sovereign since European Union law overrides any inconsistent English law.

Classification of Acts of Parliament

Acts of Parliament may be classified as being Public Acts or Private Acts.

Public Acts deal with matters of public policy and are usually introduced by a government minister. Such Bills may implement a particular stated objective of government or at least reflect general government policy. The government, which can dictate the Parliamentary timetable, will find the necessary time for the

3

measure to go through Parliament and will work to ensure that it receives support from the government's own members of Parliament.

Sometimes, Public Acts are introduced as Private Members' Bills and may reach the statute books if the government is prepared to make time available for passage through Parliament. Private Members' Bills can deal with matters of considerable importance, for example, even if Private Members' Bills fail, the mere fact that they have been introduced will have enabled the Member of Parliament to give publicity to the subject matter of the Bill. Private Acts usually deal with matters of private or local interest, for example, where local authorities, public undertakings or companies are seeking special powers, perhaps, to use land in a particular way. Private Bills are checked to make sure that notice has been given to parties likely to be affected by them but once this has been done they pass through the rest of the procedure without significant debate.

Codifying, consolidating and amending Acts

Although English law is not codified, there are some areas of the law that have been the subject of codifying legislation. Such Acts bring together all the existing law on a particular subject, whether common law or statutory, into one comprehensive statute. In doing this, law may be changed. The major codifications in English law have been the Bills of Exchange Act 1882, the Partnership Act 1890, the Sale of Goods Act 1893 and the Theft Act 1968.

A consolidating Act does not (except in minor ways) change the law but merely re-enacts, in one statute, the scattered statutory provisions dealing with a particular topic. The purpose of a consolidating Act is not to change the law, but to make it more easily accessible. The Companies Act 1985 was a consolidating Act and re-enacted the Companies Act 1948, including several other amending Acts that had altered the 1948 Act. An amending Act changes one or more sections of an existing Act.

A statute remains in force until it is repealed by Parliament even if the legislation has become obsolete.

Delegated legislation

Some Acts of Parliament give or delegate powers to institutions such as the Crown, Ministers, Public Corporations and Local Authorities to make legislation. This type of legislation is referred to variously as delegated legislation, subordinate legislation or secondary legislation. The Act of Parliament giving or delegating the power to legislate is known as the 'Parent Act'.

Unlike Acts of Parliament, delegated legislation may be challenged in the courts, eg on the grounds that it is ultra vires, and so the courts may examine the delegated legislation to see if the enabling Act actually empowered the subordinate body to make such laws. Additionally, there are arrangements for some parliamentary control of delegated legislation, often taking the form of providing for parliamentary scrutiny. Delegated legislation can save a lot of parliamentary time and is particularly appropriate if the subject matter is either very detailed, highly technical or calls for local knowledge.

Such legislation can be altered relatively quickly without the need for parliamentary debate.

Delegated legislation can take several forms.

1. The most important form of delegated legislation is the 'statutory instrument'. This legislation is not passed as a statute. Instead, an 'Enabling Act' is passed and this will give the government minister power to introduce secondary legislation. The statutory instrument will contain a preamble, that sets out the authority under which it is passed. It will also contain a statutory note that sets purpose and scope. The Deregulation and Contracting Out Act 1994 allows ministers to change certain Acts of Parliament, which are specified within the 1994 Act, by way of statutory instrument, without going through the normal parliamentary procedure. The 1994 Act is used to repeal or amend provisions in primary legislation, which impose a burden on business or others. Many statutory instruments are used to implement EC Directives.

2. The Privy Council will make Orders in Council. The Council is made up of eminent parliamentarians and can be used to introduce legislation without going through the process of enacting a statute. Orders in Council can be used to implement emergency legislation.

3. Byelaws made by local authorities and other public bodies are another type of delegated legislation. These byelaws are used to introduce local rules of minor importance. The power to enact byelaws is given by an 'Enabling Act', eg the Local Government Act 1972.

Judicial precedent

The doctrine of judicial precedent (*stare decisis*) holds that judges in lower courts are bound to follow legal principles previously established by judges in the higher courts. As such, much of the common law has been developed through the doctrine of precedent.

The courts are arranged in a hierarchical structure.

The House of Lords

The House of Lords is the most senior of the English courts. The House of Lords is not bound to follow any previous precedents but the decisions of the House are absolutely binding on all inferior courts. Until 1966 the House was bound to follow its own previous decisions. A Practice Statement in 1966, issued by the Lords, stated that the House of Lords recognized that if the doctrine of precedent was too rigidly adhered to, the development of the law might be hindered and injustice might result in a particular case. The House of Lords would therefore normally treat their own decisions as binding but would depart from such decisions where it appeared right to do so. In doing this, the Lords would bear in mind the danger of disturbing agreements previously entered into. In reality, the Lords only rarely departs from one of its own previous decisions.

The law lords also hear appeals from the courts in Her Majesty's dominions and from some commonwealth countries. When the Lords sit in this capacity, they are known as the Privy Council. Technically, decisions of the Privy Council are not binding on English courts and are only persuasive authority. In practice, they are usually regarded as having similar authority to the House of Lords decisions.

The Court of Appeal

The decisions of the Court of Appeal are binding on all lower courts and also binding on future Court of Appeal judges. In practice, decisions of the Court of Appeal are extremely important as it hears many more appeals than the House of Lords. Nevertheless, the House of Lords will hear cases of greater public importance and its decisions have the greatest authority.

Following the 1966 Practice Statement of the House of Lords, the Court of Appeal attempted to depart from its own previous decisions. The Practice Statement itself, however, stated that it was not intended to apply to any other courts. The Court of Appeal is therefore bound by its own previous decisions but exceptions have been formulated. In *Young v Bristol Aeroplane Co Ltd* [1944] KB 718 it was decided that the Court of Appeal could depart from its own previous decisions in three circumstances:

- ♦ where there were two conflicting earlier Court of Appeal decisions, the court could decide which one to follow and which one to overrule;
- ♦ if a previous Court of Appeal decision had later been overruled by the House of Lords the Court of Appeal should not follow it;
- ♦ a previous Court of Appeal decision should not be followed if it was decided with lack of care, ignoring some statute or other high ranking authority such as a previously decided House of Lords case.

Although these principles apply both to the civil and criminal divisions of the Court of Appeal, it is generally recognized that the criminal division has slightly wider powers to depart from its own previous decisions, eg where justice would otherwise be denied to the appellant.

The Court of Appeal is normally comprised of three judges known as Lord Justices of Appeal. Sometimes a full court of five judges may sit in the Court of Appeal. A full court has no greater power to depart from its own previous decision than a court of three Lord Justices of Appeal.

The High Court

Judges sitting in the High Court are bound by decisions of the House of Lords and the Court of Appeal. Decisions of the High Court bind all lower courts. High Court judges are not bound by the decisions of other High Court judges although they do tend to follow each other's decisions so as not to lead to uncertainty.

The High Court is divided into three Divisions: the Queen's Bench Division; the Chancery Division; the Family Division. Each of these three divisions of the High Court has a divisional court, staffed by three High Court judges. The divisional courts hear appeals from lower courts and decisions of the divisional courts are binding on other judges of the divisional court (subject to the exceptions in *Young v Bristol Aeroplane Co Ltd* [1946] 1 AUER 98) on High Court judges sitting alone and on all lower courts. Decisions of the divisional court are not binding on the Employment Appeal Tribunal. Divisional courts are bound by the decisions of the House of Lords, the Court of Appeal and any previous decisions of the divisional courts. In criminal cases, a divisional court may depart from the decision of a previous divisional court where it would cause injustice not to do so.

The lower courts

The decisions of the lower courts (the Crown Court, the county court and the Magistrates Court) are not binding on any other courts. Judges in these courts do not make binding precedent.

All English courts must take into consideration decisions of the European Court of Justice. The European Court of Justice does not use a system of precedent. Decisions of this court are binding on all English courts.

The binding power of a judgment

The ratio decidendi (the reason for the decision) is the part of the judgment that is binding on other courts. The 'ratio decidendi' might be described as any statement of law that the judge applied to the facts of the case and on which the decision is based. The ratio of a case will be decided by courts subsequently reviewing/applying the cases when considering whether or not they are bound by the earlier case. Cases may contain more than one ratio.

Statements of law which do not form part of the ratio of the decision are known as 'obiter dicta' (other things said). Obiter can arise as statements of law based on facts which did not exist (eg a judgment may state what the law would have been if the facts had been different in some material way). Statements of law which are wider than is necessary to deal with the facts of the particular case are also obiter dicta. Such statements are not binding on lower courts but may be considered persuasive.

Advantages/disadvantages of the system of precedent

The system of precedent is based on law reporting carried out by private firms. The law reporters are barristers and they decide which judgments they consider to be important or not. The system of precedent means that English Law is bulky. To some extent, the vast number of precedents can take away the element of certainty that the system is intended to promote. Another disadvantage of precedent is that bad decisions can remain binding law for a long time and until 1966, such decisions of the House of Lords could only be changed by Parliament.

The device of distinguishing a case means that the system of precedent is not entirely rigid. A lower court judge can refuse to follow a precedent if he can distinguish it on its facts. This gives a degree of flexibility to the system of precedent and allows judges to escape precedents that they consider inappropriate to the case in front of them. An important advantage of precedent is that it results in high quality decisions being applied in all courts. Judges in appellant courts have the time and experience to decide on often extremely complex matters, and establish and develop principles of law. These decisions are then applied in the lower courts.

Custom

In Anglo-Saxon times, custom (ie patterns of behaviour recognized and enforced by the courts) was the principal source of law. General customs (ie universally observed throughout the land) have either fallen into desuetude or become absorbed into judicial precedent or statute. A process of absorption has occurred in relation to the general customs of merchants, which were assimilated by the courts in the 17th and 18th century and developed into commercial law, as we now know it. Local custom, however, (ie customs operative in a particular locality or among a particular group of people in a locality) is even now occasionally recognized by the courts as establishing local law which may be at variants with general law, although it must not be contrary to statute or to a fundamental principle of common law.

Local customs are largely to be found in rights of way. Recognition of a local custom depends on a number of conditions being satisfied, namely that the custom must:

♦ have existed since 'time immemorial' – theoretically, the custom must go back to 1189 but in practice must have existed within living memory;

- ◆ have been continuous – the right to exercise the custom must not have been interrupted;
- ◆ not be unreasonable;
- ◆ be certain in nature and scope and prove to adhere to a defined locality or group of people;
- ◆ be recognized as compulsory.

European Community Law

The United Kingdom joined the EEC (European Economic Community) in 1973. In order to be admitted as a member of the EEC, the UK Parliament passed the European Communities Act 1972. This enacted that Community law should be applied in British courts. In 1992, the Treaty on European Union (the Maastricht Treaty) renamed the EEC as the European Community (the EC). As a matter of convenience, the Community is referred to as the EC, rather than the EEC even in relation to matters before the Maastricht Treaty.

In 1986, the 12 member states signed the Single European Act which was designed to remove all barriers to a single market by 1992. The Act also strengthened the powers of the European Parliament and created a court of first instance to work beyond the European Court of Justice. In 1992, the Treaty on European Union (the Maastricht Treaty) was signed by the then 15 member states. The Treaty proposed the creation of a European Union with the three following pillars:

- ◆ the European Community;
- ◆ a common foreign and security policy;
- ◆ co-operation in the fields of justice and home affairs.

The Treaty gave the European Parliament greater power to legislate and set a timetable for Economic and Monetary Union. The Treaty of Amsterdam was signed in October 1997 and came into force in May 1999. This Treaty aimed for closer political co-operation between the member states and incorporated much of the justice and home affairs pillar into the EC Treaty, giving the member states a greater power to veto proposals which would affect their national interests.

Sources of Community law

If EC legislation is directly applicable it automatically forms part of the domestic law of member states, but that does not necessarily mean that claimants can directly rely on the legislation in the domestic courts. In order for this to be possible, the legislation must be capable of having direct effect. Therefore, where EC legislation has direct effect an individual can directly rely on the legislation, either as a cause of action or as a defence, in the domestic courts in his country.

- ◆ Treaty articles are directly applicable, as are EC regulations but do not necessarily have direct effect. No EC legislation can have direct effect unless it satisfies the criteria laid down in *Van Gend en Loos v Nederlands Administratie der Belastingen* [1963] ECR 1 which provides that the legislation must be sufficiently *clear, precise* and *unconditional*. If the Community legislation does not meet this criterion it can only have direct vertical effect, rather than direct horizontal affect. Where the legislation has direct vertical effect, an individual against the state and governmental departments can invoke it. If it had direct horizontal effect, it can be invoked between private parties.

♦ Regulations are binding in their entirety and are directly applicable in all member states without further implementation by the member states. A regulation may specify the date on which it is to come into effect, otherwise it will come into effect 20 days after the date of its publication in the Official Journal of the Community.

♦ Directives are addressed to the government of member states and must be published in the Official Journal of the Community. Directives are not directly applicable. It is left to each member state to implement the objectives of the directive in a manner and form suited to its own particular political and economic culture. All Directives are issued with an implementation date and member states are under a duty to implement them by this date. In the UK, such implementation is generally through statutory instrument. If the Directive is not implemented by the due date, the Commission has the power to take proceedings against the member state.

Once an EC Directive has been implemented by the member state, individuals can invoke the domestic legislation against other individuals.

♦ Decisions are addressed to one or more member state, to individuals or to institutions. They are binding in their entirety without the need for further implementation by member states and can only be invoked against the person to whom they are addressed.

♦ The Commission has the power to make recommendations and opinions. They have no binding legal force. Where a member state passes legislation to comply with a decision or an opinion, a national court may refer a case to the ECJ to see whether they apply and how they should be interpreted.

The European Court of Justice (ECJ)

The judges of the ECJ are appointed by consent of the member states and hold office for a six-year renewable term. All the judges, without any indication of dissent, sign the decisions of the court. Apart from hearing appeals from the Court of First Instance, the ECJ has three separate Heads of Jurisdiction.

◆ It can express an authoritative opinion on EC Law, if requested by a national court. Once the ruling has been given by the ECJ, the case is returned to the court that requested the ruling so that that court can apply the ruling of the ECJ. Article 234 of the EC Treaty allows a national court to request an authoritative ruling in respect of the following:

  ● interpretation of the EC legislation;
  ● validity and interpretation of statutes of bodies established by an Act of the Council, where those statutes so provide. Any national court or tribunal may refer a matter within Article 234 to the ECJ. Most of the ECJ's work involves preliminary rulings. The court, not the parties to the case, seeks the ruling. Although all national courts have discretion to seek a preliminary ruling, a court of final appeal has an obligation to do so where there is a relevant point of EU law and where there has been no previous interpretation of the point by the ECJ.

◆ Article 230 of the EC Treaty allows the ECJ to review the legality of acts adopted by the European Parliament or other Community institutions. This is a form of judicial review to ensure that the government and other governmental bodies do not exceed their powers.

◆ Article 226 of the EC Treaty allows the ECJ to bring actions against member states to compel compliance with Community obligations. Article 227 allows member states to take other members to the ECJ for failure to live up to their treaty obligations.

EC law can only be effective if it overrides national law. In *Costa v ENEL* [1964] ECR 585 the ECJ stated that the EC Treaty had become a part of the legal systems of the member states and that the courts of the member states were bound to apply the treaty. The ECJ also stated that member states had, by signing the treaty, limited their sovereign rights within limited areas and created a body of law that they are bound to follow. The *Costa v ENEL* case specifically decided that Italian legislation which was incompatible with Community law and that which had been passed after Italy had signed the Treaty could have no effect. Following the House of Lords decision in *Equal Opportunities Commission v Secretary of State for Employment* [1994] 1 All ER 910 the House of Lords would appear to have the power to declare legislation invalid on the grounds that it is incompatible with Community law, even without referring the case to the ECJ.

The European Convention on Human Rights/the Human Rights Act 1998

In 1951 the UK ratified the European Convention on Human Rights. The Convention was designed to ensure that the human rights abuses, which occurred during and before the Second World War, did not happen again in signatory countries. The Human Rights Act 1998 (which gave *effect* to the Convention on Human Rights) came into effect in the UK in October 2000. Section 2(1) of the Act states that a court or tribunal determining a question arising in connection with a convention right must take into account any judgment, decision, declaration or opinion of the European Court of Human Rights. The Act preserves the sovereignty of Parliament by stating that the court is required to take these decisions into account rather than absolutely bind the UK courts by such decisions.

Section 3(1) of the Act requires that, in so far as possible, all legislation must be read and given effect in a way which is compatible with convention rights. The House of Lords, Court of Appeal and High Court can make a declaration of incompatibility in any legal proceedings in which a court determines whether or not UK legislation is compatible with a convention right. Such a declaration of incompatibility does not affect the validity of the domestic legislation and is not binding on the parties to the litigation. Where a declaration of incompatibility is made, the relevant minister has the option to revoke the offending legislation, or amend it so that it is no longer incompatible. The minister will revoke or amend the legislation, however, only if he considers that there is compelling reason for doing so.

If secondary legislation is found to be incompatible with the convention rights, any domestic court can declare the legislation invalid, unless the parent Act specifically provides that in such circumstances, the secondary legislation is to prevail.

Section 6(1) of the Act provides that 'it is unlawful for a public authority to act in a way which is incompatible with a convention right'. In other words, the Human Rights Act creates an enforceable duty on 'public authorities' to act in a manner that is compatible with the convention rights. 'Public authority' includes a court or tribunal and 'any person certain of his functions are of a public nature', but not if that person is acting privately. Parliamentary debates make it clear that 'core public authorities' (House of Lords debate 24 November 1997, COLS. 809-11) such as government departments, Home Office, Lord Chancellor's Department, Local Authorities, Social Services, Police, Crown Prosecution Service, Customs & Excise, Trading Standards, Criminal Review Commission are within the scope of s 6 of the Human Rights Act. The obligations imposed by s 6 also extend to other bodies which exercise public functions (s 6(3)) and include the Law Society, Utility Companies and Regulators. Significantly, 'courts and tribunals' are also designated as public authorities and therefore have to comply with s 6 of the Human Rights Act. This will affect the way judges exercise their discretion and may make it more difficult to obtain certain types of relief, eg applications for search orders.

Section 7 of the Act confines the class of persons who may bring proceedings against a breach of a convention right to those who are 'victims' of an unlawful act.

The European Convention on Human Rights

The Human Rights Act incorporates the European Convention on Human Rights in the UK Law. It is therefore proposed to highlight some of the more relevant articles of the Convention.

Article 5(1) provides that everyone has a right to liberty and security of person and no one is to be deprived of their liberty except:

♦ after conviction by a court;
♦ upon arrest;
♦ to prevent the spread of infection diseases;
♦ in order to treat the mentally ill;
♦ in the case of alcoholics or vagrants.

Article 5(2) provides that anyone arrested has the right to be informed promptly, in a language that they understand, the reason for the arrest and the charges against them.

Article 5(3) requires that those arrested should be brought promptly before a judge.

Article 6(1) guarantees the right to a fair trial. The trial must be a public hearing within a reasonable time of arrest by an independent and impartial tribunal established by law. The judgment must be announced publicly.

Article 6(2) holds that everyone charged with a criminal offence is presumed innocent until found guilty according to the law whilst Article 6(3) sets out the minimum rights of those charged with a criminal offence.

Article 8(1) provides that everyone has the right to respect for his private and family life, his home and his correspondence. Public authorities may interfere with this right on the following grounds:

♦ in the interests of national security, public safety or the economic well-being of the country;
♦ for the prevention of disorder or crime;
♦ for the protection of health or morals;
♦ for the protection of the rights and freedoms of others (Article 8(2)).

Article 10(1) gives a right to freedom of expression although Article 10(2) provides that this freedom is subject to formalities, conditions, restrictions or penalties required within a democratic society to: secure the interests of national security, territorial integrity or public safety; prevent disorder or crime; protect public health or morals; protect the reputation or rights of others; prevent the disclosure of confidential information; maintain the authority and impartiality of the judiciary.

The Court of Human Rights

The Court of Human Rights hears cases concerning breach of the convention on human rights. All EC member states have signed up to the European Convention as well as other states that are not EC members. Article 35 of the Convention provides that an applicant to the court must prove:

- that the complaint involves a breach of the convention by a country which has ratified it;
- that the breach occurred within the jurisdiction of that country; and
- that all domestic remedies have been exhausted and the application to the court has been made within six months of these remedies having been exhausted.

The court does not use a system of precedent.

The court system

The civil court

The civil courts are arranged in a hierarchical structure and any civil dispute coming before the courts will either commence in the county court or in the High Court. From either of these courts there is an appeal to the Court of Appeal, and from there to the House of Lords.

The county court

The county court has unlimited jurisdiction in respect of business disputes that involve a claim for breach of contract or a claim in tort. The High Court also has unlimited jurisdiction to hear contract and tort cases where the claim is for pure financial or economic loss of more than £15,000. If the claim includes one for personal injuries, the claim must be for at least £50,000. The value of the action is the amount that the claimant reasonably expects to recover. There is a presumption that even actions where the claim is for more than £15,000 should start in the county court, rather than the High Court. This presumption may be rebutted and the action commenced in the High Court if:

- it is for an amount of money which exceeds the High Court minimum limit;
- the claimant believes that the case is sufficiently complex to warrant an action in the High Court;
- the outcome is of general public importance.

The county court can also hear equity actions where the value of the trust or estate is not more than £30,000, or where claims for salvage which do not exceed £15,000, as well as certain divorce matters, and certain bankruptcy and insolvency matters.

County court judgments are registered with the Registry of County Court Judgments and the register is open to public inspection. A commercial creditor is likely to inspect this register before making a loan. Once a county court judgment has been satisfied, the judgment debtor's name will be removed from the register. If the judgment is satisfied within one month of judgment, the entry on the register is cancelled altogether. All entries are removed completely six years after the date of judgment.

The county court does not have the responsibility of enforcing its judgment. Enforcement is left to the person in whose favour the judgment was given, the judgment creditor.

The High Court

The High Court is divided into three divisions: the Queen's Bench Division, the Chancery Division and the Family Division. The Chancery Division hears matters that originated in equity, (eg bankruptcy, mortgages, trusts, wills, company law and partnership law issues). It includes two specialist courts: the Company's Court and the Patents Court. The Queen's Bench Division deals with contract and tort cases and includes the Commercial Court and the Admiralty Court. The Family Division is concerned with family matters. Any of the three divisions can transfer a case to another division. The Commercial Court hears cases involving import and export of goods, banking, insurance and financial services and may hear any case arising out of trade or commerce in general. The Commercial Court has its own specialist procedures that are less formal than those generally used in the High Court.

Appeals from the High Court go direct to the Court of Appeal and from there to the House of Lords. Permission ('leave') must, however, be obtained for appeal. Appeals from a Master (junior judge) go first to a High Court judge and then to the Court of Appeal.

The High Court also hears appeals. The Queen's Bench Divisional Court is of particular significance in relation to statutes that impose criminal liability on business (eg the Trade Descriptions Act 1968 and the Consumer Protection Act (Pts 2 and 3)). The divisional court hears appeals by way of case stated from the Magistrates Court, Tribunals or the Crown Court.

The Court of Appeal (Civil Division)

The Court of Appeal is divided into the Civil Division and the Criminal Division. The Court of Appeal (Civil Division) hears appeals from the High Court but not appeals from the divisional court. Permission ('leave') to appeal must be granted. The Court of Appeal also hears appeals from the county court. Appeals from a Master in the High Court go first, on appeal, to a High Court judge then, and only then, to the Court of Appeal. A 'leap frog' appeal can be made direct from the High

Court to the House of Lords if the parties consent and the House of Lords give their permission. Additionally, the High Court judge must issue a certificate stating that the case involves an important point of law involving either the interpretation of legislation or the case concerns a matter that has already been fully considered by the Court of Appeal or House of Lords.

The House of Lords

The House of Lords is the Supreme Appellate Court in Great Britain and Northern Ireland. The House of Lords hears appeals from the Court of Appeal. The Court of Appeal will hear an application for leave to appeal to the House of Lords and refer it to an Appeal Committee of three Law Lords. The House of Lords also hears appeals from the Scottish Court in Session and, occasionally, from the High Court when the leapfrog procedure is invoked.

Five Law Lords generally hear appeals to the House of Lords. Seven judges may sit to hear an appeal if a case is considered to be of particular importance, as happened in *Pepper v Hart* [1993] AC 593. The Law Lords always reserve their judgment. The individual judgments of the Law Lords are known as opinions.

Procedure in the civil courts

In June 1995, Lord Woolf was charged with the task of reviewing civil jurisdiction, litigation and procedure. The Woolf Report found that the Civil Justice system was slow, expensive, bound by archaic procedures, excessively complicated and ill-suited to the needs of clients. The adversarial system of litigation meant that unnecessary delays and tactics were used to run up the cost of litigation and to defeat the other side. Lord Woolf's report resulted in the Civil Procedure Act 1997 and the Civil Procedure Rules 1998. The objective of these rules is to enable the courts to deal with cases justly and expeditiously. One of the main features of the reforms is that the management of the case is passed to the judge who will first determine which of these three new 'tracks' should be used to hear the case. The judge will also set the time scale by which certain procedures must be completed.

The active management of the case by the judge requires him to encourage:

- ♦ co-operation between the parties to the case;
- ♦ encourage the parties to settle the case or part of the case;
- ♦ identify the true point at issue and ensure that issues which do not require litigation are disposed of before the case is tried;
- ♦ decide the order in which issues will be resolved;
- ♦ consider whether the taking of any step is justified by the costs involved; and
- ♦ to ensure that the case proceeds quickly and efficiently.

If the case does reach the hearing stage, the judge sets out timetables for the hearing and supervises the control of the case. Orders made by the court may be subject to conditions (eg the payment of money into court). If these conditions are not complied with the case may be struck out. The parties to a dispute are actively encouraged to consider alternative dispute resolution and the judge may suspend proceedings in order to enable the parties to try and resolve their dispute by an alternative method.

The three 'tracks' for a hearing are as follows.

♦ The small claims track generally deals with cases where a claim for damages does not exceed £5,000. The case should not involve a substantial amount of preparation before the hearing. The small claims track has been designed so that the parties have the option of conducting their case without legal representation. Personal injury cases will only be allocated to the small claims track where the total amount of the claim is not more than £5,000 and the claim for general damages for personal injuries is not more than £1,000. Generally a small claims case will involve only one hearing in front of a district judge. The parties are required to file and serve copies of all relevant documentation, including any expert's report (can be admitted with the consent of the court). Generally, each side will pay its own costs. The only costs recoverable are those involved in issuing the claim. Appeals against small claim decisions are to a circuit judge on the grounds that there was a mistake of law or a serious irregularity in the conduct of the case.

♦ Cases (other than landlord and tenant cases) for claims that include a claim for personal injury will generally be allocated to the fast track if the claim is for not more than £15,000 and there is not a substantial amount of pre-hearing preparation. Cases will not be allocated to the fast track if they are expected to last for longer than one day or if there is likely to be a substantial amount of oral expert evidence at the trial. Fast track cases should be completed within 30 weeks after allocation. On allocation to the fast track, the court will set out a timetable for matters such as disclosing documents, exchanging witness statements and expert's reports, the sending of listing questionnaires by the courts so that the date and length of the trial can be fixed, the completing of such questionnaires and the hearing itself. Financial penalties can be imposed on any party who does not comply with the timetable. Postponement of the trial is seen as a last resort. With such cases, each party can be allowed one expert per issue, with a maximum of two issues. Generally, expert evidence is given in written reports.

♦ Claims that are not suitable for the small claims track or the fast track are allocated the multi-track. The amount claimed is usually substantially over £15,000 or the case is likely to last more than one day in court or to be one where substantial expert evidence is given. A claim will also be allocated to the multi-track where the court is likely to have to decide a substantial question of fact. The multi-track allows the court considerable flexibility in dealing with the claim and although the case is judicially managed, there is no standard procedure. Multi-track cases adopt procedure to meet the needs of the case. Thus, a party may indicate in the allocation questionnaire that a case management conference is required (this is similar to an ordinary business meeting). At the conference, the judge will try to identify the issues in dispute and lawyers representing the parties must have the authority to deal with matters that arise. Litigants may be required to attend by the court and the claimant may be asked to provide a case summary (generally not exceeding 500 words to which the defendant may be asked to agree). The judge can alter the standard rules on disclosure documents and the court may order a pre-trial review in a case involving complex issues.

Alternative dispute resolution

Litigation should always be a last resort for a business. Legal action is both costly and lengthy and may lead to intrusive publicity. Alternative dispute resolution methods may therefore be a means of resolving disputes. Arbitration, mediation and conciliation are therefore alternatives that may be used to resolve disputes.

Arbitration

Parties to a dispute may agree to refer their dispute to arbitration rather than to a court. In commercial disputes arbitration may be very similar to litigation, particularly if the arbitrator is a judge or a master from the Commercial Court. The rules of procedure followed may be similar to those in the High Court and lawyers may be required to represent the parties to the dispute. The proceedings may not therefore be substantially cheaper than litigation in court but the arbitration hearing is in private. The Arbitration Act 1996 provides that the object of the arbitration is to obtain a fair resolution of disputes by an impartial tribunal without unnecessary delay or expense. The parties should be free to agree how their dispute is resolved (subject to safeguards required in the public interest); in respect of matters given by the Arbitration Act, the court should not intervene except as provided by the Act.

Section 33(a) of the Arbitration Act 1996 requires that an arbitrator should act fairly and impartially as between the parties and give each party a reasonable opportunity of putting his case and answering that of the opponent. The arbitrator is not bound to follow High Court procedures but the arbitration should adopt procedures suitable to the circumstances of the particular case so as to provide a fair means for the resolution of the dispute. Section 33 of the Act is mandatory and cannot be contracted out of. Section 44 requires the parties shall do all things necessary for the proper and expeditious conduct of the proceedings and this includes complying with procedural and evidential matters without delay, including getting a judgment on a question of law from a court if necessary.

Section 9 of the Arbitration Act allows a party to apply for a stay of proceedings if the other party brings court proceedings in respect of a matter which it has been agreed should be resolved by arbitration. The court will grant a stay unless satisfied that the arbitration agreement is null and void, inoperative or incapable of being performed. An agreement may be referred to arbitration either by the court, or by statute or by the parties themselves.

Mediation

An independent body resolves a dispute which is heard by arbitrator. In respect of mediation, the parties themselves agree to any resolution of the dispute. The mediator's role is to try to facilitate an agreement. There are no fixed rules as to how mediation might operate.

Generally, the parties will present an outline of their case to each other in the presence of the mediator and reply to the other party's case. The mediator will set out the rules and strive to identify the key issues in the dispute. The two sides will then refer to different rules and the mediator will spend time with one group, before passing on the position of that party to the other. A number of such visits may be needed before the parties move to a position of agreement.

Conciliation

Conciliation is similar to mediation except that the conciliator actually suggests a basis for settlement to the parties. Both mediation and conciliation may prove futile in that no settlement may reached by the parties.

Tribunals

It is not possible to take a dispute to a tribunal unless the dispute concerns the particular type of matter with which the tribunal has capacity to deal. If the dispute does concern such a matter then it cannot be taken before the ordinary courts and must be dealt with by the relevant tribunal. The major tribunals are: Employment Tribunals; the Employment Appeal Tribunal; the Combined Tax Tribunal; the VAT and Duties Tribunal etc.

There are a number of advantages in appearing before a tribunal namely: costs are likely to be lower than a hearing before the courts; proceedings are informal and the response is speedy.

The Criminal courts

Criminal trials are conducted in either the Magistrates Court or the Crown Court. Criminal offences are classified as follows:

♦ offences triable only on indictment are the most serious offences, eg murder and can only be tried in the Crown Court;

♦ minor offences, eg a majority of motoring offences are triable only summarily and must be heard by the Magistrates Court;

♦ other offences, eg theft can be tried either in the Magistrates Courts or in the Crown Court. The Magistrate will decide whether the case should be tried summarily by the Magistrates Court or on indictment in the Crown Court. Where the Magistrates decide on summary trial they must ask the accused whether or not he consents to be tried by the Magistrates or whether he wishes to opt for a jury trial. The Magistrates must explain to the accused that if he opts for summary trial he may nevertheless be sent to the Crown Court for sentencing.

As well as hearing cases (summary trial and most offences tried either way) Magistrates Courts also have other duties. Thus, for example, magistrates will hear applications for bail; they conduct committal proceedings if the defendant is to be committed to the Crown Court for trial; they have jurisdiction in some civil areas affecting children and families; they hear applications for various types of licenses (liquor licences) and also deal with some types of civil debts (arrears of Council Tax). Defendants have a right of appeal against conviction or sentence to the Crown Court, that has the power to increase the sentence passed by the Magistrates (not permitting the maximum for the offence).

The Crown Court

The Crown Court conducts all trials of indictable offences and some trials where the offence was triable either way. The Crown Court may also pass sentence on those summarily convicted of an offence triable either way if the Magistrates commit to the Crown Court for sentencing. A trial in the Crown Court is before a jury of lay members of the public and the jury will decide the facts (ie whether or not the defendant is guilty).

The Divisional Court

The Queen's Bench Divisional court hears appeals by way of case stated from the Magistrates court. It can also hear appeals by way of case stated from the Crown Court if the case was first tried in the Magistrates Court or subsequently appealed to the Crown Court. The appeal can only be on a point of law or on an argument that the magistrates exceeded their powers.

The Court of Appeal (Criminal Division)

The Court of Appeal hears appeals from the Crown Court, either against conviction or against sentence. Appeals from the Crown Court are allowed on grounds that:

♦ the jury's verdict should be set aside on the grounds that it is unsafe and unsatisfactory;

♦ a wrong decision was taken as to a question of law; or

♦ that there was a material irregularity in the course of the trial.

The House of Lords

The House of Lords hears appeals from the Court of Appeal (Criminal Division) and from the Queen's Bench Divisional court. The Court of Appeal will need to certify that the case involves a point of law of general public importance. Additionally, either the Court of Appeal or the House of Lords must grant permission for the appeal.

1.2 Aspects of the law of contract

Rules relating to offer/acceptance

Contracts are made through a process of offer and acceptance whereby one of the parties (the offeror) makes an offer that sets out the terms which will form the basis of a legally binding agreement, if such terms are accepted by the other party (the offeree). Generally, the offer must be made with the intention of forming legally binding relations. If the offeree accepts (by indicating consent to be bound by the terms of the offer) a legally binding contract will come into existence. An offer can be written, communicated orally, or may be inferred from the conduct of the offeror (eg where goods are bought at auction). An offer may be made to a specific person, to a group of people or to the world at large (*Carlill v Carbolic Smoke Ball Co* [1893] 1 QB 256). An offer made to a specific person can be accepted only by such a person (*Cundy v Lindsay* (1878) 3 App Cas 459).

The fact that an offer requires an expression of unequivocal willingness to contract means that quotations of rates or prices are not offers (*Scancarriers A/C Aotearoa International Ltd* [1985] 2 Lloyd's Rep 419). It also means that enquiries and replies to any such enquiries are not offers. Thus, in *Harvey v Facey* [1893] AC 552 an enquiry relating to the lowest acceptable price for a certain piece of land and the response of the other party did not lead to a binding contract. Similarly, in *Gibson v Manchester City Council* [1979] 1 All ER 972 a letter sent by Manchester City Council stating 'may be prepared to sell the house.' was held not to constitute an offer to sell but merely an invitation to treat.

An offer must, therefore, be distinguished from an 'invitation to treat' (an invitation to enter into negotiations that may lead to an offer). The main significance of an invitation to treat is that it is not an offer capable of acceptance. Examples of an invitation to treat are as follows.

Display of goods

The display of goods in a shop window amounts only to an invitation to treat. In *Fisher v Bell* [1961] 1 QB 394 a shopkeeper was charged with offering for sale a flick-knife that was on display in his shop window contrary to s 1(1) of the Restriction of Offensive Weapons Act 1959. The court held that the display of goods in a shop window was not an offer to sell but an invitation to treat. It was, therefore, for the customer to make an offer which the shopkeeper may or may not accept. The rationale behind this decision is that a shop is a place for negotiation in respect of the terms of a contract and the shopkeeper invites customers to make an offer which he is free to either accept or reject. Circulars sent to potential customers are also invitations to treat for the supply of goods or services, and not offers (*Grainger & Son v Gough* [1896] AC 325).

The display of goods on shelves in a self-service shop (like the display of goods in a shop window) is an invitation to treat. In *Pharmaceutical Society of Great Britain v Boots Cash Chemists (Southern) Ltd* [1953] 1 QB 401 the defendants were charged with the offence of selling a listed drug evident by, or under the supervision of, a registered pharmacist contrary to the Pharmacy and Poisons Act 1933. The defendants operated a self-service shop where the goods for sale were displayed on shelves. Customers entering the shop picked up the goods they wished to buy and took them to a cashier near the exit. A registered pharmacist was present near the cash desk and could prevent a customer from buying any listed drugs. The prosecution argued that the sale of the displayed goods was completed when the customers put the goods into their basket because at this stage no pharmacist supervised the act. The Court of Appeal held that the display of goods was only an invitation to treat, that the offer to buy the goods was made by the customer at the cash desk and that the contract was only concluded when the cashier accepted that offer. The contract was therefore concluded under the supervision of a pharmacist and no offence was committed.

Advertisements

Whether an advertisement is an offer or an invitation to treat depends on the intention with which it is made. If an advertisement amounts to an offer, the contract is concluded when people respond in such a way that they accept the offer (eg by conduct). If an advertisement is only an invitation to treat (usually the case) a response to the advertisement cannot form a binding contract. Thus, in *Partridge v Crittenden* [1968] 1 WLR 1204 the defendant who had placed an advertisement in the classified section of a magazine was charged with unlawfully offering for sale a bramble finch contrary to the Protection of Birds Act 1954. The words 'offer for sale' were not directly used in the advertisement. A customer posted a cheque for 25 shillings requesting a bramble finch hen and the defendant responded by sending a bramble finch hen, as requested, in a box by British Rail. The court held that the defendant was not guilty and that the advertisement was an invitation to treat, not an offer. Consequently, the defendant had not 'offered for sale' a wild bird. In *Grainger & Son v Gough* [1896] AC 325 the undesirability of treating such advertisements as offers was explained by using the example of a wine merchant sending out a wine list to customers. Lord Herschell said:

> 'the transmission of such a wine list does not amount to an offer to supply an unlimited quantity of the wine described at the price name, so that as soon as an order is given there is a binding contract... If it were so, the merchant might find himself involved in any number of contractual obligations to supply wine of a particular description of which he would be quite unable to carry out, his stock of wine of that description being necessarily limited.'

Some advertisements, however, do amount to offers and in *Carlill v Carbolic Smoke Ball Co* [1893] 1 QB 525 the defendants advertised that they would pay £100 to anyone catching influenza after using their product in a specified manner. The advertisement also stated that the defendants had desposited £1,000 in a Regent Street bank showing their sincerity. The claimant, Mrs Carlill bought one of the smoke balls on the strength of the advertisement and despite using it properly claimed she had caught the flu. The defendants claimed they were not bound by the advertisement on the following grounds:

- that the advertisement was a mere sales 'puff' rather than an offer;
- that a contract could not be made with the whole world;
- that the defendants, promise was too vague to be an offer.

The Court of Appeal held that the advertisement constituted an offer of a unilateral contract (a person who makes an offer of a unilateral contract is bound to anyone performs the required act). The offer stipulated that the acceptance could be using a smoke ball in the correct manner and catching flu. The claimant, having satisfied these requirements, had therefore accepted the offer. The defendants' reference to the £1,000 deposited with a bank indicated to the court that the promise of payment was not a mere sales puff. The case also reinforces the point that an offer can be made to the whole world (eg such as in reward cases). Such offers lead to binding contracts with anyone who comes forward and fulfils the conditions of the offer.

Tenders

An announcement that the provision of goods and services is open to tender is not an offer but an invitation to treat. Such persons who submit tenders make an offer that may be accepted or rejected by the person seeking the tenders (*Spencer v Harding* (1870) LR 5CP 561).

A person seeking tenders may indicate that he will accept the highest or lowest tender and will be contractually bound to do this. In such cases, the person inviting tenders with such an indication accompanies his invitation to treat with an offer of a unilateral contract to accept the highest or lowest tender. In such cases, the highest or lowest tender, as appropriate, will constitute an acceptance of that offer and the person seeking tenders will be contractually bound to accept that tender (*Harvela Investments Ltd v Royal Trust Co of Canada (CI) Ltd* [1986] AC 207.

Acceptance of an offer

Once an offer is accepted a contract comes into existence and both sides are legally bound. An acceptance must, however, be clear and unequivocal. Acceptance can be by words or conduct and must be communicated to the offeror. Consequently, an oral acceptance that is drowned by a passing aeroplane or is inaudible because of interference on the telephone is not effectively communicated (*Entores Ltd v Miles Far East Corpn* [1955] 2 QB 327). Telex and fax messages sent during office hours are regarded as instantaneous communications and are subject to the same principles as oral acceptances; they take effect when printed on the offeror's telex or fax machine (*Brinkibon Ltd v Stahag Stahl Und Stehlwarenhandel GmbH* [1983] 2 AC 34). This rule does not apply where the communication is not instantaneous (eg where a telex is sent out of office hours the time of acceptance will depend on the intention of the parties and sound business practice and in some cases on a judgment as to where the risk should lie (the *Brinkibon case*).

An acceptance of an offer of a bilateral contract (one where both parties exchange promises to perform) is only effective when it is received. It follows that the acceptance must take the form of some positive action and an offeree is not bound simply because an offeror has framed his offer in such terms that a contract is presumed to exist, unless non-acceptance is communicated (*Felthouse v Bindley* (1862) 11 CBNS 869).

Where the offeror requires the acceptance to be in a particular form then an acceptance in some other way may be effective so long as it is no less advantageous to the offeror than the prescribed method (*Tinn v Hoffmann* (1873) 29 LT 271; *Yates Building Co Ltd v RJ Pulleyn & Sons (York) Ltd* (1975) 119 Sol J 0370). If the offer states that the acceptance may only be made in a specified manner then the offeree must comply with that method of acceptance, unless the offeror waives the required method of acceptance. The offeree must comply with the terms of the offer for there to be a valid acceptance (*Compagnie De Commerce et Commission SALR v Parkinson Stove Co Ltd* [1953] 2 Lloyd's Rep 487).

The postal rule

It may be extremely important to know exactly when an acceptance becomes legally affective. The offer can be revoked at any time before acceptance (unless consideration is given to hold the offer open for a specific period) (*Dickinson v Dodds* (1876) 2 ChD 463). When the acceptance takes place by letter or telegram the postal rule will apply. The rules state that the acceptance of an offer by post is effective immediately the letter is properly posted or, in the case of a telegram, when sent. In *Adams v Lindsell* (1818) 1 B& Ald 681) the defendants offered by letter to sell wool to the claimants requiring an answer by return of post. The defendants misdirected the letter and it was therefore delivered two days later than it would have been had it been properly addressed. The claimants posted an acceptance which itself was received later than would normally have been expected had the offer letter been properly addressed and delivered as expected. As the defendants had not received an acceptance by the expected date (not realising that the offer letter had been delayed because it was misdirected) they sold the goods to a third party. The court held that there was a concluded contract when the letter of acceptance was posted. A letter is 'posted' when it is placed, correctly stamped, in an official letterbox or into the hand of a post office employee or agent authorized to receive letters (*Re London & Northern Bank, ex p Jones* [1900] 1 Ch 220). In *Household Fire Insurance Co v Grant* (1879) 4 Ex D 216 the Court of Appeal applied the postal rule in a case where the letter of acceptance was permanently lost in the post in *Henthorn v Fraser* [1892] 2 Ch 27 and held that the postal rule would apply not only where the offer was sent by post but whenever it was reasonable to accept that an acceptance would be made by post. An acceptance by post would be effective

> 'where the circumstances are such that it must have been within the contemplation of the parties that, according to the ordinary usages of mankind, the post might be used as a means of communicating the acceptance of an offer'.

In *Holwell Securities v Hughes* [1974] 1 WLR 155 the Court of Appeal reviewed the postal rule in a situation where the defendant had made the plaintiffs an offer to purchase his house for £45,000. The option was said to be exercisable by 'notice in writing' to the defendant within six months. The plaintiffs posted a letter exercising the option but the letter was never delivered and no further communication took place until the option had expired. The plaintiff sued for specific performance requiring the defendant to sell the house to them. The Court of Appeal held that the postal rule did not apply and therefore no contract had been concluded. The express terms of the offer stated that the acceptance had to reach the offeror and this was sufficient to exclude the application of the postal rule. Lawton LJ said that the postal rule does not apply if:

> 'having regard to all the circumstances, including the nature of the subject matter under consideration, the negotiating parties cannot

have intended that there should be a binding agreement until the party accepting an offer or exercising an option had in fact communicated the acceptance...'.

Counter offer

An acceptance of an offer must be unqualified and unconditional. Acceptance on terms which effectively amounts to a material alteration of the terms of the offer may amount to a counter offer. The effect of such a counter offer will be to reject the original offer and substitute that offer with the terms of the counter offer. In *Hyde v Wrench* (1840) 3 Deav 334 the defendant offered to sell his farm to the claimant for £1,000 requesting that a reply by return of post was required. The claimant's agent called on the defendant and offered £950 on the claimant's behalf. The defendant wrote to the claimant's agent, in due course, declining the offer of £950 and the claimant then sought to accept the original offer to sell the farm at £1,000. The court concluded there was no contract when the defendant refused to sell to the claimant for £1,000. The court concluded that the counter offer had the effect of rejecting the original offer. In business terms, it would be harsh if the offeree, having refused the original offer, could then accept it and make the offeror liable for breach of contract.

Certainty of terms

A contract will only come into existence if the offer, which is accepted, contains all the essential terms of the contract. A court must be able to identify, with certainty, what has been agreed between the parties and the basis of that agreement. In deciding whether or not the terms of the agreement are sufficiently certain, the courts take an objective approach by asking whether a reasonable man would have thought that the agreement was sufficiently certain. This allows the courts to ask not what the parties to the contract actually meant, but what they appeared to mean. If the intention of the parties cannot be discovered, however, the agreement is not a legally binding contract and cannot be enforced (*Scammel and Nephew Ltd v Ouston* [1941] AC 251). In *Bushwall Properties Ltd v Vortex Properties Ltd* [1976] 2 All ER 283 A agreed to buy from B fifty-one and a half acres of land for £500,000. Under the terms of the agreement, the price was to be paid in three instalments but on each payment a 'proportionate part' of the land was to be conveyed to A. The Court of Appeal held that the agreement was void for uncertainty because it did not provide the machinery for identifying the proportionate part to be conveyed in each phase, nor could a term be implied as to how each proportionate part was to be identified. Although price is of the essence of a contract, the lack of an agreed price for the sale of goods will not necessarily prevent a contract from coming into existence. Section 8(1) of the Sale of Goods Act 1979 provides that the price in a contract of sale of goods may be fixed by the contract, may be left to be fixed in a manner agreed by the contract, or may be determined by the course of dealings between the parties. Section 8(2) provides that where the price is not determined by any of these methods, the buyer must pay a reasonable price. Section 15(1) of the Supply of Goods and Services Act 1982 makes similar provision where the contract is for the supply of a service.

In *Hillas & Co Ltd v Arcos Ltd* (1932) 147 LT 503 the court held that an agreement entered into between the parties for the sale and purchase of timber in 1930, that contained an option to buy 100,000 standards of timber in 1931, but the size and quality of which timber was not specified, was held to be valid. The court held that any uncertainty in respect of the size and quality of the timer could be clarified by reference to the previous dealings of the parties and the usual practice in the timber trade. Another case where the court concluded there was a valid contract despite the apparent uncertainty of the terms was *Sudbrook Trading Estate Ltd v Eggleton* [1983] 1 AC 444 where the House of Lords dealt with the situation where the price of a piece of property was left to be decided by two valuers, one to be appointed by each party. The court concluded that if a fair and reasonable price could not be achieved either because the independent valuers could not agree, or because one of the parties failed to appoint a valuer, the court could substitute its own machinery to ascertain the price (eg by appointing its own valuers).

Once performance has been commenced, the courts are much more likely to hold that there is a valid contract. This is not absolutely essential, however, because in the absence of a binding contract a party who has received valuable benefits could be ordered to pay for them on the basis that a *quantum meruit* basis party receiving the benefits would therefore have to pay a reasonable price for remuneration. (*Quantum meruit* means how much the plaintiff actually deserves.)

The basis of an offer and acceptance when dealing with machines

It is common for people to buy goods or services through the purchase of a ticket from machines. In terms of recognizing the existence of an offer and acceptance this can sometimes cause difficulty. In *Thornton v Shoe Lane Parking Ltd* [1971] 1 QB 163 Lord Denning analysed the position of a customer in a multi-storey car park issued a ticket by a machine on entry to the car park. He concluded that the contract was completed not when the customer received the ticket, but as soon as the customer became irrevocably committed to the contract (ie when he put the money into the machine). In terms of an offer and acceptance, the offer is made when the proprietor of the machine displays it as ready to receive the money. The acceptance is made when the customer puts his money into the slot. It is common for goods/services to be purchased electronically through websites. In the context of such a transaction it will appear that a website that displays the prices at which a customer can buy the goods/services will be an invitation to treat. When the customer places an order this will amount to an offer to buy the goods at the displayed price and the acceptance will only be completed (and the contract concluded) when the customer receives confirmation of the order after clicking the purchase button. Within the existing common law, the website is equivalent to a display of goods in a shop window. Difficulties with electronically concluded contracts may arise, however, where the acceptance is received out of office hours or in the middle of the night. In *Brinkibon Ltd v Stahag Stahl Und Stahlwarenhandelsgesellschaft mbH* [1983] 2 AC 34 Lord Wilberforce, dealing with communication by telex, accepted that the message may not reach, or be intended to reach, the designated recipient immediately; messages may be sent out of office hours, or at night, with the intention, or on the assumption, that they will be read at a later time. Sometimes, there may be error or default at the recipient's end which prevents the receipt at the time contemplated by the sender. Taking these factors into account, Lord Wilberforce concluded that there can be no universal rule to cover all such cases and they must be resolved by reference to the intention of the parties, by sound business practice and in some cases by a judgment of where the risks should lie.

If an acceptance by telex or fax is received during office hours, however, it is effective when it is received and not when it is brought to the actual attention of the recipient (even if the recipient's computer is turned off). Lord Fraser in *Brinkibon* said that once the message has been received on the offeror's telex machine, it is not unreasonable to treat it as delivered to the offeror, because it is his responsibility to arrange for prompt handling of messages within his own office. E-commerce is now regulated by the Electronic Communications Act 2000 which clarifies the law on electronic signatures; the Consumer Protection (Distance Selling) Regulations 2000 give the buyer who has electronically bought goods the right to cancel the contract within seven days. Finally, the EC Electronic Commerce Directive 2002 regulates the moment at which an electronic contract is concluded.

Termination of offers

An offer can terminate at any time prior to acceptance, including by revocation, rejection, lapse of time or death of the offeror or offeree.

An offer can be revoked at any time before it is accepted and once revoked, the offer no longer exists and therefore is not capable of being accepted. A revocation is effective only when the offeree receives it. A revocation will generally be communicated to the offeree by the offeror or his agent although the courts have held an offer to be revoked through communication by an unauthorized but reliable third party (*Dickinson v Dodds* (1876) 2 Ch D 463). If an offer is to be revoked by rejection, that rejection by the offeree needs to be communicated to the offeror. In some cases, a counter-offer (*Hyde v Wrench* (1840) 3 Beav 334) will be treated as a rejection of the original offer. The counter offer effectively attempts to introduce new terms.

An offer may lapse if not accepted within a reasonable time. What amounts to a reasonable time will depend on the circumstances of the case including the subject matter of the offer. If, for example, a businessman makes two offers, one to sell a consignment of ripe bananas and the other to sell his business premises, the offers would not be expected to remain open for the same length of time. The courts will take into consideration that the subject matter of one of the offers is perishable goods with a short life span and therefore any acceptance must be within a reasonable time within the context of the offer and the product being dealt with.

The fact that the offeror has died before the offer is accepted will not necessarily prevent the offeree from accepting the offer. If the offer was to supply a personal service (to sing at a concert) then the offer can no longer be capable of acceptance on the death of the offeror. If the offer is not one for the provision of personal services then in *Bradbury v Morgan* (1862) 1 HC 249 it was suggested that the offeree could accept the offer until he has notification of the offeror's death.

Intention to create legal relations

The existence of an offer and acceptance will only lead to a legally binding contract if the offeror and the offeree intended to create legal relations. In such a situation, the courts will take an objective view of the intention of the parties. The question is not one of whether or not the parties actually intended to enter into a legal relationship but whether they appeared to a reasonable man to have this intention.

When deciding whether or not there is an intention to create legal relations the courts divide agreements into two classes:
♦ business and commercial agreements;
♦ social and domestic agreements.

In respect of business and commercial agreements, there is a presumption that the parties intend to enter into a legally binding contract whereas in the case of social and domestic arrangements, the presumption is that there is no such intention. Either of these presumptions can be rebutted by evidence to the contrary. In a business and commercial arrangement therefore, an offeror or offeree will need to introduce evidence to rebut the presumption that they intended to enter into legally binding relations. In *Esso Petroleum Ltd v Commissioners of Customs & Excise* [1976] 1 WLR 1 in order to promote their petrol, Esso advertised that they would give a World Cup coin (each coin bore the likeness of a member of the England squad for the 1970 World Cup) to motorists who purchased four gallons of petrol. The court held that there was an intention to create legal relations because the advertising took place in a business context and was designed to achieve commercial success. Purchase tax was not payable, however, because the agreement to supply the coins was not a sale and the consideration given by the motorists for these coins was not the payment of money but the contract to buy petrol.

If parties to a commercial contract make it clear that they do not intend their agreement to form a binding contract, this will override the presumption to enter into legal relations. In *Rose & Frank v Crompton Bros* [1925] AC 445 the defendants appointed the plaintiffs to sell their product in America under an agreement that contained an 'honour clause', ie a clause which stated that the agreement was merely recording the intention of the parties and was binding in honour only and not in law. The plaintiff sued for alleged breach of contract. Both the Court of Appeal and House of Lords held that the honour clause constituted a clearly expressed intention that the agreement was not to be legally binding.

Letters of comfort

A letter of comfort is a letter written to give reassurance to a person who is considering extending credit to a third party. Such a letter may amount to a guarantee, in which case it will provide a definite promise to answer for the debt of the third party. A letter of comfort that does not amount to a guarantee, may nevertheless give rise to a contractual obligation, but this will depend on whether or not an intention to create legal relations can be inferred from the language of the letter and the surrounding circumstances. In *Kleinwort Benson Ltd v Malaysia Mining Corpn BHD* [1988] 1 WLR 379 the claimant bank was unwilling to lend money to MMC Metals Ltd, a subsidiary of MMC BHD. The bank was not satisfied with the credit- worthiness of MMC Metals Ltd and asked MMC BHD to guarantee the loan. MMC BHD replied that it was not their policy to guarantee loans to their subsidiaries. After some negotiations, MMC BHD issued a letter of comfort which stated that it was MMC BHD's policy to make sure that MMC Metals Ltd was 'at all times in a position to meet its liabilities to you'. The bank made the loan to MMC Metals Ltd, which went into liquidation without repaying the debt. The bank sued MMC BHD on the letter of comfort. The Court of Appeal concluded that the letter of comfort did not give rise to any contractual liability since the letter contained no contractual promise intending to give rise to a legal relationship. The statement by MMC BHD was no more than a statement of present intention. Although in *Kleinwort Benson* the letter of comfort did not give rise to a contractual promise, the precise wording is likely to be a deciding factor.

The Court of Appeal distinguished *Edwards v Skyways Ltd* [1964] 1 All ER 494 where the claimant worked for the defendants as a pilot. He was made redundant, along with 15% of the workforce, and given three months notice of termination of his employment. The claimant had the right either to withdraw pension contributions he had made, or to take the right to a pension that would become payable at retirement age. At a meeting between the defendants and the claimant's trade association, the defendant said that if the redundant employees withdrew their present contributions, the defendants would make them ex gratia payments that would approximate to the defendant company's pension contributions (the ex-gratia payment merely meant that it was made without admitting any legal liability on the defendant's part. It did not mean that the agreement should have no effect in law). On the strength of the defendant's promise, the claimant decided to withdraw from the pension fund and to take his own contributions and the promised ex gratia payment. The defendant subsequently rescinded the promise to make the ex gratia payments because of financial difficulties. It was held that in a business context, there was a strong presumption that an agreement was intended to create legal relations and that the defendants had not rebutted this presumption. The claimant was therefore entitled to the ex gratia payment.

Social and domestic agreements

When considering whether or not a social or domestic arrangement amounts to a contract, the courts will presume that the parties did not intend to create legal relations. This presumption can be rebutted by evidence and the circumstances of the case will be examined to ascertain the intention of the parties. In *Jones v Padvanton* [1969] 1 WLR 328 the court concluded that in family agreements there is a strong presumption that the parties do not intend to create legal relations. Similarly, in *Balfour v Balfour* [1919] 2 KB 571 the Court of Appeal established the principle that agreements between husband and wife are unlikely to be contracted unless there is very clear evidence that this was in fact the intention. The principle set out in *Balfour* is weakened if the husband and wife are separated or are contemplating separation. In *Merritt v Merritt* [1970] 1 WLR 1121 the husband signed an agreement under which he agreed to transfer the joint matrimonial home to the wife if she paid all the charges that arose in connection with the house until the mortgage was paid off. When the wife had paid off the mortgage, she applied for a declaration that the house should be transferred to her. The court concluded that the agreement between the husband and wife had been binding on them. As they were no longer living together, the presumption that they did not intend to make a contract was greatly reduced and a reasonable person looking at the agreement would have regarded it as legally binding. Lord Denning MR stressed that in these cases, the courts will look at their apparent intentions.

Consideration

A contract is a bargain, the essence of which is that each party will give up something in order to get something they want. This concept underpins the idea that a contract will only come into existence if each party to the contract furnishes consideration. Consideration is thus the price paid to get the benefit of the contract (*Currie v Misa* [1875] LR 10 Ex 153). Consideration, therefore, consists either in the giving of a benefit or the suffering of a loss, eg in a contract of sale of goods, the buyer's consideration is the promise to pay the price whilst the giving of this promise is of benefit to the seller.

It is the requirement that consideration must move to and from each party that distinguishes contracts from gifts. If a contract is made, each side gives a benefit to the other in return for a benefit received. In the case of a gift, however, only one side gives a benefit. A contract that is not made by a deed is known as a simple

the owners of the machine by unloading the machine. It was irrelevant that stevedores had already promised someone else, the carriers, that they would unload the machine.

If a person is already under a contractual duty to do something, a mere promise to perform it is not good consideration for another promise by the person to whom the contractual duty is already owed. In *Stilk v Myrick* (1809) 2 Camp 317 several of the ships crew deserted during a voyage and the captain promised to pay the wages of the deserters to the rest of the crew if they would continue the voyage home shorthanded. On return to England, the extra wages were not paid and the seamen sued. The court held that the men were not entitled to the extra money promised to them because they had provided no consideration. They were already required to cope with normal emergencies under their existing contracts and therefore desertion by fellow crewmembers was a normal emergency. In *Williams v Roffey Bros and Nicholls (Contractors) Ltd* [1991] 1 QB 1 the Court of Appeal placed a major limitation on the principle in *Stilk v Myrick*. The court held that where A makes a further promise to B in return for B's promise to perform (or performance of) his contractual obligations already owed to A, and as a result of B's promise (or performance) A obtains a practical benefit (or avoids a disadvantage), B provides good consideration for A's further promise. The facts of the *Williams case* were that the plaintiff had been engaged by the defendants (main contractors in refurbishing a block of flats) to carry out carpentry work for £20,000. In order to avoid penalties being imposed on him the defendants promised to pay the plaintiff an additional sum if he would carry out the work on time. The plaintiff promised to do this, and completed the work in a number of flats, but was not paid the additional amount promised. The Court of Appeal held that the defendants promise was binding.

Composition with creditors

If an insolvent person owes money to more than one creditor, all of the creditors might enter into a composition agreement between themselves. Under such an agreement all the creditors agree with each other that they will settle for less than the amount owed to them individually. For example, if an insolvent businessman owes £20,000 to A, £40,000 to B and £40,000 to C when the businessman's assets only amount to £10,000, A, B and C may agree with each other that they would each accept 10 pence in the pound on the debts owed to them. Such a contract is binding on all three creditors because each has promised the other two that he will accept 10 pence in the pound, if the others will. If any of the creditors later sues for the whole amount owing to him the other creditors can prevent an action from going ahead. If the creditors change their mind and sue the businessmen for the full debt, he cannot prevent an action against himself because he has given no consideration for the composition agreement and was not a party to that agreement between the creditors.

Part payment of a debt

A debt can be extinguished either by paying it in full or by accord and satisfaction (agreement and consideration). In other words, if A owes £10,000 to B the debt is extinguished if A pays that amount to B. If, however, B agrees to forego part of the debt in return for A's part payment (there is partial repayment of an existing contractual debt) that is not sufficient consideration and B can subsequently recover the remainder of the debt. In *Folkes v Beer* (1884) 9 App Cas 605 the defendant agreed to accept repayment by instalments of a debt owed by the plaintiff. When the debt was repaid, the defendant sued for interest and the plaintiff argued that the defendant had agreed to bring no further action if the debt was paid off by instalments. The defendant argued that there was no consideration for her promise and, even if there were, that did not include a promise to waive the interest due to her. The court held that payment by instalments of the debt was not consideration for a promise not to take further action. The payment of the lesser sum (the debt due by instalments without interest) could not be satisfaction for the greater amount owed (the amount of the debt by instalments with interest). The court applied the rule in *Pinnel's case* (1602) 5 Co Rep where it was said that there are exceptions to the rule that part payment of a debt is no consideration for a promise to remit the rest of the debt. Thus, *Pinnel's case* provided that (provided it was done at the creditor's request) early payment of part of a debt, part payment at another place then that originally specified for payment, or payment in kind, even if the value of the goods is less than the debt, is good consideration for a promise by the creditor to remit the remainder of the debt. For example, if A owes B £10,000 payable on the 1 January in New York and, at B's request, A pays £1000 on the 31 December (or pays £1000 in Manchester on the correct day), or gives B a rose or a scarf on the correct day, the debt is validly discharged. At one time, it was thought that payment by cheque at the creditor's request could amount to a different form of payment and therefore would extinguish the whole debt. The Court of Appeal in *D and C Builders Ltd v Rees* [1966] 2 QB 617 rejected this argument when it held that there is no effective difference between cash and a cheque that is honoured.

Position in equity: promissory estoppel

The decisions in *Pinnel's case* and *Folkes v Beer* must be viewed in the light of the doctrine of *promissory estoppel*. In *Central London Property Trust Ltd v High Trees House Ltd* [1947] KB 130 the plaintiffs let a block of flats to the defendants that remained vacant due to the war. In 1941 the plaintiffs agreed to accept a reduced rent, which was paid quarterly until 1945 when the plaintiff demanded the full rental. Although the defendants had provided no consideration for the plaintiffs' promise to remit the rent, Lord Denning concluded that, where one party gave a promise that he intended to be binding and which was acted on, that promise could be raised as a defence by the promisee if the promisor sought to enforce his strict legal rights.

The promise to remit part of the rent was made under conditions prevailing at the time when the flats were partially let (because of the war) and that when the flats became fully let, early in 1945, the promise to remit part of the rent ceased to bind the plaintiffs. Lord Denning also suggested that a promise of this type might be terminated by notice.

Under the doctrine of promissory estoppel a promise not to enforce the contractual right may be given some effect, despite the absence of consideration, where it would be inequitable for the promisor simply to go back on his promise and enforce his rights fully. For promissory estoppel to apply the following requirements must be satisfied:

- there must be an unequivocal promise by one party that he will not (at least for the time being) enforce his strict contractual rights against the other. The promise may be expressed or implied from conduct;
- the promisor must have intended that his promise should be acted on and the promisee must have acted on it and altered his position in reliance on the promise by doing something he would not otherwise have done (*Hughes v Metropolitan Rly Co* (1877) 2 App Cas 439);
- it must be inequitable for the promisor to go back on his promise having regard to the course of dealings which have taken place between the parties.

Generally, promissory estoppel only suspends rights and does not wholly extinguish them. Where promissory estoppel operates to suspend an obligation, the promisor may, by giving reasonable notice to the promise, revert to his strict contractual rights (*High Trees case*). Further, promissory estoppel only prevents the promisor from enforcing his strict rights despite the absence of consideration from the promisee; it cannot be used to find a cause of action (*Combe v Combe* [1951] 2 KB 215).

Privity of contract

The doctrine of privity of contract is based on two rules:

- only a party to a contract can take the benefit of that contract or claim rights under it;
- a contract cannot impose obligations on a third party so that a contractual obligation cannot bind a third party or be enforced against him.

Both these rules are subject to exceptions and qualifications.

In *Tweddle v Atkinson* [1831] 1 BS 393 the claimant married the daughter of one Guy. At the time of the marriage, Guy and Tweddle (the claimant's father) agreed with each other that they would both pay the claimant a sum of money. Tweddle paid the claimant the promised money but Guy died without having paid the amount he had promised. The claimant sued Guy's personal representatives for the money. The court held that the claimant could not sue on the contract because he was not a party to it. Guy had made the contract with Tweddle and only the latter could have sued Guy for breach of contract. Tweddle would only have been awarded nominal damages, however, as the non-performance of the promise made to him had caused him no loss. The House of Lords affirmed the privity rule in *Dunlop Pneumatic Tyre Co Ltd v Selfridge & Co Ltd* [1915] AC 847. Dunlop sold tyres to Dew & Co, who were dealers in motor accessories. In return for being given a 10% discount on the price, Dew & Co agreed that they would obtain a written undertaking from any person to whom they resold the tyres that they would not sell below a certain price. Dew & Co resold the tyres to Selfridge & Co who entered into a written agreement not to resell the tyres below the agreed price. However, Selfridge & Co resold the tyres below the agreed price and Dunlop sued them on the written agreement not to do so. The House of Lords held that Dunlop could not sue Selfridge on the written agreement given by them to Dew & Co as Dunlop were not parties to the contract between Selfridge and Dew & Co.

When a contract is made on behalf of a third party it is sometimes possible for the contracting party to obtain specific performance of the contract. Where such an order is obtained, the third party may be able to enforce the performance of the contract. In *Beswick v Beswick* [1968] AC 58 a coal merchant assigned his business to his nephew in return for the nephew agreeing to pay the coal merchant an annuity for the rest of his life. The agreement also provided that if the coal merchant pre-deceased his wife, the nephew would pay the widow £5 per week for the rest of her life. After the coal merchant died, the nephew made one payment to the widow and then refused to make further payments on grounds of lack of privity of contract. The widow sued for arrears of payment and an order for specific performance in respect of future payments. The court held that the widow could not succeed in her personal capacity but could recover as the administratrix of her husband's estate. Only nominal damages were recoverable, however, because her husband's estate had suffered no loss in consequence of the nephew's refusal to make payments. The widow could have specific performance of the contract as she was, in effect, suing as her husband.

Both the rules on which the doctrine of privity is based are subject to exceptions or qualifications. The rule that someone who is not a party to the contract cannot enforce the contract is subject to significant exceptions under the Contracts (Rights of Third Parties) Act 1999. This Act does not abolish the privity rule but allows a third party, in some circumstances, to enforce a term of the contract. Section 1 sets out two circumstances in which a third party may enforce terms of a contract entered into by the promisor and the promisee. The promisor is defined as the party to the contract against whom the term is enforceable by the third party. The promisee is defined as the party to the contract by whom the term is enforceable against the promisor. Thus, for example, where a shop sells goods to X that are not of satisfactory quality, the Contract (Rights of Third Parties) Act may allow Y (third party) to sue the shop. The shop is the promisor, X is the promisee and Y is the third party. Section 1(1) of the Act provides that a third party to a contract may, in his own right, enforce a term of the contract if:

- the contract expressly provides that he may so do; or
- the term purports to confer a benefit on him (unless on a proper construction of the contract the parties did not intend the term to be enforceable by the third party).

The third party must either be expressly identified in the contract by name, or as a member of a class (eg through a reference to 'the employees' of the party) or as answering a particular description. The third party need not be in existence at the time the contract is entered into (eg an unborn child can benefit under s 1).

When a benefit is conferred on a third party by the Act, the third party can avail himself of any remedy that would be available to him had he been a party to the contract eg damages, an injunction or specific performance. The third party can also avail himself of exclusion or limitation clauses. Thus, for example, if a contract between A and B for the carriage of machinery by B provides that B's liability for damage to the machinery is limited and the machinery is damaged by the negligent driving of C, one of B's lorry drivers, C is not protected by the clause if he is sued in negligence by A. If, however, the clause expressly provides that the liability of B or any of B's employees for lawful damage is restricted C will be protected by the clause.

Section 3(6) of the Contracts (Rights of Third Parties) Act provides that where a third party seeks the protection of an exemption clause in reliance on s 1, he may not do so if he could not have relied on such an exemption clause had he been a party to the contract. Thus, for example, an exemption clause is held ineffective if because of the provisions of the Unfair Contract Terms Act 1977 between the parties to the contract, the third party cannot similarly rely on it.

Section 2 of the Contracts (Rights of Third Parties) Act provides that where the third party does gain rights under s 1 to enforce a term of a contract, the parties to the contract may not generally rescind or vary the contract in such a way so as to extinguish or alter the third party's right without his consent. This is only the case if a third party has communicated his ascent to the contract to the promisor, or if the promisor knows that the third party has relied on a term, or if the promisor should reasonably have foreseen that the third party would rely on the term and the third party has in fact done so. Further, the parties to the contract will be able to rescind or vary the contract without the consent of the third party if an express term of the contract allows them to do so, or if an expressed term sets out the circumstances in which this may be done.

Section 1 of the 1999 Act does not confer any rights on a third party in respect of a bill of exchange, promissory note or other negotiable instrument (eg a cheque). The Bills of Exchange Act 1882 entitles a third party to payment on a bill or other negotiable instrument if he is the 'holder' of it and it has been endorsed to him.

Formalities

Although most commercial contracts are made in writing, there is no legal requirement that this must be the case. Generally contracts do not need to be made in any particular way. There are, however, some exceptions to that rule:

♦ a conveyance of a legal estate in land must be by deed;
♦ the creation of a lease of over three years duration must be by deed;
♦ the promise of a gift is not enforceable unless made by deed.

An instrument shall not be a deed unless it is made clear on its face that it is intended to be a deed by the party or parties making it and is validly executed as such. Section 1(3) of the Law of Property (Miscellaneous Provisions) Act 1989 provides that for a deed to be validly executed the instrument must be signed by the individual in the presence of a witness who attests the signature. A person who attests a document by signing it shows that he has witnessed the signature of the other party. The Limitation Act 1980 provides that an action cannot be brought on a simple contract six years after the date when the right of action arose. Where the contract is made by deed, however, an action can be brought 12 years after the right to bring the action arose.

Certain types of contracts must be in writing, eg contracts for the sale or disposition of land and contracts regulated as consumer credit agreements. Contracts of guarantee under which one person assumes secondary liability to settle the debts and liabilities of another must be evidenced in writing and signed by the person giving the guarantee or they will be unenforceable (s 4 of the Statute of Frauds 1677).

Capacity

Generally everyone has full contractual capacity. Minors (persons under the age of 18) may have limited capacity in some cases (Family Law Reform Act 1969).

♦ Where necessaries are delivered to a minor, he must pay a reasonable price for them. Section 3(3) of the Sale of Goods Act 1979 defines necessaries as 'goods suitable to the condition in life of the minor …' A minor can also validly make a contract of employment as long as the contract is overall beneficial to the minor.
♦ Contracts giving a minor an interest of a permanent nature (eg which impose a continuing liability on a minor) avoidable by the minor either before he reaches 18 or within a reasonable time (eg contract of partnership; contracts to buy shares; contracts to take a least of land).
♦ All other contracts are not binding on a minor. A minor will only be able to recover any money paid or property delivered under such a contract if there has been a total failure of consideration.

Corporations

Corporations have full contractual capacity (see Chapter 3).

Contractual terms

The terms agreed by the parties will define the scope of the obligations and promises contained in the contract. Express terms are those which are actually agreed between the parties either in words or in writing. Sometimes these may amount to representations although not all exchanges between the parties form part of the legally binding contract. Additionally, terms may be implied into the contract either by the courts or by statute. Where there has been a breach of a contractual term that will give the injured party the right either to sue for damages or, even, repudiate the contract. The nature of the remedy will depend upon the class of term that has been reached. Where there is a breach of:

◆ warranty – the breach is not so serious that it goes to the route of the contract and the injured party is entitled to sue for damages;
◆ condition – the injured party may repudiate the contract and sue for damages because the breach is sufficiently serious to undermine the whole contract. The injured party may, however, treat the breach of condition as a breach of warranty and merely sue for damages;
◆ an innominate term – whether or not the injured party is entitled to repudiate the contract will depend on the severity of the consequences, which flow from the breach.

Exemption or exclusion clauses are terms in a contract that try to exclude or exempt a party's liability for breach of contract. The Unfair Contract Terms Act 1997 has limited the effect of exemption and exclusion clauses and the Unfair Terms in Consumer Contract Regulations 1999, SI 1999/2083 have provided additional protection to consumers faced with unfair terms. The courts may also render an exclusion clause invalid, either by holding that the clause is not a term of the contract in question or by finding that the clause did not exclude liability for the particular breach which occurred. The common law rules should, therefore, not be overlooked.

Judicial control of exclusion clauses

One of the fundamental rules of contract law is that parties are free to contract on whatever terms they so agree. Additionally, where the parties enter into a written agreement freely, which contains an exclusion clause, then following the doctrine of freedom of contract that exclusion clause is binding. The courts did recognize the unfairness of exclusion clauses and the fact that it is the party with the greater bargaining power that, in reality, inserts exclusion clauses into contracts. The courts have therefore tried to limit the effect of exclusion clauses as follows.

♦ The courts might decide that the clause was never incorporated into the contract. Customers of a bank may, therefore, be able to argue that the bank's written terms have not become part of the contract (eg *Burnett v Westminster Bank Ltd* [1966] 1 QB 742). In such a situation the bank would have to establish that customers were given adequate notice (either before the contract was concluded or before the term became part of normal banking practice) and the burden of proof is heavy if unusually wide or onerous conditions are sought to be imposed on the customer (*Tai Hing Cotton Mill Ltd v Liu Chong Hing Bank Ltd* [1986] AC 80). Such cases usually involve a consideration of what is customary in a trade, or what are the reasonable expectations of a party in order to determine whether a clause is unusually wide or onerous.

♦ Where exclusion or exemption clauses are incorporated in a contract they may still be construed against the bank so as to be ineffective to exclude liability for the breach that has occurred. Clauses that may be construed against a bank may include those clauses imposing bank charges. Such clauses must be clear in respect of the obligation of the customer to pay. Further variation of any contractual terms is subject to an implied term that it is not to be exercised for an improper purpose, dishonestly, arbitrarily or so unreasonably that no reasonable lender would act in that way (*Paragon Finance plc v Nash and Staunton* [2002] 2 All ER 248).

The Unfair Contract Terms Act 1977

Despite the attempts of the courts to restrict the scope of the exclusion or limitation clauses, the Unfair Contract Terms Act 1977 (UCTA) was passed to give additional protection to control the effect of exclusion clauses. The 1977 Act is not confined to consumer contracts and this is particularly relevant to the provision of banking services.

Liability for negligence

Section 2(1) of UCTA provides that a person cannot, by reference to a contractual term or to a notice, exclude or restrict his liability for death or personal injury resulting from negligence. Section 2(2) provides that liability for other types of loss or damage caused by negligence (eg damage to goods) cannot be excluded except in so far as the term or notice satisfies the requirements of reasonableness. The result of s 2(2) is that a bank cannot, by reference to any contract or term, or to a notice given to customers generally or to particular customers, exclude or restrict its liability for negligence unless the reasonableness test is satisfied. Negligence is defined to mean any breach arising from the express or implied terms of a contract to take reasonable care or to exercise reasonable skill in the performance of a contract, or of any common law duty to take reasonable care or to exercise reasonable skill (eg as an agent). Thus, in *Smith v Eric S Bush* [1989] 2 All ER 514 the claimant applied to a building society for a mortgage to buy a house. The building society employed a firm of solicitors (the defendants) to undertake the survey for which the claimant paid £39 to the building society. The building society supplied the claimant with a copy of the surveyor's report, which contained a disclaimer to the effect that neither the building society nor the surveyors would be liable for any inaccuracies. The surveyor's report gave a valuation for the house and stated that no major building work was necessary. The claimant sued the defendant for negligence when the chimneys fell through the room because the two chimneybreasts had been removed without proper supports being fitted. The House of Lords held that the defendants were liable for negligence and the disclaimer was invalid.

Contractual performance

Section 3 of UCTA applies to two categories of persons:

♦ those who deal as a consumer;
♦ those who deal on the other party's written standard terms of business (commercial contracts are potentially caught under this category).

A party to a contract deals as a consumer in relation to another party if (A) neither enters into the contract in the course of a business nor holds himself out as doing so; and (B) the other party does make the contract in the course of a business; and the goods are of a type ordinarily supplied for private use or consumption. In *R and B Customs Brokers Ltd v United Dominions Trust Ltd* [1988] 1 All ER 847 the Court of Appeal held that a company could deal as a consumer having bought a second hand car for a director to use both on company business and privately. A term in the contract which excluded s 13 of the Sale of Goods Act 1979 was not effective as the company was a consumer. UCTA does not define written standard terms of business. Written terms would, however, appear to be standard where the same terms are used when supplying all customers of the business or where the same terms are always used when the two parties in question contract with each other. Where a person deals as a consumer it will not be necessary to decide whether or not the consumer deals on the other's written standard terms of business.

Where s 3 applies (unless the term is reasonable), the other party cannot by reference to any contractual term exclude or restrict liability in respect of a breach of contract claim to be entitled to render a contractual performance substantially different from that which was reasonably expected; or claim to be entitled to render no performance at all. Where s 3 applies, a bank cannot by reference to any contractual term (unless it dissatisfies the requirement of reasonableness) claim to be entitled to render a contractual performance, which is substantially different from that which was reasonably expected. The provision can apply where there is no breach of contract (eg where a clause enables the bank to terminate a facility (on demand) or with a variation clause).

Also caught in relation to ss (2)(ii) and (3) are attempts to subject the right of enforcing remedies to restrictive or onerous conditions, excluding or restricting rights or remedies available to the injured party, and using the rules of evidence or procedure to avoid liability. A clause in a banking contract excluding or restricting a right of set off would therefore be subject to the test of reasonableness (*Stewart Gill Ltd v Horatio Myer & Co Ltd* [1992] QB 600).

Indemnity clauses

Section 4(1) of UCTA provides that a person dealing as a consumer cannot by reference to any contractual term be made to indemnify another person (whether or not a party to the contract) in respect of liability which may be incurred by the other for negligence or breach of contract, unless the term satisfies the requirements of reasonableness. In non-consumer contracts, indemnity clauses are not affected by the Act.

The requirements of reasonableness

A term that excludes or restricts liability can only be effective if it satisfies the requirements of reasonableness. The term must have been a fair and reasonable one to include having regard to the circumstances that were, or should reasonably have been, known to or in contemplation of the parties. Whether the provisions are reasonable is to be determined at the time the contract is made so that the extent of any loss cannot itself be taken into account (s 11(1)). The onus is on the bank to establish that the test is satisfied (s 11(5)). In deciding whether the terms are reasonable, the courts will have regard to a wide range of factors, including those set out in Sch 2 to the Act. Thus, the respective bargaining power of the parties, whether the terms were negotiated (not necessarily between the parties themselves but between representatives, eg of the banks and of consumer interest), the degree of notification given to the customer and the length of the contract are relevant factors. Section 11(4) of UCTA allows the courts to take into account the resources and other factors (eg ability to obtain insurance) to be considered in the reasonableness of limitations on the amounts payable on liability for damages. The courts are more likely to declare clauses in contracts involving consumers to be unreasonable than clauses in contracts involving commercial parties like banks of equal bargaining strengths (*National Westminster Bank plc v Utrecht-America Finance Co* [2001] 3 All ER 733).

Exclusions

Schedule 1 to UCTA provides that ss 2 and 3 of the Act do not extend all contracts, including any contracts relating to the creation or transfer of securities or any right of interest in securities. Where commercial parties choose as the governing law of a bank in contract a system of law other than English law, UCTA does not apply (s 27(2): *Centrax Ltd v Citibank NA* [1999] All ER (Comm) 557).

The Unfair Terms in Consumer Contracts Directive

The Unfair Terms in Consumer Contracts Regulations 1999, SI 1999/2083 (UTCC Regulations) implement the EU Directive on Unfair Terms 1994. The regulations leave in place existing UK law and add an additional layer of regulation to consumer contracts. As such they affect the regulation of consumer banking contracts, but not commercial contracts. The UTCC regulations do not therefore apply to corporate customers.

The UTCC Regulations apply to any term in a contract between a supplier and a consumer. A consumer is defined as a natural person (and not therefore a company) who is acting for purposes that are outside his trade, business or profession. Since the regulations do not require a consumer to be acting wholly outside the business, it would appear that so long as one or more purposes are outside that person's business, he could still be a consumer despite there being a business purpose to the transaction. Thus, in the banking context a small trader with just one current account for both his business and personal matters will still be treated as a consumer. Additionally, a professional person borrowing for home renovations which are to include a new study so that he does not have to travel to work everyday, or a wife who holds shares in her husband's business, giving the bank security over her share in the matrimonial home for his business, will be treated as a consumer.

Regulation 5(1) provides that 'a contractual term which has not been individually negotiated shall be regarded as unfair if, contrary to the requirement of good faith, it causes a significant imbalance in the party's rights and obligations arising under the contract, to the detriment of the consumer'. Regulation 5(2) then goes on to state that a term shall always be regarded as not having been individually negotiated where it has been drafted in advance and the consumer has therefore not been able to influence the substance of the term. Even if a specific term or certain aspects of it have been individually negotiated, the regulations apply to the rest of the contract if an overall assessment of it indicates that it is a pre-formulated standard contract. Under the regulations, the onus of establishing that a term was individually negotiated is on the bank. Clauses from precedents, manuals, or even one previous agreement would be treated as drafted in advance and therefore be regarded as not having been individually negotiated under the regulations.

Exclusion of core provisions

Regulation 6(2) of the UTCC Regulations provides that the core provisions of a contract cannot be questioned. In other words, it is only the subsidiary terms of a contract that can be challenged as unfair, although in assessing the fairness of a particular contractual term, the courts may refer to all the other terms of the contract, including core provisions. The unfair terms which are, therefore, not capable of review under the regulations are those that relate to 'the definition of the main subject matter of the contract' or to 'the adequacy of the price and remuneration'.

Excluded also from the scope of the regulations are terms incorporated in a consumer contract in order to comply with (a) mandatory statutory or regulatory provisions of the UK or European Community or (b) the provisions or principles of international conventions to which the member states are party.

Statutory provisions cannot therefore be subject to the unfairness test under the regulations.

Unfair terms

To be unfair under the UTCC Regulations a term must be contrary to the requirement of good faith, and cause a significant imbalance against the customer; the requirement of good faith in this context is one of fair and open dealing. Openness requires that the terms should be expressed clearly and legibly. Appropriate prominence should be given to terms, which might operate at a disadvantage to the customer. Fair dealing requires that a supplier should not, whether deliberately or unconsciously, take advantage of the consumer's necessity, lack of experience of unfamiliarity with the subject matter of the contract, weak bargaining position or other factors listed in Sch 2 to the Regulations (*Director General of Fair Trading v First National Bank plc* [2001] AC 481 at 494).

The lack of good faith must cause a significant imbalance in the party's rights and obligations under the contract, to the detriment of the consumer. The obvious imbalance between a bank and a consumer is not the immediate focus of the enquiry, although it may be the reason for the imbalance in the rights and obligations. What the courts are interested in is the imbalance in contractual rights and obligations (eg in a default clause in a loan agreement, the scope of the bank's rights must be assessed in terms of the clause itself and other aspects of the facility).

Misrepresentation, mistake, duress and undue influence

Even if all the requirements of a valid contract are satisfied, the contract may nevertheless be voidable or void. A contract that is voidable creates contractual obligations between the parties but one of the parties may have the option to have the contract set aside. A contract, which is void, however, is a nullity and confers no rights on either party. A contract may be voidable due to misrepresentation, duress or undue influence. Contractual mistake, however, may render the contract void. Although a number of vitiating factors are explored in this section the emphasis is on the effect of undue influence.

Misrepresentation

A misrepresentation is a false statement or fact made by one party to a contract to the other during negotiations for the contract. To entitle the other party to release, the misrepresentation must induce him to enter into the contract. Mere sales talk or exaggerated commendations as to the value of the goods or services do not afford any grounds for relief. Thus, to describe land as 'fertile and improvable' (*Dimmock v Hallett* (1866) 2 Ch App 21) is a mere commendation and does not provide a ground for relief if the land is barren. For a statement to constitute an effective misrepresentation, the following requirements must be satisfied.

♦ An actionable misrepresentation must be an untrue statement of fact, as distinct from an expression of opinion or intention or statement of law. A misstatement of opinion or of intention, however, may involve an implicit statement of fact and thus be a ground for avoiding the contract. In *Smith v London and House Property Corpn* (1884) 24 Ch D 7 the Court of Appeal held that the purchaser was entitled to rescind a contract to purchase certain property when it was discovered that a tenant who had been described as 'most desirable' was, in fact, badly in arrears with his rent and the claimants were threatening legal action against him. The court took the view that the vendor could not possibly have entertained the opinion he expressed. Generally, a statement of intention cannot amount to a misrepresentation because it is not a statement of fact. Where a person makes a statement of intention knowing that it is false, then the statement may be regarded as one of fact. In *Edgington v Fitzmaurice* (1885) 29 Ch D 476 there was said to be a fraudulent misrepresentation when the company issued a prospectus inviting the public to subscribe for debentures stating that the company intended to use the money raised to develop the company's trade. In fact the real purpose of issuing the debentures was to raise money to pay off the company's debts.

♦ If the misrepresentation is to be a ground for relief it must have operated on the mind of the representee and actually have induced him to enter into the contract. If, therefore, the representee was unaware of the statement or if he was not induced to enter into the contract by the statement being made to him then he has no remedy. In *Redgrave v Hurd* (1881) 20 Ch D 1 a solicitor agreed to become a partner in a firm when he was informed that the business produced an income of £300 per annum. The solicitor was offered the chance to check the business accounts but declined the offer. On discovering the truth, the solicitor refused to go ahead with the agreement and raised misrepresentation as a defence in an action against him. The court held that the solicitor had no duty to check the truth of the statements made to him and the fact that he did not check them indicated that he had been induced to rely on such statements when entering into the contract. If, however, a person does check the truth of a statement made to him then he cannot later say that the statement induced him to make a contract.

Types of misrepresentation

Once it is established that there is an actionable misrepresentation, which has induced the contract, it then becomes necessary to determine the nature of the misrepresentation. The classification of the misrepresentation will depend on the state of mind of the party who makes the misrepresentation.

Innocent misrepresentation

A statement made by a person in the belief that it is true, when in fact it is not, is an innocent misrepresentation. At common law an action for damages did not lie for a mere innocent misrepresentation unless it had become a term of the contract.

Negligent misrepresentation

A negligent misrepresentation is one which is made carelessly, or without reasonable belief in its truth, and the person responsible for the misrepresentation owed a duty of care because of the special personal relationship between them under the rule in *Hedley Byrne & Co Ltd v Heller and Partners Ltd* [1964] AC 465. An action for negligent misstatement at common law is not generally pursued where it is possible to sue for damages under s 2(1) of the Misrepresentation Act 1967 which provides that a person who has entered into a contract after a misrepresentation has been made to him, and as a result of it has suffered loss, can sue for damages if the misrepresentor would be liable to damages for misrepresentation if the statement had been made fraudulently. In such circumstances, the misrepresentor is liable not withstanding the fact that the misrepresentation was not made fraudulently, unless he can prove that he had reasonable grounds to believe, and did believe up to the time the contract was made, that the facts represented were true.

Fraudulent misrepresentation

A representation is fraudulent if it is made in the absence of an honest belief that it is true. In *Derry v Peek* (1889) 14 App Cas 337 the House of Lords defined a fraudulent misrepresentation as a full statement made (a) knowingly, or (b) without belief in its truth, or (c) recklessly whether it be true or false. A plaintiff who alleges fraud on the part of the other party must show the absence of an honest belief by the other in the statement he made.

Remedies

All three types of actionable misrepresentation can give rise to the right to rescind the contract. In cases involving fraudulent misrepresentation rescission is a right, subject to the rule that any equitable remedies are available at the discretion of the court. In cases of negligent or wholly innocent misrepresentation, rescission is not available as of a right. In cases of negligent or innocent misrepresentation s 2(2) of the Misrepresentation Act 1967 allows the court to award damages in lieu of rescission. As rescission is an equitable remedy the right to rescind may be lost in a number of circumstances:

♦ where the person who has the right to rescind the contract affirms the contract either expressly or impliedly. Mere lapse of time may be sufficient to indicate that the contract has been affirmed;
♦ where it is impossible for the courts to restore the parties to their original position;
♦ where a third party has acquired a title to the goods in good faith and without notice of the seller's defect of title.

Damages for misrepresentation

The measure of damages available in respect of an actionable misrepresentation would differ according to the type of misrepresentation.

Fraudulent misrepresentation

If a fraudulent misrepresentation is proven then damages will be assessed on the basis of fraud. Such damages will attempt to restore the parties to the position they would be in if the tort had never been committed and so all expenses and losses subsequently incurred will be recoverable. In *Doyle v Olby* [1969] 2 QB 158 Lord Denning said that in the case of a fraud the defendant is bound to make restitution for all actual damages flowing directly from the fraudulent inducement (cf the assessment for damages in contract where damages are limited to what may reasonably be supposed to have been in the contemplation of the parties).

Negligent misrepresentation

Before the Misrepresentation Act 1967 was enacted, damages were available for a misrepresentation, which was not made fraudulently (unless damages could be claimed for the tort of negligent misstatement). Section 2(1) of the 1967 Act allows damages for negligent misrepresentation and states that where a person has committed a negligent misrepresentation he shall 'be so liable' as if the misrepresentation had been made fraudulently. In *Royscot Trust Ltd v Rogerson* [1991] 3 All ER 294 the Court of Appeal therefore assessed the award of damages for negligent misrepresentation on the basis of deceit. Balcombe LJ said 'in my judgment the wording of the subsection is clear: the person making the innocent [negligent] misrepresentation shall be 'so liable', ie liable to damages as if the representation had been made fraudulently'.

Wholly innocent misrepresentation

There is no right for damages for a wholly innocent misrepresentation but the court does have a discretion to award damages under s 2(2) which allows the award of damages in lieu of rescission in cases of non-fraudulent misrepresentation (ie in cases of negligent or wholly innocent misrepresentation). In such cases there must have been a non-fraudulent misrepresentation that would have entitled the claimant to rescind the contract, and the claimant must claim that the contract has been or ought to be rescinded. Further, the court must consider it equitable to award damages rather than rescission.

Mistake

A mistake on the part of the parties to a contract will not generally invalidate it. Certain types of mistake are regarded as being so fundamental that they may operate to nullify consent and so prevent a contract coming into existence. In such circumstances no legal rights are conferred on the parties and if the contract relates to property title will not pass to the buyer. Some of these mistakes have no effect at all on the validity of the contract. The different kinds of mistake recognized by the common law are as follows.

Common mistake

When common mistake occurs, the parties to the contract reach agreement, but they make the same fundamental mistake. Such a mistake can make the contract void, although this may not necessarily be the case. The courts have expressed the view that common mistake can arise as follows.

(a) **Mistake as to the existence of the subject matter:** There is no contract where either one or both of the parties are mistaken as to the existence of the subject matter of the contract. The contract is thereby avoided for mistake. This situation should be contrasted to one where the goods ceased to exist after the contract was made but before the buyer took delivery of them. In this situation, the contract is not void for mistake and the courts will then have to determine where the risk of loss lies.

(b) **Mistake as to ownership:** If the seller of the property does not in fact own the property at the time when the contract is entered into it may be possible to avoid the contract for mistake. Mistake as to ownership is only capable of making the contract void at common law where the contract is not one into which a statute implies a term but where the seller has the right to sell, eg *Cooper v Phibbs* (1867) LR 2 HL 149 where A agreed to take a lease of a fishery from B but unknown to both the parties, A was already the tenant for life of the fishery and B had no ownership at all.

(c) **Mistake as to quality:** It is unlikely that a common mistake as to the quality of goods being sold will have any effect on the contract. In *Bell v Lever Bros* [1932] AC 161 the defendants who wished to make Bell redundant entered into a compensation agreement under which Bell was entitled to receive £30,000 for the early termination of his contract of employment. In fact, Bell could have been dismissed without any compensation because of earlier breaches of his contract of employment. At the time the redundancy agreement was entered into the defendants were not aware that Bell had broken company rules which would have entitled them to dismiss him. The jury concluded that Bell had either not appreciated that he had breached company rules or had forgotten his breach of these rules at the time the contract for compensation was entered into. The court therefore concluded that Bell was entitled to receive the compensation agreed and the contract was not void for mistake.

Mutual mistake

There is said to be a mutual mistake when the parties to the contract are at cross purposes so that there is never any real agreement. The offer made relates to one thing and it is accepted under the belief that it relates to something quite different. If the court concludes that a reasonable man would not infer that the view of either the offeror or the offeree was objectively what was intended, then the contract can be void for mistake. In *Raffles v Wichelhaus* (1864) 2 H C 906 a contract for the sale of goods, due to arrive in Liverpool on the ship 'Peerless' from Bombay, was entered into. In fact, two ships by the same name sailed from Bombay to Liverpool. The defendants had in mind the ship that set sail in October, whilst the claimant had in mind that which set sail in December. The court held that there was never a binding contract because there was no consensus ad idem (that is agreement on the timing).

Unilateral mistake

A unilateral mistake occurs where only one of the parties is mistaken in respect of either the identity of the other contracting party, or as to the terms of the contract. Such a mistake may render the agreement void. Unilateral mistake can occur as follows.

(a) **Mistake as to identity:** a mistake as to the identity of the parties may be held to negate consent. Thus, where a seller intends to make an offer to B the contract will be void if C accepts the offer by inducing the seller to believe that he is, in reality, B. It may, however, be difficult to prove mistaken identity where the parties are in each other's presence at the time the contract is made. Where the parties enter into a contract when both are personally present there is a presumption that the parties enter into the contract with each other irrespective of their correct names. In *Phillips v Brooks Ltd* [1919]

2 QB 243 a rogue called North agreed to purchase jewellery from the plaintiff, and as he was about to make payment by cheque, he represented that he was Sir George Bullough and gave the correct address for this person. The plaintiff checked a telephone directory which confirmed the information given by North. The plaintiff then allowed North to take the jewellery in return for a cheque on which North had forged Sir George Bullough's signature. The cheque was dishonoured, and the plaintiff claimed the return of the jewellery, which had been pledged to a third party, who had acted in good faith. The court held the plaintiff sold and intended to sell the jewellery to the person who came into the shop (North) and therefore there was no mistake as to identity when the contract was made. The *Phillips case* was affirmed in *Lewis v Averay* [1972] 1 QB 198 where it was held that the plaintiff intended to contract with the person before him when he sold goods to a rogue who represented himself as Richard Green, the actor. The court concluded that there was no mistake as to identity since the plaintiff had intended to contract with the person before him.

Where the parties enter into a contract by correspondence and are not in each other's presence when the contract is concluded, mistake as to identity can void the contract, but only if the mistake is as to identity of the other party. It is not enough that there is a mistake as to the attributes of the other party. In *Cundy v Lindsay* (1878) 3 App Cas 459 a rogue called Blenkarn ordered goods by post and signed the letter containing his signature so that it looked like 'Blenkiron Co', a respectable firm known to the plaintiffs. The plaintiff sent the goods at the address given by the rogue but they never received payment. The rogue then sold the goods to a third party and in an action by the plaintiffs the court held that there was no valid contract between the claimant and the rogue. The contract was void for mistake because the claimants were mistaken as to the identity of the person with whom they were dealing.

A mere mistake as to the credit-worthiness or other attributes of one of the parties is not sufficient to void the contract (*King's Norton Metal Co Ltd v Edridge Merrett & Co Ltd* (1897) 14 TLR 98.

(b) **Mistake as to the terms of the contract:** a mistake as to the terms of a contract may negate the consent of the other party. In *Hartog v Colin & Shields* [1938] 3 All ER 566 it was held that there was a fundamental mistake when the defendants agreed to buy rabbit skins at a certain price per pound when, in fact, they were offered for sale with the price being quoted for each piece. The court concluded there was no contract and the claimants could not reasonably have supposed that the offer expressed the true intention of the defendants. Again, a mistake as to the terms of the contract were not sufficient to set aside the contract (*Smith v Hughes* (1871) LR 6 QB 597).

Non Est Factum (It is not my deed)

A party who signs a document is bound by the legal obligations embodied in it regardless of whether or not he read the document. Where a party signs a document that turns out to be entirely different from the document he believed he was signing, however, he can plead that the document is not binding on him. The plea is not available to a person who negligently fails to enquire into the nature or effect of the document, but has been applied to assist persons who due to some infirmity did not appreciate the nature of the document executed. Thus, in *Foster v Mackinnon* (1869) LR CP 704 an elderly and nearly blind man was induced to endorse a bill of exchange under the belief he was executing a guarantee similar to the one he had executed on previous occasions. It was held that the document should be set aside because it was executed under a mistaken belief as to its character even though to a person with normal sight its character would have been readily apparent. In *Saunders v Anglia Building Society* [1970] AC 1004 an old lady signed a document that she thought was a deed making a gift of a house to her nephew when, in fact, the document amounted to a transfer of the house to her nephew's business associates. The court held that the transaction would not be set aside because the document she intended to execute was not fundamentally or radically different from the one she in fact signed, and she could easily have seen from the beginning of the document that the transfer was expressed to be made to a person other than her nephew.

A person who signs a blank document is likely to be regarded as having been careless if incorrect figures are subsequently entered (*United Dominion Trust Ltd v Western* [1776] QB 513).

Duress

Historically, the common law would only hold a document voidable for duress if the contract was entered into as a result of the threat of unlawful physical violence. A threat to goods was not enough. In recent years, however, a doctrine of economic duress has sometimes led to the contract being held voidable because the person coerced into making the contract did not really consent. Further, if one of the parties to the contract exerts undue influence over the other the contract may be voidable in equity. The basis of both duress and undue influence is that no real consent is given to the contract.

In recent years the doctrine of economic duress has been recognized and in *Occidental Worlwide Investment Corpn v Skibs A/S Avanti* [1976] 1 Lloyd's Rep 293 Kerr J rejected a claim of economic duress because, although there was commercial pressure, there was nothing under the law that could be regarded as 'a coercion of will so as to vitiate consent'. In other words, for the courts to recognize duress it must be shown that the victim's consent is negated or destroyed so that consent to the contract does not really exist. Generally, in order to amount to economic duress the threat must be to do an unlawful act (eg break a contract) although an immoral but lawful act may suffice. Thus, in *Atlas Express Ltd v Kafco (Importers and Distributors) Ltd* [1989] 1 All ER 641 the defendants imported basketware and distributed it to retailers. They entered into a contract with the claimants, a national carrier, under which the claimants were to distribute the basketware to Woolworths shops nationwide. The claimant's depot manager subsequently sought to renegotiate the contract of carriage and the defendants agreed because they were heavily dependant on the contract with Woolworths and could find no alternative carrier. The court held that the defendants did not have to pay the additional amount under the renegotiation contract. The court held that consent to the new terms was vitiated by economic duress. Economic duress is unlikely to lead to banking contracts being vitiated. In *Crescendo Management Pty Ltd v Westpac Banking Corpn* (1988) 19 NSW LR 40 the court held that in the absence of causation, economic duress is not made out. In that case the bank had refused to hand over moneys unless the security document was signed and although the court regarded the pressure that the bank applied as being unlawful, it concluded that it had played no part in the execution of the mortgage, which had occurred before the pressure was applied. Further, the courts have held that commercial pressure that is not of itself unlawful or unconscionable, even to the point where the party subjected to the pressure has little choice but to act as he did, cannot have the transaction set aside for duress. Thus, in *CTN Cash & Carry Ltd v Gallagher Ltd* [1994] 4 All ER 714 the court held that it is possible that a threat to perform a lawful act coupled with a demand for repayment might amount to economic duress. It would be extremely difficult for such an action to succeed when the agreement is made between two commercial companies and the person making the demand believes it to be valid.

Undue influence

Historically, the limits of duress have been very narrow and the courts of equity have therefore developed the doctrine of undue influence that will allow equity to set aside gifts or contracts on the basis of undue influence. A distinction needs to be drawn, however, between actual and presumed undue influence.

Actual undue influence

Actual undue influence is similar to duress, since it is necessary for the person seeking to have the contract set aside to firmly establish excessive pressure. There is no need to establish either a special relationship of any type or previous dealings between the parties. Thus, in *Williams v Bayley* (1866) LR 1 HL 200 a mortgage agreement under which a colliery owner mortgaged his colliery to a bank was set aside because the bank indirectly threatened the owner that, if he did not enter into the arrangement, his son would be prosecuted for forgery. The court concluded held that the colliery owner did not voluntarily enter into the agreement. Although the person alleging the undue influence must prove such pressure was exerted, he does not have to show that the agreement subsequently entered into was manifestly disadvantageous to him. In *CIBC Mortgages plc v Pitt* [1993] 4 ALL ER 433 the Lords held that actual undue influence is a species of fraud and that just as a person who perpetrated a fraud cannot argue the transaction was beneficial to the person defrauded, so a person exercising actual undue influence cannot argue that the contract was beneficial to the person influenced. The agreement will be set aside as a matter of justice, because the wrong-doer's conduct prevented the wronged party from exercising free will and a properly informed choice.

Actual undue influence has become less important as duress has become easier to establish, with the result that the boundaries between the two are increasingly blurred.

Presumed undue influence

Presumed undue influence falls into two categories as follows.

(1)   Certain types of relationship give rise to an irrefutable presumption of undue influence, eg parent and child, solicitor and client, trustee and beneficiary, religious adviser and disciple but not husband and wife. In cases where there is a presumption of undue influence and it can be shown that the contract was manifestly to the disadvantage of the party influenced, the contract will be set aside unless the dominant party can prove that there was no undue influence (*Allcard v Skinner* [1887] 36 Ch D 145). The justification for there being no presumption of undue influence of a husband over his wife are said to be commercial reality, domestic harmony and the ordinary expectation that wives will make gifts, and transfer property, to their husbands.

(2)   Where the relationship is not within those that give rise to a presumption of undue influence, undue influence may still be presumed if the influenced party proves as a matter of fact that there existed a relationship of trust and confidence between himself and the other party. There is no reason why the other party in whom trust is reposed cannot be a bank (*Lloyd's Bank v Bundy* [1975] 1 QB 326). Additionally, although there is no automatic presumption of undue influence between husband and wife, undue influence may be presumed in cases where either party has proven that they placed trust and confidence in their spouse. In such cases, the party subject to the influence must prove the contract was manifestly disadvantageous. In such a situation it will then be for the other party, in whom trust has been reposed, to disprove that undue influence actually existed. Presumed undue influence can occur where the relationship is between a bank and its customer. Thus, in *Lloyd's Bank v Bundy* [1965] QB 326 the bank obtained from one of its customers a guarantee covered by a charge over land to secure an overdraft granted to the customer's son. The father was elderly and naïve in business

matters, and the property charged by him was his home and only valuable asset. The branch manager did not disclose to him the extent of the financial problems faced by his son, and failed to suggest that the father seek independent advice before executing the guarantee. The charge under guarantee was set aside on the basis that the relationship between the defendant and the bank was one of trust and confidence and the court could intervene to prevent this relationship from being abused. The bank had breached its fiduciary duty of care by not advising the defendant to obtain independent legal advice. The *Bundy case* is unusual and the bank's failure to volunteer advice does not normally lead to the creation of a fiduciary relationship. The court held, however, that a fiduciary relationship exists where the customer has placed such trust and confidence in the bank as to give it influence over him. The principle was clarified in *National Westminster Bank plc v Morgan* [1985] AC 686 where the House of Lords held that in order to establish undue influence, the customer must show that the bank had exerted a dominant influence over the customer and that the contract entered into was manifestly disadvantageous to the customer. In the Morgan case, the wife, who was also a customer of the bank, expressed her unwillingness to execute a charge covering the husband's business ventures. The branch manager reassured her erroneously, though in good faith, that the charge secured only the amount advanced to refinance the original mortgage over the matrimonial home. The branch manager failed to advise the wife to seek independent legal advice. On the husband's death, the bank sought to sell the property in order to recover the balance outstanding under the refinancing arrangement. The Lords held that the bank had not committed a breach of a duty of care or of a fiduciary duty owed to the wife. The relationship between the parties had remained that of banker and customer and, on the facts, the branch manager had not exercised undue influence in order to induce the wife to execute the charge.

Sometimes a husband may exert undue influence over or make a misrepresentation to his wife, who then agrees to give the matrimonial home, or other assets, as a security for a loan made to the husband's business. The wife can have the agreement set aside, as against the husband, if either undue influence or misrepresentation can be shown. The question whether or not the wife can have the loan set aside against the bank was looked at in *Barclays Bank plc v O'Brien* [1993] 4 All ER 417 where the House of Lords held that where a wife agreed to stand surety for the debts of a company in which the husband had a direct financial interest but in which the wife did not have such an interest and the creditor knew that they were husband and wife, the creditor could enforce the surety unless it was procured as a result of undue influence, misrepresentation or other legal wrong committed by the husband. Where the wife entered into the transaction only because of the undue influence, misrepresentation or other legal wrong committed by the husband, the creditor would be unable to enforce the security, on account of having constructive notice of the wife's right to set aside the transaction. In all but exceptional circumstances the creditor would not be fixed with constructive notice if he had warned the wife of the risks involved, at a meeting not attended by the husband, and advised her to get independent legal advice. On the facts, the bank knew that the couple were husband and wife and should have been put on enquiry as to the circumstances under which the wife agreed to stand surety. The legal charge on the home could therefore be set aside because the bank had not warned the wife of the risks and had neither advised her to obtain independent legal advice. The rule in *O'Brien* applied not only to husband and wife but to any co-habitees and other vulnerable parties.

In *Royal Bank of Scotland plc v Etridge (No 2)* [1998] 4 All ER 705 the Court of Appeal reviewed the situation where a wife charges the matrimonial home by way of security for a loan to the husband's business as follows.

(1)   Where the wife deals with the bank through a solicitor, the bank is not ordinarily put on enquiry: the creditor is entitled to assume that the solicitor has considered whether there is a sufficient conflict of interest to make it necessary for him to advise the wife to obtain independent advice.

(2)   Where the surety does not approach the creditor through a solicitor, then it will be normally sufficient if the creditor (bank) urges her to obtain independent legal advice before entering into the transaction.

(3)   Where the solicitor gives the surety advice he does so exclusively as her solicitor. The creditor (bank) is entitled to assume that the solicitor is acting entirely in her interests even if the solicitor is also acting for the principle debtor. If the solicitor accepts the creditor's instructions to advise the surety, he still acts as her solicitor and not the creditor's solicitor when he interviews her.

(4)   The creditor is not fixed with imputed notice of what the solicitor learns in the course of advising the surety even if he is also the creditor's solicitor.

(5)   The creditor is entitled to rely on the fact that the solicitor undertook the task of explaining the transaction to the surety as indication that he considered himself sufficiently independent to give advice. The creditor is not required to question the solicitor's independence, even if he knows that the solicitor is also the principle debtor's solicitor. The creditor need not question the sufficiency of any advice given by the solicitor.

(6)   Exceptionally, the creditor will still be fixed with constructive notice of vitiating factors even though the surety has sought legal advice. These factors are:

(a)   the proposed transaction is so manifestly disadvantageous to the surety that no competent solicitor could possibly advise her to enter into the transaction;

(b)   the bank has material information that is not available to the solicitor;

(c)   the creditor asks the solicitor to explain the transaction to the surety and to confirm that he has done so and the solicitor fails to supply the necessary confirmation that he has advised her.

The creditor (bank) will be fixed with constructive notice of the vitiating factor if he proceeds with the transaction.

The issue ultimately, at the time when value is given and in the light of all the information in the creditor's possession, including its knowledge of the state of the principle debtor's account, the relationship of the parties and the availability of legal advice for the surety, is that there is still a risk that the surety has entered into the transaction as a result of the principle debtor's misrepresentation or undue influence.

Following the *Etridge case*, the responsibility for protecting sureties in transaction of this nature has effectively passed from the bank to the solicitor advising the wife or other vulnerable surety. In the majority of cases, therefore, a bank can be certain of enforcing its security after it has received a certificate from the surety's solicitor confirming that the surety has been advised as to the nature and effect of the transaction.

Illegal contracts

A contract, although otherwise valid, may be made unenforceable if it is illegal either because the purpose of the contract is unlawful or the method of performance intended is illegal. A contract the purpose of which is illegal is unenforceable and therefore void, with the result that neither party can enforce it. A contract that is lawful at its inception may be carried out in an unlawful manner; in such a case, whether an innocent party who enters into the contract or lawfully performs his part of the contract can maintain an action depends largely on the purpose of the role of law or statute that makes the performance of the contract in a certain manner unlawful. Moreover, an innocent party who refuses to participate in the illegality is not deprived of his rights. The following types of contracts can be affected by illegality.

♦   The courts held at common law held certain types of contracts to be illegal on the grounds of public policy (eg contracts entered into between parties the purpose of which is to commit a crime or tort). Thus, an agreement tending towards the maintenance of litigation is illegal unless the party giving financial assistance has a genuine and financial interest in the case. In *Trendtex Trading Corpn v Credit Suisse* [1980] 3 All ER 721 it was held that a guarantee held by Credit Suisse to pay the legal costs of an action brought by Trendtex against the Central Bank of Nigeria was not void for maintenance. Credit Suisse had shown it had a substantial interest in the outcome of the legal proceedings since that was the only possibility it had of recovering amounts owed to it by Trendtex.

♦ The common law treats certain types of contracts as void, eg contracts to oust the jurisdiction of the courts are void on grounds of public policy; contracts in restraint of trade (whether it be a restraint on the freedom of an employee to use his skills or set up a rival business) are void if these restrictions are unreasonable.

♦ Certain types of contract are made illegal by statute and in such cases the statute itself will impose the penalty, eg the Gaming Act 1845 provides that all gaming and wagering contracts, whereby one party is to win and the other is to lose on the accounts of an uncertain future event, are null and void and so neither party can enforce the agreement.

1.3 Regulating competition

Competition law

Competition law regulates the way businesses compete and is intended to promote open competition in the interests of economic efficiency and the protection of consumers. It regulates three main areas:

♦ agreements between businesses which restrict competition, eg cartels to fix prices;
♦ the exercise of market power by a business which enjoys either a monopoly or a large market share;
♦ takeovers and mergers which reduce the number of competitors in a market and which may create a new business with considerable market power.

Political factors, eg employment policies and encouraging inter-state trade, can be important considerations in regulating competition.

The main source of UK competition law is the Enterprise Act 2002 which supercedes the Competition Act 1998 and the Fair Trading Act 1973. The Competition Act 1998 came into force on 1 March 2000 with the twin objective of improving the effectiveness of domestic competition law and bringing UK law in line with EC law. The Act introduced two new prohibitions (based on the provisions of Articles 81 and 82 of the Treaty of Rome) on anti-competitive agreements and abuse of dominant position. There are criminal and civil sanctions for breach of the prohibitions. Additionally, any person injured by a breach of the legislation may seek damages so that competitors and consumers injured by anti-competitive behaviour may be entitled to compensation. The 1998 Act prohibits 'agreements between undertakings, decisions by associations of undertakings or concerted parties which:

(a) may affect trade within the UK; and

(b)   have as their object or effect the prevention, restriction or distortion of competition within the UK' (s 2).

The Enterprise Act 2002 applies these prohibitions to both informal and formal agreements, whether or not they are in writing. Agreements to which the prohibitions apply are automatically void. The European Commission has rejected the notion that banking is somehow different and does not fall within this rule. Thus, the Commission has applied Article 81(1) to various inter-bank agreements eg the Commission objected to provisions in agreements between European Savings Banks under which they undertook not to extend business into each other's geographical territories; or agreements where banks were given exclusive rights to market distribution of common products (European Commission, 21st Report on Competition Policy (EC Commission, Brussels, 1991)). The Commission has also monitored the target system (the real time gross settlement system) operated for the Euro by the European Central Bank, since it competes with the Euro Payment Scheme of the European Bankers Association (Commissioner van Miert, EU Competition Policy in the Banking Sector, Speech to Belgian Bankers Association, 22 September 1998).

The Enterprise Act 2002 is intended to apply to 'horizontal' agreements, ie agreements between businesses operating at the same level in the production and distribution chain (OFT 401, the Chapter 1 Prohibition).

The Enterprise Act 2002 sets out a non-exhaustive list of the types of agreements covered by the prohibition (the list is identical to that contained in Article 81) that prohibits, as incompatible with the common market, all agreements between undertakings, decisions where associations of undertakings and concerted parties may affect trade between member states and which have their object as or effect the prevention, restriction or distortion of a competition, and in particular those that: directly or indirectly fix purchase or selling prices or any other trading condition; limit or control production, markets, technical development or investment; share markets or sources of supply; apply dissimilar conditions to equivalent trading transaction with other trading parties, thereby placing them at a competitive disadvantage; make the conclusion of contracts subject to the acceptance by other parties of supplementary obligations which, by their nature or according to commercial usage, have no connection with the subject of such contracts.

There is no minimum size below which a market is too small to be covered by the prohibition on agreements etc which may affect trade. The Director General of Fair Trading takes the view that in relation to agreements etc that have as object or effect the prevention of competition, the prohibition will not be breached unless the agreement has an appreciable effect (where the combined market share of the parties to the agreement, decision or practice is less than 25% the agreement is unlikely to have appreciable effect). Additionally, agreements in breach of the prohibition between businesses whose combined turnover does not exceed £20 million are exempt from penalty.

The Enterprise Act 2002 contains a list of cases in which the application of the prohibition is excluded. They include mergers, agreements etc subject to scrutiny under other legislation, planning restrictions and professional rules. As a result of the Financial Services and Markets Act 2000 there are now specific powers in respect of bank mergers in the UK. Prior to scrutiny by the courts, a certificate of the bank's regulator must be filed with the court stating that the transferee has adequate financial resources (ss 106, 111, Sch 12, Pt 2). A merger or acquisition will only be blocked on prudential grounds where the merger or acquisition is for a quick investment gain or for the purpose of sale or of breaking up the target bank in ways which are detrimental to depositors. The Cruickshank Report (*Competition in UK Banking* (London, HMSO, 2000)) 'called for UK merger law to be tightened to ensure effective competition in promoted, to allow the entry of new providers and to improve services'. The report recommended that as an interim measure, all proposed mergers with banks, with material shares in a particular market or related markets, should be referred to the Competition Commission for investigation (in 2001, the Competition Commission judged a merger between one of the four big banks and a former building society anti-competitive by eliminating an important force for change in the market for personal deposit accounts and the highly concentrated market for banking services for small and medium-sized enterprises (Competition Commission, Lloyd's TSB Group plc and Abbey National plc, Cm 5208, 2001)).

Individual or block exemptions to agreements may be granted if they comply with criteria set out (identical to those set out in Article 81(3) of the Treaty of Rome) which provide: that, before an exemption can be given, the agreement must be shown to contribute to the production or distribution of goods, or for promoting technical or economic progress; that the agreement allows consumers a fair share of the resulting benefit; that the agreement does not impose restrictions which are not indefensible to the attainment of the first two conditions; that competition is not eliminated in the substantial part of the relevant products market). Individual exemption may be granted to a particular agreement on the request of one of the parties to it (a detailed analysis of the relevant market and the effect on it of the agreement in question will normally be required).

Where a party to an agreement thinks it may infringe the prohibition they may notify the agreement to the Office of Fair Trading for guidance or decision as to whether or not it infringes the prohibition. This effectively amounts to an application to the Office of Fair Trading for an opinion on whether or not the agreement is exempt. After giving such guidance, the Office of Fair Trading may take no further action in respect of such an agreement unless: he believes there has been a material change of circumstances since giving his guidance; there is reasonable suspicion that the information on which his guidance was based was incomplete, false or misleading in a material particular; one of the parties applies to him for a decision in relation to the agreement; a complaint is registered by a person who is not a party to the agreement.

Abuse of dominant position

Chapter II of the Enterprise Act 2002 covers 'any conduct on the part of one of more undertakings which amounts to the abuse of a dominant position in a market is prohibited if it may affect trade within the UK' (this prohibition reproduces Article 82 of the Treaty of Rome except that it prohibits abuses that have effects on trade within the UK. The prohibition does not prohibit dominance but the abuse of a dominant position. The prohibition came into effect on the 1 March 2000 under the preceding legislation. There are exclusions from this prohibition that include: conduct which results in a merger covered by the Fair Trading Act 1973 or which is subject to the jurisdiction of the European Commission under the EC merger regulations; undertakings entrusted with the operation of 'services of a general economic interest' or a 'revenue producing monopoly'; conduct engaged in to comply with a legal requirement; avoidance of conflict with international obligations; conduct relating to coal or steel products where the European Commission has exclusive jurisdiction under the European Coal and Steel Treaty; and on the order of the Secretary of State 'exceptional and compelling reasons of public policy'. Infringement that consists of 'conduct of minor significance', where the annual turnover of the business involved does not exceed £50 million, is exempt from penalty. It is intended that the interpretation and application of this prohibition should follow closely the implementation of Article 82.

The principle test of dominance is the ability of a business to act independently of competitive pressures. A number of factors may be relevant in assessing whether a business enjoys a dominant position (Article 82). They include: market share; customer power, which may balance the power of an otherwise dominant business; barriers to the entry of new businesses into the market, which may include regulatory barriers such as licensee requirements, intellectual property rights, strategic advantages enjoyed by a business being the first in a particular market, and any evidence of predatory behaviour designed to exclude or deter new market entrants (*United Brands v Commission* [1978] 1 CMLR 429). The Office of Fair Trading has indicated that a business with a market share of less than 40% is unlikely be considered 'dominant', but dominance may be established with a smaller market share in appropriate circumstances. Cases of joint dominance are also covered under the prohibition, eg where two or more businesses are jointly dominant in a particular market and act in a concerted fashion to abuse that dominance.

The Act gives a non-exhaustive list of types of conduct that may amount to abuse of a dominant position and include: directly or indirectly imposing unfair purchase or selling prices or other unfair trading conditions; limiting production, markets or technical development to the prejudice of consumers; applying dissimilar conditions to equivalent transactions with other trading parties, thereby placing them at a competitive disadvantage; making the conclusion of contract subject to acceptance by the other parties of supplementary obligations which, by their nature or accordance to commercial usage, have no connection with the subject of the contracts.

There is no scope for exemption from this prohibition but a person may apply to the Office of Fair Trading for their conduct to be considered for guidance or decision as to whether or not it infringes the prohibition. The DGFT is not obliged to give such guidance, but if he does so, he may not subsequently take action in respect of the conduct in question unless: he has reasonable grounds for believing that there has been a material change of circumstances since his guidance was given; he has reasonable suspicion that the information on which his guidance was based was incomplete, false or misleading in a material particular; a complaint about the conduct is made to him.

Powers of investigation

The Office of Fair Trading has extensive powers of investigation to help determine whether there has been a breach of either of the above prohibitions. They include powers to require the production of documents and/or the supply of information and to enter premises with or without a court warrant.

Control of monopolies under the Enterprise Act 2002

Part IV of the Fair Trading Act 1973 contained provisions to control the abuse of monopoly power. These provisions were largely unaffected by the Competition Act 1998 except that the new Competition Commission took over the powers formerly exercised by The Monopolies and Mergers Commission and the DGFT have enhanced investigatory powers.

The Enterprise Act 2002 requires the Office of Fair Trading and the Competition Commission to keep under review the carrying on of commercial activities in the UK and to collect relevant information with a view to becoming aware of monopoly situations and anti-competitive practises. Under the Act, a monopoly exists in relation to the supply of goods of any description where at least one quarter of the goods of that description are supplied by or to:

(1) one person;

(2) members of a single group of companies;

(3) members of group of persons who, either voluntarily or otherwise, so conduct their affairs as to prevent, restrict or distort competition in connection with the production or supply of goods of that description or where as a result of one of more agreements, goods of that description are not supplied in the UK.

Where it appears to the Office of Fair Trading that there are grounds for believing that a monopoly situation exists in relation to the supply of goods or services of any description, the Office has the power to require any person who produces or supplies goods or services of that description, or to whom such goods or services are supplied, to provide him with information on a number of issues in order to enable him to decide whether or not to refer the monopoly to the Competition Commission. The Secretary of State also has the power to make a reference to the Competition Commission where it appears to him that a monopoly situation exists or may exist.

After a reference, an investigation is undertaken by a group of at least three members of the Competition Commission who may take oral and written evidence and who have wide discretion in respect of procedure. On completion of its investigation the Competition Commission will produce a report for the Secretary of State on whether or not a monopoly situation exists, and where the reference so requires, whether it operates against the public interest. If the Competition Commission reports that a monopoly exists, the Secretary of State can make a number of orders relating to the future behaviour of the monopolist. Where the Office of Fair Trading considers that a monopoly situation exists and operates against the public interest, he may recommend to the Secretary of State that he accepts an undertaking in lieu of making a reference to the Competition Commission if the Office believes that such undertakings would be sufficient safeguard to deal with the adverse affects of the monopoly.

Control of mergers under the Enterprise Act 2002

Mergers are controlled under Act, which gives the Secretary of State power to refer a merger to the Competition Commission. The Secretary of State has discretion to refer a merger to the Competition Commission when two or more enterprises cease to be distinct and either (a) the value of the assets taken over exceed £70 billion or (b) a market share of 25% for the supply of goods or services in the UK or a substantial part thereof is created or strengthened. The most important factor taken into consideration in deciding whether to make a reference to the Competition Commission is the effect of the merger on competition. Once a reference is made, the Competition Commission is required to produce a report on the question (1) whether a merger situation has been created and, if so, (2) whether it operates contrary to the public interest. The reference must specify a time limit (not exceeding six months) for production of the report by the Competition Commission, and no action may be taken in respect of the merger unless the report is made before the end of a period. The Secretary of State may, however, extend the time limit by up to a further three months if there are special reasons why the report cannot be produced within the six-month period. If the Competition Commission concludes that there is a merger situation, that operates contrary to public interest, it must consider what action should be taken to remedy or prevent adverse effects, and include any recommendations as to such action.

The Enterprise Act 2002 provides for a system of formal pre-notification of a merger. The parties to the merger must give information as to the parties involved, the financial details of the merger, the proposed timescale, and whether the merger is subject to the city code on take-overs and mergers. The Secretary of State then has 20 working days in which to consider the merger in order to decide whether to seek undertakings or to make a reference to the Competition Commission.

Confidentiality

When information is disclosed in confidence, the law may impose on the recipient an obligation to respect that confidence and may restrain the use or disclosure of that information without the consent of the person confiding. Protection of confidential information is governed by the common law and the boundaries of the law are unclear. The law is flexible and protects trade secrets, commercial information (eg customer details or marketing plans (as in *Marshall (Export) Ltd v Guinle* [1976] FFR 345). It may also protect personal information (*Stephens v Avery* [1988] 1 Ch 457) and government information. In protecting business and commercial information, confidentiality operates as adjunct to the statutory intellectual property regimes, especially patterns and copyright. Thus a business may use confidentiality to protect details of a secret invention or process, as an alternative to patenting it.

Where the parties are in a contractual relationship, an obligation of confidentiality may arise as a result either of an express or implied term of the contract (*Tournier*). A duty of confidentiality may be imposed where the parties are not in a contractual relationship and the protection of confidential information is then said to rest on broad equitable principles (*Seager v Copydex* [1967] 2 All ER 415). In order for information to be protected as confidential two conditions must be satisfied:

♦ the information must have the 'necessary quality of confidence', ie the information is not in the public domain;
♦ it must have been imparted in circumstances importing an obligation of confidence.

In certain relationships a duty of confidentiality is imposed automatically by the law so that any information (or some) received during the course of the relationship must be regarded as confidential: eg banker and customer; solicitor and client; employer and employee. The duty of confidentiality is broken either where the information is used by the recipient for his own benefit or is disclosed by the recipient to any other person. It is irrelevant that the use or disclosure was entirely innocent. The only defences to a claim for breach of confidentiality is either to deny that the information was confidential or the claim that the disclosure was justified (within the banker/customer relationship and under the *Tournier* case there are a number of circumstances where disclosure of confidential information obtained by a bank may be justified. The burden, however, is on the bank to bring itself within the exceptions. Disclosure may thus be justified on the grounds of: public policy;

compulsion by statute; in the interest of the bank, eg where disclosure is required because the bank is involved in litigation; express consent (implied consent no longer being sufficient).

The remedies available for breach of confidential information are for the courts to grant an injunction to restrain a further or continued breach of confidential information. Where a breach of confidence puts trade secrets or commercial information into the public domain, other businesses may be free to make use of such information and in such a situation damages may be the only remedy. An injunction may be granted to prevent the person who disclosed the confidential information exploiting that information. The injunction will be limited in time in accordance with the 'springboard principle' which means that the defendant is restrained from using the information to gain a head start over other businesses (*Terrapin v Builders Supply Company (Hayes) Ltd* [1967] RPC 375). Damages may be assessed in the same way as for conversion and will reflect the market value of the information (the fee a consultant would have charged for supplying it or the price a willing buyer would have paid the claimant for the information (*Seager v Copydex Ltd (No 2)* [1969] RPC 250). Alternatively, the claimant may seek an account of profits made by the use of the information.

The Takeover Panel and the Takeover Code

Established in 1986, the Takeover Panel is the regulatory body that publishes and administers the City Code on Takeovers and Mergers. The Code is designed to ensure fair and equal treatment of all shareholders in relation to takeovers and to provide an orderly framework within which takeovers are conducted. The Code, in general, applies to offers for all listed and unlisted public companies considered by the Panel to be resident in the UK, the Channel Islands and the Isle of Man.

The Code does not have (nor does it seek to have) the force of law but it represents the collective opinion of those professionally involved in the field of takeovers regarding business standards and how fairness to shareholders should be achieved.

Two

The banker-customer relationship

2.1 Creation of the banker-customer relationship

In *Joachimson v Swiss Bank Corpn* [1921] 3 KB 110 the court expressed the view that the contract on which the banker-customer relationship is founded comes into existence in the same way as any other contract, ie by an offer and acceptance. An offer is made by the person who seeks to open an account, whether a current or deposit account, and an acceptance takes place when the bank opens an account or agrees to open an account.

It is trite law that although there is a consistent course of dealings between the bank and its customer, there is in fact a single contract existing between the parties.

Although in the normal course of events several amounts are paid into the credit of the customer's account and several withdrawals routinely made, there is a single and indivisible contract entered into between the parties (*Joachimson v Swiss Bank Corpn* [1921] 3 KB 110; *Barclays Bank Ltd v Okenarhe* [1966] 2 Lloyd's Rep 87). Nevertheless, the banker-customer relationship is rarely reduced to a single document. It usually consists of a variety of written forms, supplemented by terms implied by the law. Often standard forms will govern specific aspects of the relationship, eg borrowing or security transactions including guarantees. Banks have also adopted voluntary Codes of Practice that the courts have accepted as minimum standards of good practice.

Contractual terms applicable to corporate customers are almost entirely and inevitably reduced to writing. The contract will clearly set out the bank's terms and conditions of business so that there is little or no reliance on the implied terms that have previously underpinned the banker-customer relationship (eg as in the *Joachimson* and *Tournier* cases).

Large corporate customers, in turn, have considerable bargaining power in respect of any terms and conditions introduced into the contract. They will thus have a greater say in any express terms to which the contract is made subject.

Although the banker and customer relationship is contractual, the question that needs to be explored is what sort of contract is involved? Historically, bankers acted as depositors of plate and gold for clients (a bailment). This, however, does not explain the relationship in the context of deposits of money held by a bank where the relationship is one of debtor and creditor (*Foley v Hill* [1848] 2 HLC 28 and the bank is required to return an equivalent sum in money to the customer, on demand. Nor in this context is the relationship one of bailor and bailee under which the bank would be expected to maintain the money deposited in specie. In *Foley v Hill* the court also rejected the argument that the customer was entitled to a remedy as the beneficiary of a trust, as the bank's principals or under a fiduciary relationship.

Apart from duties arising under the contract (eg duty of care, conforming to the mandate etc), special circumstances may constitute the bank a fiduciary (is then subjected to the core fiduciary duties of loyalty and fidelity). Fiduciary duties are based on a proximate relationship with a given customer. Such proximity may arise either from the bank's assumption of the role of a fiduciary or from its awareness of circumstances that have induced the customer to regard it as having assumed such a role (*Bristol and West Building Society v Mathew* [1998] Ch 1).

In contrast, the bank's liability as a constructive trustee is incurred as a result of its nexus with the trustee or agent who has committed a breach of trust. Liability by a stranger who intermeddles with trusts property arises where (i) the bank has been accessory to, or assisted in, the trustee's breach of trust, or (ii) where the bank has received trust property in breach of trust. The bank is liable as an accessory where it has acted dishonestly and is liable for receipt if the state of its knowledge is such as to make it unconscionable for it to retain the benefit of the receipt.

Duty to exercise reasonable skill and care

A customer may attempt to recover his losses from the bank by pleading a breach of an implied duty of care in contract. This duty is implied into the banker and customer relationship by the common law or by s 13 of the Supply of Goods and Services Act 1982 which implies a term to this effect in contracts for the supply of a service in the course of a business. The duty of care may also arise concurrently in tort. Indeed, tort may impose wider obligations that are not inconsistent with obligations imposed by contract (*Tai Hing Cotton Mill Ltd v Liu Chong Hing Bank Ltd* [1986] AC 80).

The scope of the duty of care in contract has been looked at in a number of recent cases. In *Selangor United Rubber Estates Ltd v Cradock (No 3)* [1986] 1 WLR 1555 a bank produced financial assistance in connection with a takeover bid. Because of the inexperience of bank officials, the bank failed to realize that the company was, in fact, indirectly financing the acquisition of its own shares. In respect of the duty of care the court held that a bank

> 'has a duty under the contract with its customer to exercise reasonable skill and care in carrying out its obligations under the contract'.

The standard of skill and care is an objective standard applicable to bankers and an infinite variety of factors will be taken into consideration in deciding whether that standard has been discharged. These considerations include:

- ◆ prima facie the assumption that men are honest;
- ◆ the practice of bankers;
- ◆ the limited time that banks have to decide on the course of action to be taken;
- ◆ the extent to which an operation is unusual, or out of the ordinary course of business.

Where a bank is required to make enquiry (eg as to the authenticity of a signature on a cheque) then failure to make enquiry is not excused on the basis that the enquiry would prove to be futile.

The *Selangor* case was considered in *Lipkin Gorman v Karpnale & Co* [1989] 1 WLR 1340 where an action was brought against the second defendants, Lloyd's Bank plc, to hold the bank liable as constructive trustee for funds that had been misappropriated from a client account by the fraudulent drawing of cheques. The Court of Appeal held the bank was liable neither as a constructive trustee nor for negligence. A bank should only be held liable for breach of the duty of skill and care if the circumstances are such that any reasonable cashier would hesitate to pay the cheque without a referral to his supervisor who, in turn, would hesitate to authorize payment without further enquiry. Moreover, a bank cannot be expected to review individual accounts on a continuing or periodic basis. A bank's duty of care does not arise in respect of ordinary or usual transactions involving the drawing up of cheques on the customer's account by a duly authorized signatory.

In reviewing earlier authorities, the court in *Barclays Bank plc v Quincecare Ltd* [1992] 4 All ER 363 recognized that a balance has to be struck between the bank's delegation to conform to its customers mandate and (at the same time) discharging its duty of care. A bank

> 'must refrain from executing an order if and for so long as the bank was "put on enquiry" in the sense that it had reasonable grounds for believing that an order was an attempt to misappropriate funds'.

Further, in discharging its duty of skill and care the bank is required to follow no more than its normal procedure and practices (*Schioler v National Westminster Bank Ltd* [1970] 2 QB 716). Moreover, a bank is not in breach of the duty of care if it fails to inform customers of new products (*Surveyor & Douglas v Midland Bank plc* [1999] 1 All ER (Comm) 612).

Whether the bank owes a duty of skill and care to third parties in tort will depend on the proximity of the relationship (*Hedley Byrne v Heller & Partners* [1964] AC 465).

Attempts to impose express obligations in banking contracts

A person who opens an account with a bank in the UK will normally be asked to complete and sign a bank mandate form instructing the bank to open an account. While the mandate form will contain some of the terms of the contract, such forms do not attempt to define the features of the banker and customer relationship. Indeed, the Jack Committee (Banking Services: Law and Practice Report, Cm 622) in 1989 rejected the idea of a 'model contract' even for business customers on the grounds that the general mandate form signed by the customer on opening his account gives the banks flexibility to respond to competition.

Implied obligations arising under the account arrangement

The common law recognizes that a number of obligations arise when a current or deposit account is opened. In *Joachimson v Swiss Bank Corpn* [1921] 3 KB 110 Atkin LJ held that a number of implied terms arise as a result of entering into the banker and customer relationship as follows.

The duty to conform to the customer's mandate

The bank's duty to its customer to fulfill the customer's mandate, either with regard to the payment of cheques or the collection of such instruments, has both positive and negative aspects.

The bank must pay a cheque or other instrument drawn by the customer if it appears to be proper (ie it is properly drawn and dated by the customer) and there is a sufficient credit balance on the customer's account or the amount of the instrument is within any agreed overdraft limit. In *Fleming v Bank of New Zealand* [1900] AC 577 a bank was guilty of wrongful dishonour, and thereby guilty of a breach of duty, when it dishonoured a cheque drawn by its customer who had overdrawn on his account with the bank's consent and who specifically paid into the credit of his account cash and cheques for the purpose of meeting the cheque drawn shortly before the dishonour. The bank could not set off the amount of the payments into the account against the overdraft because the payments were made to the credit of the account for the specific purpose indicated by the customer.

The bank's duty to conform to the customer's mandate requires the bank to ensure that it does not exceed the customer's mandate. It is imperative that the bank does not exceed the customer's mandate because a failure to comply with the mandate will prevent the bank from debiting the customer's account with the amount of the payment. An obvious example of where the bank has exceeded its mandate and, therefore, cannot debit the customer's account is where it pays a cheque or bill of exchange and the drawer's signature has been forged (*Greenwood v Martins Bank Ltd* [1933] AC 51). More recently, in *Barclays Bank plc v Quincecare* [1992] 4 All ER 363 the bank was held to be under a duty to refrain from executing an order to transfer funds from the customer's account if it has reasonable grounds to believe that the customer's funds are being misappropriated.

Another example where a bank may discover that it has exceeded its authority is where an agent in excess of his authority draws cheques. In the same way as with forged cheques, the customer is not liable if an agent (bank) exceeds his authority. Where the bank pays cheques drawn in excess of the agent's actual or ostensible authority the bank may be liable for breach of contract and for negligence. A bank will be liable for negligence in paying a cheque that although drawn within the scope of the agent's actual authority (eg the amount of the cheque is within express limits imposed on the agent and notified to the bank) is in excess of the agent's ostensible authority (eg where the amount of the cheque is paid into the agent's private account). In *B Liggett (Liverpool) Ltd v Barclays Bank Ltd* [1928] 1 KB 48 it was held that a bank exceeded its mandate when paying a cheque drawn on a company's account signed merely by one director although the company had given express instructions to the bank only to honour cheques signed by two directors.

In *Lloyds Bank Ltd v Chartered Bank of India, Australia and China* (1929) 1 KB 40 cheques fraudulently drawn by employees of the plaintiff bank that had ostensible authority were held to have been paid negligently and in excess of the mandate conferred on the defendant bank. Scrutton LJ said that a third party dealing in good faith with an agent acting within his ostensible authority is not prejudiced by the fact that, as between the customer (principal) and his agent, the agent is using his authority in such a way that the customer (principal) can complain that the agent acts for his own benefit. Where the third party has notice of the irregularity or is put on inquiry as to whether the agent is exceeding his ostensible authority, the paying bank is not protected. In *Morison v London County and Westminster Bank Ltd* [1914] 3 KB 356 the court examined the question of the bank's negligence and said that (apart from the rule of whether or not the evidence established that the bank acted without negligence) it is a question of fact and the following principles must be established namely:

(1) the question should, in strictness, be determined separately with regard to each cheque;

(2) the test of negligence is whether the transaction of paying any cheque was so out of the ordinary course that it ought to have aroused doubts in the bank's mind and given cause to make inquiry;

(3) in order for the bank to raise estoppel against the customer negligence must be the proximate cause of the loss.

Damages for wrongful dishonour of cheque

If the bank fails to conform to the customer's mandate, and either makes payment when it should not have or fails to make payment when payment should have been made, the customer is entitled to sue the bank for breach of contract. In assessing the award of damages the courts previously distinguished between a customer who was a trader and a personal customer, on the basis that a trader was more likely to suffer loss of reputation if a cheque issued by him were wrongfully dishonoured. That distinction is now abolished. In *Kpohraror v Woolwich Building Society* [1996] 4 All ER 119 the court held that the issue of credit rating could now be deemed to extend to personal, as well as trade, transactions and a presumption of damage could be said to arise in every case of wrongful dishonour.

Duty to obey the customer's countermand

The bank has a duty to conform to the customer's mandate not merely in making payment but in accordance with any countermand given by the customer. The customer's instructions to countermand payment must be clear and unambiguous so that where a customer who countermands a cheque gives the wrong cheque number by mistake, the bank can pay the cheque intended to be countermanded and debit the customer's account. In *Westminster Bank Ltd v Hilton* [1926] 43 TLR 124 the court held that in making payment from the customer's account the bank acts as the customer's agent. Where, therefore, the customer gives instructions that are open to ambiguity and equally capable of interpretation in one of several ways, the bank is not liable if it adopts an interpretation that is reasonable, although not the one intended by the customer.

For the countermand to be effective it must come to the knowledge of the branch manager where the customer's account is maintained. In *Curtice v London City and Midland Bank Ltd* [1908] 1 KB 293 a notice of countermand sent by telegram was placed in the bank's mailbox but, due to a delay in clearing the mailbox, the countermand did not come to the attention of the branch manager where the cheque was drawn until after it had been paid. The doctrine of constructive notice does not apply to a countermand of a cheque; only actual notice will suffice with the result that the cheque was properly paid and the cheque was not countermanded until it was brought to the attention of the branch manager. The bank, however, will be liable for negligence for failing to ensure that its mailbox is regularly checked and cleared.

The countermand will only be effective if it is given before the cheque is paid and within a reasonable time prior to payment in order to enable the bank to take appropriate action. The bank will not, however, countermand payment of cheques guaranteed by a cheque card. The whole system of cheque cards is based on the principle that such a cheque will not be countermanded if the amount does not exceed, in most cases, £50.

The Jack Committee on Banking Services recommended that the right to countermand should be protected when possible. It therefore recommended that a standard of best practice should require banks to make available an explanation of the rights and obligations of the parties to transactions effected through the Bankers' Clearing Company, including the rules of countermand. This recommendation was given effect in the Code of Banking Practice.

Duty to collect instruments

The bank is under a duty to collect amounts payable to the customer, by the use of normal banking methods, when the customer delivers them for collection to the credit of his account (*Joachimson v Swiss Bank Corpn* [1921] 3 KB 110). Such instruments obviously include cheques (although drawn on a bank that is not a member of the Bankers' Clearing Company), bills of exchange accepted by another bank, credit transfers, direct debits, payments made through electronic funds transfers and payments made through the Post Office giro services.

In *Hare v Henty* (1861) 10 CBNS 66 the court held that when a bank receives from a customer an instrument for collection, it must present such instruments for payment by the bank, or other institution on which they are drawn or on which they are issued, as expeditiously as possible. If the instrument is presented through the London Daily Clearing it is sufficient for the bank to present it or send it to its head office or clearing agent in London, for collection through the clearing, either on the day it receives the instrument from its customer or on the following day. The bank is only under an obligation to allow the customer to draw against a cheque once it has been cleared but, if the bank voluntarily credits the customer's account with the amount of an unpaid cheque, the customer may draw against the uncleared amounts immediately (see Lord Lindley in *Capital and Counties Bank Ltd v Gordon* [1903] AC 240).

Bank's duty to render an account

A bank is under a duty to render accounts to its customer either on demand or periodically, as agreed. If a bank fails to supply the customer with a statement of account, the customer's legal remedy is to seek an order for specific performance or, if the account is a current account, to close his account and to demand immediate payment of his credit balance, so compelling the bank to give an account.

73

A more significant question is whether a statement that is incorrect and shows either a larger credit or an over-debit binds a bank, or indeed the customer. This arises where, for example, amounts that should have been debited have not been deducted, so the credit balance is erroneously increased in favour of the customer, or where the value of a cheque has been debited twice so that the credit balance is erroneously reduced. Whilst attempts have been made to render a statement of account conclusive and to restrict the right of the customer to check and verify statements within an agreed time the courts are reluctant to hold such terms valid (*Tai Hing Cotton Mill Ltd v Liu Chong Hing Bank Ltd* [1986] AC 80).

Under the existing law a credit or debit entry in a statement of account is not conclusive; it is merely prima facie evidence of the state of the account and it can be rebutted by proof to the contrary. Additionally, the rules of estoppel apply to the correctness of bank statements. In *Holland v Manchester and Liverpool District Banking Co Ltd* (1909) 25 TLR 386 the court held that, where the customer acts in good faith on a wrong entry made in a passbook and alters his position accordingly, the bank is estopped from claiming that the error be rectified. In *Skyring v Greenwood and Cox* (1825) 4 B&C 281 the bank over-credited the customer's account with salary payments over a number of years and the plaintiff accordingly maintained a higher standard of living. It was held that it would be prejudicial to the customer to allow the bank to recover the amounts of the mistaken credits.

The customer's belief as to the accuracy of the statement is essential so that if the customer is aware of the bank's mistake the bank is not estopped from adjusting the error. In *British and North European Bank Ltd v Zalzstain* [1927] 2 KB 92 the court held the customer could not object to having his account debited with amounts of which he was unaware until after his account had been debited. The bank is only estopped from disputing the accuracy of the statements of account where the customer honestly believes the statement to be correct and acts on it accordingly.

Further, in *United Overseas Bank Ltd v Jiwani* [1977] 1 All ER 733 the defendant customer was wrongfully advised of the credit balance on his account. The defendant, being aware of the bank's mistake, used the money towards the completion of a transaction into which he had already entered and with which he would have proceeded in any event. The bank sought to recover the amount wrongfully credited to the customer. The court held that the defendant customer was in a position to repay the money without any hardship being imposed on him and without prejudice to him. For a bank to be estopped from re-claiming the amount wrongfully credited to the customer's account three conditions had to be satisfied, namely:

(i)   the bank must be under a duty to give accurate information about the state of the customer's account and in breach of that duty it gives inaccurate information or in some other way misrepresents the state of the customer's account;

(ii) the customer must show that the inaccurate information misled him about the balance standing to the credit of his account;

(iii) the customer must show that because of his mistaken belief he changed his position in such a way as would make it inequitable to require him to repay the money wrongly credited to his account.

A statement of account is, therefore, not a final settlement of the account between the bank and its customer. It is only conclusive against the bank if the customer has relied on the statement to his detriment.

Bank's duty of confidentiality

Many countries have a statutory law relating to the banker's duty of confidentiality. In the UK the duty is implied and the common law imposes a duty of secrecy or non-disclosure in respect of the customer's affairs. Where a breach of the duty of confidentiality is threatened by the bank, the customer can obtain an injunction to prevent the bank from disclosing information relating to the customer's affairs, but where disclosure has already been made without authorization the only remedy available to the customer is to sue for damages for breach of contract.

In *Tournier v National Provincial and Union Bank of England* [1924] I KB 461 the Court of Appeal held that there is an implied term of the contract between a bank and its customer that the bank will not divulge to a third party, without the express or implied consent of the customer, information either about the state of the customer's account or information about any transactions entered into with the bank. Any disclosure constituted a breach of the bank's duty to the customer not to disclose information in respect of the customer and acquired in the course of the banker and customer relationship.

Exceptions to the Tournier rule

In *Tournier* Bankes LJ examined the limits of the duty and qualifications of the implied duty of secrecy.

Where disclosure is under compulsion by law

The duty of confidentiality is a contractual obligation that arises from the implied contract. A contractual duty is unenforceable if there is a statutory duty to the contrary; thus, where a statute can compel disclosure, any contractual agreement to the contrary will not be enforced. This exception can be examined in two categories.

Compulsion by order of the court

An order of the court will usually take the form of a *subpoena duces tecum* that, when served on a bank official, orders him to attend court and to bring with him books, documents or letters relating to the customer's affairs specified in the subpoena.

In *Robertson v Canadian Imperial Bank of Commerce* [1994] 1 WLR 1493 the Privy Council held that as a bank manager had disclosed information about one of its customers under a subpoena it had not acted in breach of the duty of confidentiality, although the manager had failed to notify the customer of the subpoena ordering the bank to give evidence and to produce bank statements in respect of the customer's affairs. The bank was not under an absolute duty to inform the customer of the subpoena.

Alternatively, an order may be made under s 7 of the Bankers' Books Evidence Act 1879. The Act provides that

> 'on an application of any party to a legal proceeding a court or judge
> may order that such party be at liberty to inspect and take copies of
> any entries in a bankers' books for any purposes of such proceedings'.

The Act aims to prevent banks from being compelled to produce its books in legal proceedings to which it is not a party.

An order under the Bankers' Books Evidence Act can relate to both criminal and civil proceedings. In *Williams v Summerfield* [1972] 2 QB 512 an order was made compelling disclosure of bank records to enable a police inspector to inspect and take copies of certain bank accounts. Lord Widgery said in respect of criminal proceedings:

> '... justices should warn themselves of the importance of the step which
> they are taking in making an order under s 7; should always recognize
> the care with which the jurisdiction should be exercised; should take
> into account among other things whether there is other evidence in
> the possession of the prosecution to support the charge...'.

Moreover, the courts should not encourage 'fishing expeditions' such as when 'a police officer seeking to make investigations of a suspect bank account started legal proceedings for that purpose and no other.'

In respect of civil proceedings the Bankers' Books Evidence Act 1879 does not give any new powers of discovery or alter the law or practice of discovery (*Waterhouse v Barker* [1924] 2 KB 759). Discovery is a pre-trial examination of the evidence and documents by parties to legal proceedings. A bank must comply with an order of discovery made if the information is relevant to the litigation and not privileged from production. In *Bankers' Trust Co v Shapira* [1980] 1 WLR 1274 an order for discovery was made against the defendants who held accounts for persons who had fraudulently deprived the plaintiffs of a considerable sum of money and allegedly placed it in accounts with the defendant bank. The court held that the person guilty of fraud couldn't rely on the confidential nature of the banker and customer relationship to hide the proceeds of fraud. Such an order should only be made in exceptional circumstances where strong evidence is available showing that misappropriated funds are held to the credit of a bank account. Moreover, a plaintiff may have to give an undertaking to compensate the bank for any damages it becomes liable to pay to its customers.

Compulsion by statute

The Jack Committee listed 19 statutory provisions in England that, at that time, required or permitted disclosure of confidential information by banks without the consent of the customer. The list, although not exhaustive, is contained in Appendix Q of the Report.

The Criminal Justice Act 1993 (supplemented by the Money Laundering Regulations) was intended to fulfill the UK's obligations under the 1991 EC Money Laundering Directive. These regulations compelled financial institutions to put into place systems to detect and deter money laundering by placing obligations in the following key areas:

♦ systems and training to prevent money laundering;
♦ the establishment of identification procedures;
♦ record keeping procedures;
♦ internal reporting procedures.

Under the Regulations (Money Laundering Regulations 1993, SI 1993/1933) financial institutions were required to establish and maintain internal procedures to prevent money laundering, and to provide employees with sufficient training to comply with their legal obligations. A failure to comply with these regulations is a criminal offence, punishable on indictment. Regulation 5 places a substantial burden on financial institutions. Such institutions must be able to show that employees are aware of the relevant law, including the criminal offences under the statutory framework, and of their own responsibilities and duties under the regulations. Employers must provide specific training for those employees who are directly involved with customer accounts so that they can discharge their legal obligations adequately. Furthermore, such training must be continuous.

At institutional level, reg 14 necessitates the instigation and maintenance of internal reporting procedures. The regulation requires that a person be assigned the function of receiving internal reports of suspicious transactions. It is the function of this person to assimilate the information when suspicion of money laundering arises, before determining whether the information is reported to the NCIS.

Additionally, statutory guidance notes have been issued to provide a practical interpretation of the Regulations and give examples of good practice. These guidance notes are issued by the Money Laundering Steering Group, which includes representatives of the Bank of England, the British Bankers' Association, building societies, banks, investment businesses and the National Criminal Intelligence Services. Although these guidance notes are not mandatory, it is unlikely that a deposit-taking institution will be deemed to satisfy the requirements that the business be carried on with skill and integrity if the institution fails to comply with money laundering guidance notes.

The Proceeds of Crime Act 2002 established a number of money laundering offences. These are as follows:

♦ concealing, disguising, converting, transferring or removing from the UK, criminal property;
♦ entering into, or becoming concerned with an arrangement which facilitates the acquisition, retention, use or control of criminal property;
♦ acquiring, using or having possession of criminal property;
♦ failing to disclose knowledge or suspicion of money laundering that came to his attention through the course of a business in the regulated sector;
♦ failing to disclose knowledge or suspicion of money laundering that came to his attention by virtue of his position as the nominated officer in the regulated sector;
♦ failing to disclose knowledge or suspicion of money laundering where the offender is a nominated officer;
♦ the disclosure of information prejudicial to an investigation, ie 'tipping off'.

Sections 343–379 of the Proceeds of Crime Act empower the Crown Court to make a variety of orders in connection with the confiscation investigations or money laundering investigations. These include: requiring a person to produce any material that is in his possession or control that is relevant to a confiscation or money laundering investigation (ss 345–351); a search and seizure warrant where a production order would not be satisfactory (ss 352–356); a disclosure order requiring any person to give to the Director of Assets Recovery Agency any relevant information (ss 357–362); a customer information order that will require a bank to provide information relating to the affairs of a customer (ss 363–369); an account monitoring order that will require a bank to provide details of transactions on a particular account over a specified period of time (ss 370–375); a letter of request relating to accessibility of evidence available outside the jurisdiction (ss 376). The 2002 Act and the Money Laundering Regulations 2003, SI 2003/3075 supercede and replace the earlier money laundering regime which extended to estate agents, casinos, high value dealers etc.

Duty to the public to disclose

In *Weld-Blundell v Stephens* [1920] AC 956 Lord Finlay said that the bank will be justified in disclosing information relating to the customer's affairs:

> 'where a higher duty than the private duty is involved as where danger to the State or public duty may supersede the duty of the agent to his principal.'

If the bank has information, that leads it, with some confidence, to believe that the customer is using his account for the purpose of committing criminal acts, then it must decline to hold the account and it must notify the proper authorities.

The Jack Committee recommended that this exception should no longer be recognized and that the exception had been affected by legislation to such an extent that it could not envisage a situation where it might be relied upon. Nevertheless, the exception was successfully relied on in *Libyan Arab Foreign Bank v Bankers Trust Co* [1988] 1 Lloyd's Rep 259 where, following discussions with the Federal Reserve Board on 8 January 1988 (resulting from a Presidential Order freezing Libyan assets held by US nationals, including artificial entities), Bankers Trust in New York was held entitled to disclose confidential information. Further, in *Price Waterhouse v BCCI Holdings (Luxembourg)* [1992] BCLC 583 the court held that disclosure of confidential information by Price Waterhouse (BCCI auditors) to the Bingham inquiry was in the public interest when made in the investigation of the Bank of England handling its supervisory duties in respect of BCCI.

This exception continues to be recognized and appears in the Voluntary Code of Banking Practice.

Where interests of the bank require disclosure

In *Tournier* Bankes LJ said that a simple illustration of the third category of disclosure that is justified is

> 'where a bank issues a writ claiming payment of an overdraft stating on the face of the writ the amount of the overdraft.'

Obviously, disclosure by the bank of the customer's affairs will be justified if the bank is a party to legal proceedings either against the customer or a third party, eg where the bank sues the guarantor on the amount of the guarantee.

The bank may also be justified in disclosing the customer's affairs if the disclosure is necessitated by an attack on its reputation (*Sunderland v Barclays Bank Ltd* (1938) 5 LDB 163).

The Jack Committee recommended that this exception should permit disclosure about the customer's affairs where the bank is a party to legal proceedings, or within the banking group for defined purposes, but not for the purposes of marketing banking services. Moreover, the disclosure should be limited to what is necessary for the purposes of protecting the bank and its banking subsidiaries against loss, in relation to the provision of normal of banking services. This view is at variance with the *Bank of Tokyo v Karoon* [1987] 1 AC 45 which held that each corporate entity within the banking group must be viewed as a separate entity for the purposes of complying with the duty of confidentiality.

The Code of Banking Practice provides that disclosure should be permitted in the interests of the bank, eg banks may pass on information about defaulting customers when necessary to recover the money owed. The voluntary code, however, allows disclosure in two additional circumstances.

(a)   Within the group to prevent loss or fraud. This goes further than the government White Paper published in response to the Jack Report in which it was proposed that disclosure should be permitted in case of loss or potential loss. The disclosure would not be permitted to a subsidiary outside the banking group.

(b)   Banks may pass on information about a customer to banking, financial and investment members of the groups so that relevant information about the group's services can be supplied to the customer. Banks are required to ensure that those receiving the information about the customer observe the same degree of confidentiality regarding the customer as banks themselves.

Disclosure with the customer's consent

Disclosure with the customer's consent is only now permitted where the customer gives express consent. In *Turner v Royal Bank of Scotland* [1999] 2 All ER (Comm) 664 the Court of Appeal rejected the idea that a customer gives implied consent allowing the bank to disclose confidential information when he opens an account.

Continuation of the duty after the banker-customer relationship is terminated

Atkin LJ in *Tournier v National Provincial and Union Bank of England* [1924] 1 KB 461 said the duty

> 'clearly goes beyond the state of the account, that is, whether there is a debit or a credit balance, and the amount of the balance.'

It extends to all transactions that go through the account and to any securities or undertakings given in respect of the account. The duty exists not merely for the duration of the account but even after the banker-customer relationship has ceased. Atkin LJ said that it is inconceivable that the bank be at liberty to divulge confidential information after the termination of the banker-customer relationship.

Further, the duty of secrecy extends to information obtained from sources other than the customer's actual account if the information was obtained in the course of the banker and customer relationship, eg where the information is obtained with a view to assisting the bank in conducting the customer's business or in coming to decisions relating to its treatment of the customer.

Duties of the customer towards the bank

The implied duties owed by the customer to the bank are fairly certain although attempts have been made in a number of cases to expand the scope of such duties. The duties that a customer owes to the bank, whether he has a current or deposit account, are:

(i) a duty to pay reasonable charges for the services rendered by the banks;

(ii) a duty to repay any sums overdrawn on the current account.

Both of these duties can be regulated by express agreement between the parties to the banker and customer relationship. Thus, it may be agreed that the customer can overdraw up to a limited amount and it may also be agreed that the bank will give reasonable notice before demanding repayment. The scale of charges for providing banking services are available on inquiry and a customer who instructs the bank to undertake business is deemed to have agreed to pay the charges.

The Jack Committee recommended that the customer should be given full details of the method of calculation of fees and charges when these are applied to his account, including where the overdraft occurs without prior agreement.

Additional duties

If the customer fails to observe certain additional duties owed by him to the bank, the customer will provide the bank with a defence to any action. These self-regarding (to the extent that the bank can raise an estoppel against the customer) duties are as follows.

Allegation of breach of mandate

The paying bank is under a contractual obligation to conform to the customer's mandate, ie the bank must make payment in accordance with the customer's mandate if it is to be entitled to debit the customer's account. A forged cheque (whether the forgery consists of a forged drawer's signature or an unauthorized alteration of the amount) is wholly inoperative and the bank will be unable to debit the customer's account. The common law rules of estoppel may protect the bank against an allegation of breach of mandate and thus entitle the bank to debit the customer's account. Where the bank is to rely on the common law rules of estoppel it must be established that the bank was misled into believing, either by the customer's representations or his conduct, that forged or altered cheques were, in fact, genuine.

Misleading statements

In *Brown v Westminster Bank Ltd* [1964] 2 Lloyd's Rep 187 the defendant bank, suspecting an irregularity on its customer's account, requested several times that the customer verify that certain cheques were genuine. The customer, an elderly lady, confirmed some of the cheques as having been properly drawn and bearing her signature and confirmed that other cheques were drawn under her authority, for cash, by her servant. Eventually, the bank became so concerned with the number of cheques being drawn for cash by the customer's servant that the branch manager decided to discuss the matter with the customer's son, who held a power of attorney. The son brought an action in respect of a large number of forged cheques. The court held the customer was estopped from denying that the cheques were genuine even in respect of cheques drawn on the customer's account before the bank's initial inquiry. The bank relied on her statements and accordingly took no action against the servant.

Duty to notify of known forgeries

There is a duty to inform the paying bank of known forgeries. This duty is imposed on anyone, whether a customer of the bank or not, eg endorser of a cheque who knows that his name has been forged on the cheque.

In *Morison v London County and Westminster Bank Ltd* [1914] 3 KB 356 the plaintiff's employee over a number of years paid into his own account cheques drawn for the purposes of the business. The plaintiffs eventually brought an action against the bank challenging its right to debit the amounts of the forged cheques. Since the customer had for a considerable length of time known of the forgeries the court held there was a breach of duty in failing to notify the bank of the forgeries and the bank was entitled to debit the customer's account.

The *Morison Case* was affirmed in *Greenwood v Martins Bank Ltd* [1933] AC 51. In *Greenwood* the customer's wife had over a period of time forged cheques on his account. When the husband discovered this he failed to notify the bank. He subsequently, however, threatened to inform the bank and the wife committed suicide. The husband then brought an action against the bank to recover the amount of the forged cheques. The court held that, although mere silence cannot amount to a representation for estoppel to operate, deliberate silence when there is a duty to disclose may amount to a representation and thereby estop the customer from succeeding against the bank. A customer of the bank who discovers forgeries against his account owes a duty to notify the bank for two reasons:

(i)   to safeguard against further forged cheques or instruments being paid;

(ii)   to enable the bank to take steps towards recovering the money wrongfully paid under the forged instruments.

In the *Greenwood Case* a failure by the customer to notify the bank of the forgeries when they were first discovered prevented it from taking steps to recover amounts wrongfully paid. Consequently, the customer was estopped from asserting that the cheques were a forgery.

Duty to draw cheques so as not to facilitate alteration

The customer also owes an implied duty to draw cheques in such a way so as not to facilitate fraud or alteration. Again, failure to comply with this duty will entitle the bank to debit the customer's account with the full amount of the altered cheque, provided the paying bank acts in good faith and without negligence. In *Young v Grote* (1827) 4 Bing 253 the customer was said to be in breach of a duty of care to ensure that when he draws a cheque he does it in a manner so as not to allow subsequent alteration. In *Young v Grote* the plaintiff customer left blank cheque forms with his wife. The wife instructed an employee to complete one of the cheque forms. The employee filled in the cheque form and after showing it to the plaintiff's wife, altered the amount of the cheque by adding an extra figure between the '£' sign and the first number representing the amount to be withdrawn. He then proceeded to complete the amount of the cheque in words and received payment. The court held that the customer was estopped from denying the bank's right to debit the full amount of the cheque. The customer being in breach of his duty of care to ensure that cheques drawn by him cannot subsequently be altered was liable for the full amount of the altered cheque. The case was followed in *London Joint Stock Bank Ltd v Macmillan and Arthur* [1918] AC 777 where the court said that it is beyond dispute that the customer is bound to exercise reasonable care in drawing the cheque to prevent the bank from being misled. If the customer draws the cheque in a manner that facilitates fraud, he is guilty of a breach of duty as between himself and the bank and he will be responsible for any loss sustained by the bank as a natural and direct consequence of this breach of duty.

The courts have, however, refused to extend the application of this rule in *Slingsby v District Bank Ltd* [1932] 1 KB 544 where the fraudulent alteration took the form of inserting the words 'per Cumberbirch and Potts' after the name of the payee. It was said that the customer was not negligent in leaving a blank space after the payee's name and could not reasonably anticipate the form of the alteration.

In *Kepitagalla Rubber Estates v National Bank of India Ltd* [1909] 2 KB 1010 the court similarly refused to extend the scope of the self-regarding duties owed by the customer and it was held that a customer is not under any duty to take precautions to prevent persons, having access to his cheque book, from forging cheque forms by forging his signature.

Is the customer under a duty to refrain from altering the printed parts of the cheque form?

In *Burnett v Westminster Bank Ltd* [1966] 1 QB 742 it was established that a customer does not owe a duty to abstain from altering the printed parts of the cheque forms issued to him. In that case a customer held two accounts with the different branches of the same bank and, because he had no cheque forms issued by the one branch, he substituted the name and address for the other branch on a cheque form issued by it. It was said the customer could validly countermand payment of the cheque he had issued by notifying the substituted branch, although the cheque never reached that branch. This was because the cheques were mechanically sorted by reader-sorter machines at the bank's head office after presentation and since the machines relied on the magnet ink character pre-printed at the bottom of each cheque, the cheque in question was consequently sent to the branch whose address was printed on it. This branch did not dishonour the cheque because the customer's countermand had been sent to the other branch.

The unwillingness of the courts to place a duty on the customer not to make alterations on the face of the cheque places on the bank an express obligation to warn the customer against making alterations. This is sometimes done by placing a warning on the inside cover of the cheque book to the effect that pre-printed cheque forms 'should not be used for any other account indicated – please do not permit their use on any other account.'

Whilst the instructions as to the permitted use of the cheque forms are clear, whether they form part of the contractual terms is questionable. The banker and customer relationship is entered into when the bank opens an account or requests the completion of an application form for an account to be opened. This is usually done in person at the bank and, since the customer does not normally receive a chequebook until a later stage, it is doubtful whether this warning is actually binding on the customer. Such terms, however, may become part of the contract if the bank can establish a course of dealings during which such terms can be deemed to have come to the attention of the customer.

2.2 Constructive trusts

Third party claims

A bank will normally owe obligations to a customer with whom it has been entered into contractual relations. In some circumstances, however, a bank that is given instructions by a customer may have to have regard to third party claims. This may happen in the following circumstances.

- ♦ Where an employee, agent, company director, or trustee misuses his authority for his own benefit, eg where an employee misappropriates employer's funds to his own personal account, or where a director misappropriates company funds and makes a personal profit (*Selangor United Rubber Estates Ltd v Cradock (No 3)* [1968] 1 WLR 1555). In such cases, the claimant may hold the bank liable for breach of contract or equitable duty of care if he banks with the same bank as the person responsible for the misappropriation. Where the wrongdoer banks with another bank, the bank receiving the funds will owe no contractual obligations to the claimant and an action may therefore lie in conversion (if a cheque is used for the misappropriation) or, in other cases, an action for money had and received, or by holding the bank liable as constructive trustee. The action in restitution will be defeated if the bank changes its position following receipt of the funds; the alternative is to opt for an action to hold the bank liable as a constructive trustee.

- ♦ Third party claims may need consideration where the bank wishes to set-off a debit balance against the customer's personal account with a credit balance maintained by the same customer in a special account. The third party may claim title to the credit balance either because of a special appropriation or because the funds are subject to a trust.

- ♦ Alternatively, the third party may claim to have an equitable title to the funds. This type of action is based on the fact that the money was obtained from him by fraud or trick.

In some cases, the claimant will attempt to hold the bank liable as a constructive trustee, or alternatively try to assert a proprietary claim and trace the funds.

In *Barnes v Addy* (1874) LR 9 Ch App 244 Lord Selborne distinguished two categories of constructive trusteeship:

(i) where a person [stranger to a trust] receives trust property and deals with it in a manner inconsistent with the trust, he may be liable even if he acted innocently (known as liability for 'knowing receipt');

(ii) a person who, while not receiving the trust property, assists the trustees in a dishonest design will not be liable as a constructive trustee unless he assists with knowledge of the improper design (previously known as liability for knowing assistance but since *Royal Brunei Airlines v Tan* [1995] 2 AC 378 referred to as liability for 'dishonest assistance').

Liability for dishonest assistance

Such liability will be imposed on anyone who has dishonestly been an accessory to, or assisted in, a disposition of property in a breach of trust. The accessory is liable for all the losses caused to the fund by the dishonest assistance, whether the fund actually comes into his hands. Liability is imposed because his conduct in relation to the trust property has been such that he ought to be liable in damages as if he were a trustee who disposed of the property in breach of trust (*Arab Monetary Fund v Hashim* 29 July 1994, unreported).

The requirements for accessory 'liability' are as follows.

♦ There must have been a trust or other fiduciary relationship. The scope of *Barnes v Addy* has been extended to include breaches of fiduciary duties. In *Agip (Africa) Ltd v Jackson* [1991] Ch 547 an offer of the company (chief accountant) was held liable for breach of fiduciary duty when he misappropriated funds from the company's bank account by altering the payment order after it has been duly drawn up. The defendants, accountants based in the Isle of Man, assisted in laundering the misappropriated funds and were held liable for knowingly assisting in the breach of fiduciary duty.

♦ There must have been a misfeasance or breach of trust. Since *Barnes v Addy* the courts had specifically required a dishonest and fraudulent design in order to impose liability. In *Royal Brunei Airlines v Tan* [1995] 2 AC 378 the Privy Council expressed the view that liability under the accessory category required a breach of trust or other fiduciary duty, but that such conduct did not have to be dishonest. In *Brown v Bennett* [1999] BCLC 649 the Court of Appeal held for liability to be imposed as for a constructive trustee under the dishonest assistance category any breach of fiduciary duty will suffice, and not merely a breach of trust in relation to property.

♦ The person on whom liability is to be imposed must have been an accessory or assisted in the misfeasance or breach of trust. This is a question of fact and banks run the risk of being accused of providing assistance to the dishonest fiduciary by transferring money between accounts. Thus, payment by a bank on the instructions of fraudulent directors of moneys belonging to the company to another person may impose accessory liability (*Selangor United Rubber Estates Ltd*).

♦ The accessory must have been dishonest. In *Royal Brunei Airlines v Tan*, Lord Nicholls confirmed, 'dishonesty is a necessary ingredient of accessory liability'. Dishonesty is to be assessed objectively and equates to conscious impropriety. Dishonesty simply means not acting as an honest person would in the circumstances. In assessing the state of knowledge of the third party, the court will have regard to personal attributes of the third party such as his experience and intelligence, and the reason why he has acted as he did. When these factors have been identified the defendant's conduct will be judged objectively. The *Tan* test of dishonesty has been refined in a number of cases.

(a) In *Twinsectra Ltd v Yardley* [2002] 2 AC 164 T agreed to lend money to Y on the condition that he give a solicitor's undertaking that money would be used to acquire property. Y's solicitor (L) refused to give such an undertaking but S did so and the money was paid to him. S allowed the money to be used for other purposes. The Court of Appeal held L liable. The dishonesty requirement was satisfied because L knew the terms of S's undertaking, shut his eyes to its implications, and acted in reckless disregard of T's rights.

(b) In *Mortgage Corpn v Newman* [2000] Lloyd's Rep 745 the question was whether a solicitor had been dishonest. Aldows LJ said where honesty is an issue, the mind of the person responsible, the understanding and practice of solicitors at the relevant time and the events that took place are all relevant. Once the facts have been determined the judge must decide, according to the standards of the right-thinking members of society, whether the act or omission was merely due to incompetence or to dishonesty.

(c) In *Grupo Torras SA v Al-Sabah* [2000] Lloyd's Rep Bank 36 involved a fraudulent misappropriation by directors of company funds. The Court of Appeal made a number of observations on the issue of dishonest assistance including that there is no need, on the facts of the case, to show knowledge by the defendant of facts giving rise to the breach of trust or fiduciary duty.

Knowing receipt

The liability of a recipient of property disposed of in breach of trust is generally known as liability for 'knowing receipt'. There are three requirements for liability to be imposed under this head. In *El Ajou v Dollar Land Holdings* [1994] 2 All ER 685 Hoffmann LJ stated that the claimant must show:

♦ a disposal of his assets in breach of fiduciary duty;

♦ the beneficial receipt by the defendant of assets that are traceable as representing the assets of the claimant;

♦ knowledge on the part of the defendant that the assets he received are traceable to a breach of fiduciary duty.

The two main types of 'knowing receipt' were identified in *Agip (Africa) Ltd v Jackson* [1940] 1 Ch 265 as follows:

(a) person who receives for his own benefit trust property transferred to him in breach of trust: liability as a constructive trustee will be imposed if he receives property with notice (actual or constructive) that it was trust property and the transfer to him was in breach of trust;

(b)   if he received it without notice but subsequently discovers the facts.

In (a) the recipient is liable to account for the property from the time he received the property. Under (b) the recipient will be required to account from the time he acquired notice.

In *Brown v Bennett* [1999] 1 BCLC 649 the court held that the receipt had to be the direct consequence of the alleged breach of trust or fiduciary duty of which the recipient was said to have notice. In *Brown*, O had acquired the property bona fide from the administrative receiver.

Liability depends on beneficial receipt of the property disposed of in breach of trust. Agents who receive trust money in a ministerial capacity (eg for the benefit of the principal, and not for their own benefit) are not made liable for 'knowing receipt'. In *Agip (Africa) Ltd v Jackson* [1990] Ch 265 Millett J expressed the view that paying and collecting banks could not be brought within the 'knowing receipt' category since they do not normally receive money for their own benefit. The position would be different if the bank used the money to reduce the customer's overdraft, or paid its fees, commission or other charges out of trust funds. In *Polly Peck International v Nadir (No 2)* [1992] 4 All ER 769 it was held that sterling transfers had not been beneficially received by the Central Bank of Northern Cyprus but as a banker, and in that capacity had credited the funds to CBK, in Northern Cyprus. The Central Bank then undertook the conversion of currency in its own right.

On the basis of the *Agip* reasoning if a bank receives trust property into an account in credit, knowing that it has been paid in breach of trust, the bank is not liable under 'knowing receipt', but the bank may be liable under the 'dishonest assistance' category.

Level of knowledge required

Liability depends on the recipient's knowledge of the breach of trust and is assessed by reference to the five categories identified in *Baden v Societe Generale* [1993] 1 WLR 509n.

(a)   Actual knowledge or notice of the trust and the agent is aware of the breach.

(b)   Knowledge that he would have obtained but for willfully shutting his eyes to the obvious.

(c)   Knowledge that he would have obtained but for willfully failing to make such inquiries as an honest and reasonable man.

(d)   Knowledge of circumstances that would indicate that there has been a breach to an honest and reasonable man.

(e)   Knowledge of circumstances that would put an honest and reasonable man on inquiry.

Some cases support the view that the liability only arises if the recipient's knowledge falls in the first three *Baden* categories and others suggest negligence is enough for receipt-based liability. With regard to banks, the customs and practices of bankers, including the demands of commercial dealings where speed and security are essential, must be taken into account. The conduct of a bank receiving a deposit of misappropriated trust money should be measured against the standard of enquiry that could reasonably be expected of a banker (*Macmillan Inc v Bishopgate Investment Trust plc (No 3)* [1995] I WLR 978). The issue of knowledge was looked at again in *BCCI v Akindele* [2000] Ch 437 where BBCI liquidators claimed that A, a Nigerian businessman, was liable to pay the proceeds of an investment agreement that had been executed by BCCI's directors in breach of trust. Only the 'knowing receipt' claim reached the Court of Appeal where the issue of the recipient's state of knowledge was discussed. The court concluded:

(i)   dishonesty is not a necessary ingredient of liability in knowing receipt;

(ii)   there should be a single test of knowledge for knowing receipt;

(iii)   all that is necessary is that the recipient's state of knowledge must be such as to make it unconscionable for him to retain the benefit of the receipt.

The test in (iii) should avoid the difficulties that have resulted from the other categories of the requisite degree of knowledge (eg the scale of knowledge in the *Baden* case).

Applying the new test in the *Akindele* case, A's state of knowledge was such as to have made him liable under the 'knowing receipt' category to impose liability as a constructive trustee.

Combination of accounts

A customer may maintain more than one account with a bank for a number of reasons, eg a person acting in a fiduciary capacity will be required to keep client funds separate from his own (a solicitor or trustee will be required to keep client or trust funds in separate accounts from his own). In other circumstances a customer may decide to maintain separate accounts for personal reasons, eg the customer may maintain a current and deposit account with the bank.

Despite operating separate accounts for a customer, the bank may decide to treat all the customer's accounts as one and combine the balances so as to produce a single debit or credit balance payable to, or from, the customer. The situation is likely to arise where, eg the customer is either unwilling or unable to repay the overdraft on one of his accounts although he has another account that is in credit or where the customer is bankrupt or insolvent. Alternatively, the bank may decide to combine two or more accounts where a customer draws a cheque against an account with an insufficient credit balance but the deficiency can be met by combining the balances standing to the credit of the other account.

Where the bank decides to combine two different accounts on the bankruptcy or insolvency of the customer, it basically acts for its own benefit to reduce the amount of the overdraft on one account against the credit balance standing against another account. This is especially significant where the insolvent customer has an overdraft of, for example, £500 on account A, but at the same time he has a credit balance on account B of, for example £1,000. If, on the insolvency or the bankruptcy of the customer the bank were to hold the credit balance of £1,000 for the trustee in bankruptcy, the bank would clearly be disadvantaged. As an unsecured creditor it will be repaid a dividend with the other general creditors. In that situation the bank is very likely not to recover the full amount of the debit balance on the overdrawn account. If the bank, however, were to combine the accounts it would be entitled to set-off the entire amount of the overdrawn account against the credit balance on account B immediately and will be under an obligation only to pay the remaining £500 to the trustee in bankruptcy. The bank will, therefore, receive payment in full of the amount of the overdraft in priority to the other unsecured creditors.

There are a number of issues that have to be resolved in respect of the banks right to combine the accounts, and it is intended to examine these.

The right to combine the accounts

The basic rule is that a bank may combine two or more accounts at any time without notice to the customer, even though the accounts are maintained at different branches of the same bank. The rule was explained in *Garnett v McKewan* (1878) 3 App Cas 325 at 333 where it was held that the bank was justified in dishonouring the cheques as the customer is not entitled to expect his cheques to be honoured at one branch of a bank where he has an account in credit, if at the same time the credit balance is counterbalanced by a debit against him at another branch. Kelly CB thought it important that there was a course of mutual dealings between the bank and its customer, and as the customer had the power to order the bank to transfer amounts from one of his accounts to another, so the bank had a similar right. In such a case although the bank cannot be said to be acting under express instructions from the customer, such a mandate may be implied by the fact that, as a customer is assumed to know the state of his accounts, drawing a cheque on an account that is overdrawn implies an instruction to the bank to transfer funds from the account in credit to the overdrawn account. Similarly, in *Greenwood Teale v William, Williams, Brown & Co* (1894) 11 TLR 56 the senior partner of a firm of solicitors opened three accounts: an office account, a deposit account, and a private account. The bank was informed that client money would be paid into the deposit account but it was subsequently closed. Thereafter the firm's money and client money was credited to the office account. As the private account was overdrawn the bank resolved to combine the private and office accounts. The court held that the bank has the right to combine the customer's accounts subject to three exceptions:

♦ where the right to combine has been abrogated subject to agreement;
♦ where a special item of property was remitted to the bank and appropriated for a specific purpose;
♦ where the bank has knowledge that the customer holds a trust account.

The fact that the bank had knowledge that one of the accounts was a firm account was immaterial since funds held by a firm through an office account are not trust property.

The rule in *Garnett v McKewan* has been approved in a number of cases including *Halesowen Pressworks & Assemblies Ltd v Westminster Bank Ltd* [1971] 1 QB 1 where Lord Denning held the bank was entitled to combine accounts so as to be liable only for the remaining balance unless it has made some agreement, express or implied to keep them separate.

In *Re K (Restraint Order)* [1990] 2 All ER 562 it was said that the bank could exercise its right to combine accounts without infringing a restraining order under the Drug Trafficking Act 1986. More recently, in *Hong Kong and Shanghai Banking Corpn v Kloeckner & Co AG* [1990] 2 QB 514 Hirst J rejected the argument that the doctrine of the autonomy of the letter of credit led of necessity to the conclusion that a set-off could not be permitted.

There can, therefore, be no doubt that the bank has a right to combine accounts and to discharge its obligation to the customer by repaying any remaining credit balances. In *Greenhalgh & Sons v Union Bank of Manchester Ltd* [1924] 2 KB 153 the court rejected the bank's right to combine where the bank receives money that has been appropriated for a specific purpose.

Does notice have to be given?

The question as to whether a bank is required to give notice to the customer of its intention to combine the accounts was considered in *Garnett v McKewan* (1878) 3 App Cas 325 where the court unanimously answered it in the negative. Kelly CB said:

> 'In general it might be proper or considerate to give notice to that effect, but there is no legal obligation on the bankers to do, arising either from express contract or the course of dealing between the parties.'

Thus, in *British Guyana Bank v Official Receiver* (1911) 104 LT 754 it was said that the agreement to keep the accounts apart remained in effect only whilst the accounts were 'alive' and was terminated if the customer became insolvent. The issue was discussed in *Halesowen Presswork and Assemblies Ltd v National Westminster Bank Ltd* [1972] AC 785 and the House of Lords held that an agreement not to combine accounts had only been intended to be operative during the existence of the banker and customer relationship, and that relationship having terminated with a winding-up resolution having been passed by the company customer, the bank could combine the accounts without giving notice. A requirement imposing notice of the intention would have served no purpose since the banker and customer relationship had been terminated.

In such circumstances the issue that needs to be resolved is whether the bank is required to honour cheques drawn by the customer but not yet presented. A period of notice could in fact defeat the advantages gained by the bank's combining credit and debit balances. A customer who receives notice of the bank's intention to combine accounts may decide to withdraw the credit balance against which combination is sought. To protect the bank against this situation arising, Lord Chelsea of Cross (*National Westminster Bank Ltd v Halesowen Pressworks & Assemblies Ltd* [1972] AC 785) expressed the view that

> 'the choice lies between a notice taking immediate effect and no notice at all. On any footing the bank would be obliged to honour cheques drawn up to the limit of the apparent credit balance before the company became aware that the bank was consolidating the accounts and so it might be said that notification to the customer was not a condition precedent to the exercise by the bank of its right of consolidation but only a measure of precaution which the bank might take to end its liability to honour cheques.'

Special rules relating to insolvency

Probably the most frequent use by the bank of its right to combine a credit balance with a debit balance is where the customer is declared bankrupt or insolvent. In such circumstances the right to combine accounts exists not merely at common law but also under statute, namely s 323 of the Insolvency Act 1986 (replaced s 31 of the Bankruptcy Act 1914). Section 323 of the Insolvency Act permits a set-off between amounts due to the creditor from the bankrupt individual or insolvent company or vice versa, provided there has been a course of 'mutual dealings' between the parties, including 'mutual credits, mutual debts or other mutual dealings'.

The effect of the bank's right to combine accounts in the event of the customer's insolvency was discussed in *National Westminster Bank Ltd v Halesowen Presswork and Assemblies Ltd* [1972] AC 785. The bank sought to set-off the credit balance on the No 2 (trading account opened for the company) account against the debit on the No 1 (current) account. The liquidator argued that it had been agreed to keep the accounts separate and that by agreement the bank had contracted out of s 31 of the Bankruptcy Act 1914 (the predecessor to s 323 the Insolvency Act 1986). The House of Lords dealt with two main issues.

(1) Whether the dealings between the bank and its customer were 'mutual' and expressed the view that 'mutual dealings would not cover a transaction in

which property is made over for a 'special (or specific) purpose' (*Re Pollitt, ex p Minor* [1893] 1 QB 175; In *Re Mid-Kent Fruit Factory* [1896] 1 Ch 567; *Re City Equitable Fire Insurance Co Ltd* [1930] 2 Ch 293). He took the view that every payment of money, or contractual provision is for a special or specific purpose in the ordinary sense of those words and something else is required to take the transaction out of the concept of 'mutual dealings'. He then went on to define the concept of 'mutual dealings' as follows.

> 'Money is paid for a special (or specific) purpose so as to exclude mutuality of dealing within s 31 (of the Bankruptcy Act 1914) if the money is paid in such circumstances that it would be a misappropriation to use it for any other purpose than that for which it is paid.'

The effect of s 31 remains unaltered under the Insolvency Act 1986, although the new section provides that any sums due from the bankrupt to the party seeking to exercise the set-off are not to be included in the account if the other party had 'notice at the time they became due that a bankruptcy petition relating to the bankrupt was pending'.

(2) Whether it was possible to contract out of s 31 of the Bankruptcy Act 1914. The majority concluded that it was not possible to contract out of s 31 of the Act, the section being of a mandatory nature. They based their decision on the nature of the wording used in the section and took into account that the change in terminology between the Bankruptcy Act 1849 (s 171) and the Bankruptcy Act 1869 (s 39) from 'may' to 'shall' must have been intended to avert doubts. Lord Cross, however, reached a different conclusion and said that the word 'shall' was intended to give the creditor a definite right to 'set-off' as opposed to giving s 31 a mandatory effect. Section 323 of the Insolvency Act supports the view that the right to set-off is mandatory in subs 2 that provides that an account 'shall' be taken of what is due from each party to the other. It therefore follows that a set-off follows automatically regardless of any agreement to the contrary between the parties.

A question that did not arise in the *Halesowen* case [1972] AC 785 is whether allowing the bank a right of set-off actually amounts to a voidable preference as regards the creditors under ss 239 and 340 of the Insolvency Act (s 239 applies to the winding up of companies and s 340 applies to the bankruptcy of individuals). Where a preference is given to a creditor within the 'relevant time' (normally six months before the winding up or bankruptcy) the court has the power to set aside the preference if the debtor was desirous of conferring a benefit on the creditor. Where the customer arranges for a sum to be credited to his account under pressure the rule is inapplicable.

Limitations to the right to combine

Mocatta J recognized the following exceptions to the bank's right to combine in *Barclays Bank Ltd v Okenarhe* [1966] 2 Lloyd's Rep 87.

(a) There is no right to combine in relation to accounts maintained with a bank by one person but in two different capacities, eg where the customer maintains an account in his personal capacity and also holds a trust account. In *Union Bank of Australia Ltd v Murray-Aynsley* [1898] AC 693, however, the Privy Council held that where there are several accounts in the name of the same customer with a bank, but the customer does not make it clear to the bank and the bank does not know which of those accounts is a trust account, the bank is entitled to combine all the accounts.

(b) The right to combine does not arise if there is an express or implied agreement not to combine the accounts. For example, in the *Bradford Old Bank Ltd v Sutcliffe* [1918] 2 KB 833 the right to set-off was not permissible where the bank had agreed with the customer that the two accounts would be kept separate. In that case the bank had opened a current account and Scrutton LJ said that amounts paid into that account cannot be used by the bank in discharge of the loan account without the customer's consent. Similarly, in *Buckingham v London & Midland Bank Ltd* (1895) 12 TLR 70 it was held that the bank had no right to combine, a loan account (secured) with a current account. Again, In *Re EJ Morel Ltd* [1961] 1 All ER 796 the court recognized the right of the bank to combine, but this time only to a limited extent as the bank was not allowed to combine all three accounts. In the *Morel* case a company maintained a No 2 account and a wages account, and the arrangement was that the credit balance on the No 2 account would always be sufficient to cover the wages account. It was held that the No 2 account and the wages account were in substance one as between the bank and the company.

(c) If money is deposited with the bank for a special purpose the bank cannot combine. In the *Greenhalgh* case [1924] 2 KB 153 the bank had knowledge of the ultimate destination of the proceeds of certain bills deposited by the customer to the credit of his account and for that reason the court held the bank had no right to combine accounts. In *Barclays Bank Ltd v Quistclose Investments Co* [1970] AC 567 it was held that money paid into a bank account was paid in with the knowledge of the bank for a specific purpose, ie payment of a dividend, and that purpose having failed due to the liquidation of the customer, the bank could not claim a set-off against other indebtedness of the customer.

(d) Combination is not possible for contingent liabilities. In *Jeffreys v Agra & Mastermans Bank* (1886) LR 2 Eq 674 a customer being indebted to the bank handed to it certain bank receipts issued by another bank representing deposits lodged with that other bank. The court held that the bank could only set-off such sums as were due and payable immediately. It could not retain the balance as security for amounts the customer might owe the bank in future.

(e)   Set-off is not available where there is any doubt as to the identity of the account-holder. In *Bhogul v Punjab National Bank* [1988] 2 All ER 296 it was held that the right of set-off against funds held in several different accounts depends on the several different accounts belonging to the same person (see also *Uttamchandami v Central Bank of India* (1989) 139 NJL 222 where the Court of Appeal held that:

> '... Set-off has never been allowed save where the accounts are of the same customer, held in the same name, and in the same right ... What is unusual about the present case is that the bank is seeking to set off accounts held in different names...').

Bankers references

Status enquiries

Bank references are supplied where, for example X, a customer of Bank A wishes to undertake business with one Y, a customer of Bank B. To satisfy himself about the credit-worthiness of Y (person being investigated), X (the enquirer) may request a confidential financial report. X will normally ask Bank A (reference seeking bank) to obtain the necessary information from Bank B (the referee bank). Alternatively, if X is made aware of Y's bank (Bank B) in the course of business negotiations, Y may request Bank B to provide Bank A with a reference.

The rights of the person being investigated: rights of Y

The person who forms the subject matter of the enquiry, Y, will have contractual remedies against his bank, B, if the bank either fails to supply the reference or it is inaccurate. If Bank B gives an unfavourable reference, Y may have three alternative forms of action.

Breach of the duty of confidentiality

The Banking Code (2001, 4th Ed) expressly provides that '[I]f we are asked to give a banker's reference about you, we will need your written permission before we give it'. In *Turner v Royal Bank of Scotland* [1999] 2 All ER (Comm) 664 the bank relied on the customer's implied consent to the release of confidential information (in the form of a banker's reference) as a defence. The Court of Appeal held that the claimant could not be deemed to have given implied consent since he was unaware of the practice of providing bankers' references. There was evidence to suggest that bank policy, in fact, was not to inform customers of the practice. The bank could only bind a customer who was not aware of the practice if it was sufficiently notorious to make it an implied term of the banker-customer relationship. The court focused on the claimant's status as a personal customer and ignored the fact he also had a business account. The Business Banking Code (which came into effect April 2002), which covers bank dealings with business customers but not personal customers, provides

> 'if we [the bank] are asked to respond to a status enquiry about you, we will make sure we have your written permission before we give it.'

The Banking Code adopted the Jack Committee recommendation that banks be required to obtain specific consent from the customer in respect of each enquiry. The *Turner* case reiterated this view.

Breach of duty to exercise skill and care

Where a bank receives a reference request (Bank B) it must exercise reasonable skill and care in complying with this request. In this context, the bank's duty to exercise skill and care is on the same basis as the provision of financial advice to a customer. In *Woods v Martins Bank Ltd* [1959] 1 QB 55 the court held that giving such advice was part of the banking business and the bank therefore could not escape the consequences of carelessness. Further, once the bank has complied with this duty, it does not assume a continuing obligation to keep the advice under review, or, if necessary, to correct it in the light of supervising events (*Fennoscondia Ltd v Clarke* [1999] 1 All ER (Comm) 365). Further the House of Lords has distinguished between the duty to supply the information for the purposes of enabling someone else to make the decision, or to assess the information and to advise on how the information should be used. In the first instance, the bank discharges its duty if it takes reasonable steps to ensure that the information is correct (*South Australia Asset Management Corpn v York Montague Ltd* [1997] AC 191).

An action in defamation

Such an action is likely to be met with the defence that any communication is privileged. This defence is likely to be available only where the bank has asked without malice. In most cases this is likely to be the case. In *Robshaw v Smith* (1878) 38 LT 423 the bank showed the enquirer an unfavourable anonymous letter about the person being investigated. The court concluded that the disclosure was privileged and the bank had acted properly to a request for information. In *London Association for Protection of Trade v Greenland Ltd* [1916] 2 AC 15 the view was expressed that the communication of information is privileged whenever an organization has a contractual or business duty to provide it. Therefore, the bank may be able to plead privilege as a defence since supplying references is a duty recognized by the business world.

The position of the enquirer: rights of X

In some circumstances the enquirer may be able to sue his own bank, eg if that bank inaccurately conveys information obtained. In such a case the enquirer may abandon negotiations resulting in loss or be lulled into a false sense of security. Where the customer requests information, his bank has an obligation to convey to him the available information in full and accurately.

The question of the enquirer's rights against the referee bank is more difficult. There is no contractual relationship between the enquirer and referee bank and therefore an action based on fraudulent statements may be the only remedy. The enquirer's right to bring an action based on the referee bank's dishonesty is affected by s 6 of the Statute of Frauds Amendment Act 1828. The section provides that an action

> 'for any representation or assurance concerning the credit, character, ability, or trade conduct of another person, made with the intent that the person concerned may obtain money, credit, or goods, lies if the statement is made in writing and signed by the party charged...'.

Section 6 of the Statute of Frauds Amendment Act 1828 extends to any kind of misrepresentations and not merely fraudulent statements. The person responsible for the misrepresentation must sign the statement personally. Bankers' references are usually unsigned.

Moreover, the question that arises is how can a body corporate sign individually? In *UBAF Securities Ltd v European American Banking Corpn* [1948] QB 713 the signature of the company's authorized assistant secretary was treated as that of the company for the purposes of s 6.

The enquirer also has a right to recover damages from the referee bank by suing in negligence. In *Hedley Byrne & Co Ltd* [1964] AC 465 the court held that the bank had assumed a duty of care owed to the advertising agency (the enquirer). The referee bank was aware that the information was required for a person other than the bank requesting the reference and that knowledge established a relationship of proximity between the referee bank and the advertising agency. The referee bank must, therefore, be shown to have made the statement in circumstances where the referee bank assumes responsibility for the accuracy of the statement. The test is objective and the proximate relationship places the bank under a duty of care. In *Caparo Industries plc v Dickman* [1990] 2 AC 605 the court held the auditors liable for any loss resulting from reliance placed on the accounts by individual investors or in a take-over situation by a bidder. Thus, there is an assumption of liability if the information is used for the purposes it was intended. Further, the court has to consider whether, on the facts, it would be just, reasonable and fair to impose on the representator or the provider of the information a duty of care towards a third party. The court will take into account:

- the purpose for which the statement was made: the representor will be liable to the third party if the statement was made for the purpose of it being communicated to the third party;
- the purpose for which the statement was communicated: in other words, was the statement communicated for information only or with the expectation that it will be acted upon;
- the nature of the relationship between the representor, the person to whom the advice is given, and the third party;
- whether the statement was made for the use of a restricted class;
- the state of the adviser's knowledge: in other words did the representor know the statement would be communicated to a third party and the purpose for which the statement was communicated?

Thus, in the majority of cases the maker of the statement owes a duty of care only to the person for whose immediate use the information is intended.

Further, the claimant must show he has placed reliance on the information supplied to him. In *Mutual Mortgage Corpn Ltd v Bank of Montreal* (1965) 55 DLR (2nd) 164 a bank that was not prepared to extend further credit to a customer introduced him to a mortgage company that was known to extend credit to risks declined by banks. The loan was used to reduce a bank overdraft. An action by the mortgage company to recover losses sustained as a result of the customer's failure was dismissed. There was no evidence to show that the mortgage company, which had its own policy and experience in dealing with high risk cases, would have refused to grant the loan had it been familiar with the customer's record.

Finally, the advice on which reliance is placed must be one in which the referee has adequate expertise to justify reliance by the enquirer.

Where there is a contractual relationship between the bank supplying the reference and the enquirer the bank may rely on the effectiveness of any disclaimer of responsibility. Any such disclaimer will be subject to the test of reasonableness under the Unfair Contract Terms Act 1977 and the Unfair Terms in Consumer Contracts Regulations 1999, SI 1999/2083.

2.3 Some consequences of the banker-customer relationship

Bailment

A bailment occurs when one person (the bailor) transfers possession of a personal chattel to another (the bailee) on the basis that the chattel will be returned to the bailor or dealt with by the bailee as instructed. The bailment usually arises as a result of the voluntary possession of the goods or other chattels although the possession may be actual or constructive. Bailment may either be gratuitous or for reward, with the degree of care required of the bailee depending on whether remuneration is provided.

A bank that accepts valuables for safe custody becomes a bailee of the valuables for the customer. In the absence of agreement to the contrary, the deposit of valuables with a bank for safe custody, by a customer, is subject to the law of bailment. It is possible, however, to exclude liability by express clauses in the contract of bailment. The effect of the Unfair Contract Terms Act 1977 (s 2 (liability for negligence) and s 3 (liability arising in contract)) is that such clauses will be ineffective unless reasonable.

Bank as bailee

The nature of the bank's duty of care as bailee of the customer's valuables depends on whether the bailee is held as a gratuitous bailee or as bailee for reward. In *Houghland v R Low (Luxury Coaches)* [1962] 1 QB 694 the court held that it is unecessary to put different types of bailment into water tight compartments, such as gratuitous bailments on the one hand and bailments for reward on the other. A bailee is under a duty to exercise a degree of care, therefore, warranted by the circumstances. In *Morris v C W Martin & Sons Ltd* [1966] 1 QB 716 Lord Denning expressed the view that a more stringent duty of care will usually be expected from a bailee for reward than from a gratuitous bailee. Banks usually advertise safe custody facilities in order to attract customers and it therefore stands to reason that they derive a general pecuniary benefit from the provision of these services (even if they do not specifically charge for the service). Therefore, a high degree of care would be expected of banks.

The bank's duty of care as bailee covers both the exercise of skill in the custody of the items and also in the appointment of persons charged to ensure safe handling. A bank that negligently, or in breach of any agreement with the customer as to the deposit, loses or damages an item deposited, will be liable in negligence or for breach of contract for the value of the items or the amount of damage. An action in such circumstances will lie in the tort of conversion. Similar liability will also be imposed if the item deposited is handed over to someone not entitled.

Even if the customer's own negligence has contributed to the item being mis-delivered, the bank cannot plead contributory negligence in defence (Torts (Interference with Goods) Act 1977, s 11(1)). Circumstances may arise, however, in which the customer's conduct may stop him from claiming against the bank, eg where the customer has led the bank to believe that delivery to the person concerned would be proper.

Refusal by the bank to deliver the goods to the customer amounts to conversion of the item deposited. Where there is any doubt as to the customer's right to delivery, the bank is entitled to refuse to hand over the item until reasonable enquiries have been made to establish the true position. In *Clayton v Le Roy* [1911] 2 KB 1031 the court said

> 'a man does not act unlawfully in refusing to deliver up property immediately upon demand made. He is entitled to take adequate time to enquire into the rights of the claimant.'

Where a bank is faced with conflicting claims by two or more persons to items held for safe custody, the bank may seek relief from the court by way of inter-pleader summons (RSC Ord 17 CPR, Sch 1). In such circumstances, the court determines the validity of the rival claims and the bank is relieved from further liability. In this situation, the bank need not wait for an action to be brought by the claimants and it is enough that the bank expects to be sued.

Where the goods are misappropriated by an employee of the bank, it will be vicariously liable (*Morris v C W Martin & Sons Ltd* [1966] 1 QB 716). But if a customer authorizes the bank to deliver up the items deposited to a third party, such instructions should be clear and unambiguous to protect the bank from claims in conversion. Authority to allow a third party 'access' to the items deposited is not considered sufficient to allow removal of such items. Third party authority is cancelled by the customer's debts, insanity or bankruptcy.

Appropriation of payments

One of the features of the current account is that the credit/debit balance will alter on an almost daily basis because mutual dealings will be transacted through it. For most purposes it is adequate to determine the net credit or debit balances on the account, although in some cases it may become important to determine which of the debit entries have been discharged by the credit entries that have taken place. The problem occurs in two types of cases eg:

♦ where the bank seeks to enforce a security in relation to the overdrawn current account;
♦ where the issue is that of a partner's liability on the dissolution of the firm.

Thus, a situation may arise where a third party guarantees an overdraft facility for an agreed period. On the expiration of that agreed period the bank decides not to freeze the account on the final date for which the security is given and the account is continued in the ordinary manner, with further credits and withdrawals being made against the account. Where, in that situation, the bank subsequently seeks to enforce the guarantee, a dispute may arise as to the extent of the debts covered by the guarantee. The bank may argue that the guarantee extends to the full amount overdrawn including any amounts withdrawn after the account should have been frozen or ruled off, whilst the guarantor will seek to reduce the amount of his liability by any sums paid to the credit of the account after that date. The issue may also arise where a partnership firm is dissolved eg on the retirement of a partner, and the partnership account continues to be operated in the ordinary way. In that situation it becomes necessary to determine the liability of the retired partner in relation to partnership debts incurred after his retirement and after notice of retirement has been published in the *London Gazette*.

The principal used by the courts to solve disputes of this nature is known as 'the rule of appropriation of payments' or as 'first incurred first discharged'. The effect of this rule is that each item paid to the credit of the customer's account is deemed to discharge the earliest of the debit items on the account. The rule was established in *Devaynes v Noble; Clayton's Case* (1816) 1 Mer 572 where one of the partners in a banking partnership died, and consequently the partnership was dissolved. The remaining partners continued the business as a going concern. Eventually, the bank became insolvent and a customer sought to recover the balance due to him from the deceased partner's estate. At the time of the partner's death there was a substantial credit balance in the account, but during the period following it the surviving partner withdrew amounts exceeding the credit balance. The surviving partner also paid credits to the account, so that the balance in the account was higher than the original balance in favour of the partnership at the time of the partner's death. The court held that the deceased partner's estate was not liable for debts incurred by the bank in respect of money deposited by the customer to the credit of the account. The money paid out by the bank had discharged the initial balance due to the customer at the date of the relevant partner's death.

The rule in *Clayton's Case* is based on a presumption as to the probable intention of the parties and if a creditor wishes to depart from the arrangement he must make his intention clear to the debtor. In this case, there was no indication of any such intention and the amounts paid out by the bank after the death of the partner had discharged the initial balance due to the customer. The presumption of intention on which the rule in *Clayton's Case* is based is not readily displaced. In *Deeley v Lloyds Bank Ltd* [1912] AC 756 a bank obtained from its customer a first mortgage to secure an overdraft. When the bank received notice that the customer had granted a second mortgage over the property, it failed to freeze the balance as it stood, and instead allowed the customer to continue operating the account in the ordinary manner. The amounts paid in by him were higher than the balance of the overdraft at the date of the notification of the second mortgage although further fresh withdrawals had left the account in debit. The second mortgagee claimed that he had priority to the bank, as credits (applying the

Clayton's Case) to the customer's account had discharged the earlier indebtedness. The Court of Appeal held that the rule in *Clayton's Case* had been displaced by the intention of the parties and Fletcher Moulton LJ contended that it was absurd to attribute to a bank an intention to appropriate payments into a secured rather than unsecured debt. He ridiculed the recognition of a legal rule that the bank could circumvent by the 'simple formality of drawing two horizontal lines in their books and making believe to commence a new account'. The House of Lords, however, reversed the decision on the grounds that the rule in *Clayton's Case* was not excluded by the conduct of the parties. It held that primarily the right to appropriate a payment made to the credit of an account rested with the debtor, but if he did not evince an intention, the creditor ought to do so, and in the absence of a specific appropriation the position was governed by the rule in *Clayton's Case*. Indeed, if either the bank or creditor had intended to appropriate the payments made to the credit of the account after notification of the second mortgage, it should always rule off the account where it is desired to preserve a security on which further advances cannot be charged. An alternative course of action would be for the bank to strike a balance in the account and then open a fresh account in the name of the customer (see *Royal Bank of Canada v Bank of Montreal* (1976) 67 DLR (3d) 755).

The rule in *Clayton's Case* has also been applied in cases where a partnership firm is dissolved. In *Royal Bank of Scotland v Christie* (1841) 8 A & Fin 214 a partner in a trading firm mortgaged his own land to secure advances made to the firm by its bank. At the date of the partner's death the firm had overdrawn on its account, but on the death of the partner the account continued unbroken. The surviving partners paid into the account amounts, which exceeded the debit balance at the deceased partner's death, and then withdrew an even larger balance. The court held that the rule in *Clayton's Case* required payments into the account by the surviving partners to be credited first against the earlier debit items in the account; the account being overdrawn, the payments into the account after the death of the partner went to pay off the mortgage.

In *Re Yeovil Glove Co Ltd* [1965] Ch 148 a company created a mortgage over the whole of its assets by way of a floating charge to secure its existing and future indebtedness to the bank. The company went into liquidation within 12 months of the creation of the charge with the result that the charge was void except as security for 'cash paid to the company at the time of, or subsequently to the creation of, and in consideration for, the charge'. The Court of Appeal held that the floating charge was valid security for advances made by the bank after it was created, but not for earlier advances. Because the company had paid amounts into its current account since the creation of the charge, those amounts went towards satisfying its existing indebtedness under *Clayton's Case* and the advances made since the creation of the floating charge were still owing and secured by the charge.

The rule in *Clayton's Case* applies only to current accounts (*The Mecca* [1897] AC 286) and there are a number of instances where it is likely to be displaced.

(1) Slade J expressed the view in *Siebe Gorman & Co Ltd v Barclays Bank Ltd* [1979] 2 Lloyd's Rep 142 at 164 that the opening of a fresh account displaces the rule in *Clayton's Case*. He also recognized two further exceptions to the rule. Firstly, the rule does not apply in respect of secured transactions where the second mortgagee agreed to the making of fresh advances by the first mortgagee. Secondly, the rule does not apply where the fresh advances are made under a contractual obligation arising under the mortgage deed.

(2) Where a trustee pays trust money into his personal account, thus mixing trust funds with his own funds. In *Re Hallett's Estate* (1880) 13 Ch D 696 a solicitor, who misappropriated funds from a client account and had them transferred into his account (so trust and personal funds were mixed in the account), was deemed to withdraw his personal savings first thus leaving the trust funds intact.

(3) The rule does not apply to separate bank accounts even if maintained with the same bank. In *Bradford Old Bank Ltd v Sutcliffe* [1918] 2 KB 833 a customer had a loan account and a current account and it was held that payments to the credit of the current account must be appropriated to that account. Accordingly, a guarantor for the loan account could not claim that such payments should be used to reduce the loan account.

Moreover, the rule does not apply where the account has been stopped, ie where payments in and out do not take place.

(4) The rule does not apply where the parties have merely entered into a series of transactions without a current account (*Cory Bros Co v Mecca Turkish SS (Owners), The Mecca* [1897] AC 286) or where it is clear from the circumstances that the creditor intended to reserve the right.

(5) The rule does not apply where the bank agrees not to apply the first-in, first-out rule. Thus, in *Westminster Bank Ltd v Cond* (1940) 46 Com Cas 60 the guarantor argued that because the bank had continued the account unbroken after making a demand on him, the loan had been paid off by subsequent payments into the account. The court rejected this argument on the grounds that the guarantee form contained an express clause to prevent the operation of the rule.

Termination of the banker and customer relationship

The banker and customer relationship may be terminated in a number of different ways namely: (i) by agreement between the parties; (ii) by the unilateral conduct of one of the parties, eg by the customer giving notice to terminate; (iii) by operation of law.

By agreement between the parties

A demand for repayment of the full credit balance on an account when the customer has no other accounts with that bank will suffice to terminate the banker and customer relationship. If the customer has more than one account with the bank the relationship will not be terminated until all the accounts maintained with the bank or building society are closed. The effect of the termination is that the bank's mandate to honour cheques and to collect cheques and other instruments is withdrawn and the whole of the credit balance becomes immediately repayable either to the customer himself or in accordance with the instructions. Conversely, on termination of the relationship by the bank any debit balance (eg where the customer is overdrawn) becomes immediately payable and the bank can recover the amount by bringing an action in debt. Where the bank has made a loan to the customer that is repayable in the future, the termination of the relationship does not advance the date for repayment of the loan.

A demand for repayment of the credit balance must be made at the branch where the account (*Leader & Co v Direction-Gessellschaft* (1914-15) 31 TLR 83) is kept if the customer wants repayment of the credit balance immediately. It is advisable for a bank to obtain in writing any indication of the customer's intention to close the account (*Wilson v Midland Bank Ltd* (cited in Milnes Holden, *The Law and Practice of Banking* vol 1 Banker & Customer. 5th edn Pitman, 1991, p 117).

A customer who wishes to close a deposit account or other account where notice has to be given must give the necessary notice. If, however, the deposit is for a fixed period then it becomes automatically payable at the end of that period.

A bank may terminate the banker and customer relationship by giving notice to the customer and tendering the credit balance held in favour of the customer. Unless, otherwise agreed the bank must give a reasonable length of notice of its intention to terminate the account so as to enable the customer to make alternative arrangements and to allow any outstanding instruments to be presented (see *Joachimson v Swiss Bank Corpn* (1872) LR 8 EX 10). In *Prosperity Ltd v Lloyds Bank Ltd* (1923) 39 TLR 372 the court held that the bank could not lawfully close an account forthwith but should give the customer sufficient notice of its intention to close the account. The court took the view that the question of what constitutes reasonableness:

> 'must depend on the special facts and circumstances of the case. An account might be a small account drawn upon only by cheques cashed by the customer for his own purposes. In that case a comparatively short notice might be all that was needed.'

> But if the customer uses the account for cheques that are remitted overseas, then a longer period of notice is required to be given by the bank.

If, however, the bank decides to close the current account without giving any, or a reasonable period of, notice of its intention, the customer's only remedy is to sue for damages for any inconvenience and any loss of business he suffers.

This requirement to give notice does not apply to a deposit account and, unless otherwise agreed, a bank may repay a balance on a deposit account at any time. Where notice is required to be given prior to closing an account in respect of a deposit account the bank would appear to satisfy its obligations if instead of the necessary notice the bank pays interest for the period of notice.

Death of the customer

The death of the customer terminates the contract between him and the bank because of the personal nature of the relationship (*Farrow v Wilson* (1869) LR 4 CP 744). The credit balance on the customer's current or deposit account vests in his personal representatives but such persons cannot sue the bank to recover the amount credited to his account until they have obtained a grant of probate. A bank's duty to pay cheques on the deceased's account is terminated when the bank receives notice of the customer's death and not merely by the fact of the death if that is unknown to the bank (*Tate v Hilbert* (1793) 2 Ves 111; Bills of Exchange Act 1882, s 75(2)). This actually increases the period during which a bank is protected, if it continues to operate the customer's account after his death but the fact of the death is unknown to the bank.

Although, the personal representatives of a deceased customer may demand repayment of the deceased's account, they are not entitled to operate it by drawing cheques on it. For this purpose they are required to open a fresh account in their own names and, on the production of the grant of probate to have the balance of the deceased's account transferred to the new account. If the deceased customer's account was overdrawn the personal representatives must discharge the debit balance out of the estate but they are not personally liable for it.

Mental disorder

If the customer suffers from a mental disorder to such an extent that he is unable to manage his own affairs properly, the banker and customer relationship is terminated in the same way as if the customer had died. In *Drew v Nunn* (1879) 4 QBD 661 Brett J said:

> 'where such a change occurs as to the principal that he can no longer act for himself, the agent whom he has appointed can no longer act for him.'

The court may appoint a receiver to administer the property of such a person. By such an order the receiver may be empowered to operate the customer's account, and in such a situation the proper course is for a new account to be opened in the receiver's name, indicating that it is a fiduciary account, and the credit balance in the customer's account is then transferred to this account. In honouring cheques drawn by a receiver the bank must be aware and comply with any limitations on his powers.

Bankruptcy or insolvency

If no receiver is appointed to administer the affairs of the customer of unsound mind, then there is no one who can give the bank a good discharge if it closes the account. It has been held that if a bank makes advances out of the customer's account at the request of a relative or custodian, and the advance is used to pay for goods or services necessary to the customer, then the bank is entitled to debit the customer's account with the amount of the advance (*Re Bevan, Davies, Bank & Co v Bevan* [1913] 2 Ch 595.

If a person is adjudged bankrupt by the court, the contract between him and the bank is terminated and all his property vests in the trustee in bankruptcy appointed to administer the estate (Insolvency Act 1986, s 306). On the production of a certificate of appointment the trustee is entitled to receive the balance standing to the credit of the customer's account. Under s 267 of the Insolvency Act 1986 a person may be adjudged bankrupt if he is indebted to the petitioner for £750 or more and he appears either 'unable to pay or to have no reasonably prospect of being able to pay' his debts. A particular problem that may arise in relation to banks is whether a bank should continue to pay its customer's cheques after it learns that a petition has been presented to the court but before it learns that a bankruptcy order has been made. The answer to this question depends on s 284 of the Insolvency Act 1986. Where a person is adjudged bankrupt any disposition of property made by that person in the period to which the section applies is void except to the extent that it was made with the consent of the court, or except to the extent the court subsequently ratifies it. The period to which the section applies is the period beginning with the day of the presentation of the petition for the bankruptcy order and ending with the vesting of the bankrupt's estate in a trustee.

Where the customer's account is overdrawn the payment of a cheque against the overdrawn account is something the bank could prove against under s 382 of the Insolvency Act. The section defines a 'bankruptcy debt' in relation to a bankrupt as any debt or liability to which he is subject at the commencement of the bankruptcy.

If the customer of a bank is a company, the mandate given by it to the bank may terminate in one of a number of ways, namely: by the board of the company passing a resolution to that effect and notifying to the bank; by the appointment of a receiver or administrative receiver; by the making of an administration order; or by the company going into liquidation.

Resolution of the board of directors

A resolution appointing a bank to act in that capacity for a company usually remains in force until the resolution is amended by the board of directors and a copy sent to the bank. Accordingly, the original mandate may be amended or determined by a subsequent resolution. A company may close its account by withdrawing its credit balance or by repaying its overdraft without formally passing a resolution determining the mandate. In such a situation written evidence should be obtained, from those authorized to operate the company's account, that the account has been closed.

Where the customer is made bankrupt or goes into liquidation the issue of the bank's mandate to pay cheques drawn against the account will become important. The Insolvency Act 1986 has consolidated the law on company insolvency and winding-up and the law on the bankruptcy of individuals.

The basic effect of the customer's bankruptcy is to vest his property in the trustee in bankruptcy (Insolvency Act 1986, s 306). For bankruptcy purposes, the customer's estate includes all the property belonging to or vested in him at the commencement of the bankruptcy or acquired by him before his discharge (Insolvency Act 1986, ss 283 and 307(1)). For the purposes of the bankruptcy any credit balance in the customer's bank account is treated as an asset of the customer, although the bank is entitled to a set-off where appropriate.

Section 278 of the Insolvency Act 1986 provides that the bankruptcy of an individual 'commences with the day on which the bankruptcy order is made' and unless the bank obtains an unfair preference from the bankrupt it is not concerned with transactions preceding the date of the bankruptcy order. Section 278 resolves a problem that was created by the Bankruptcy Act 1914 in respect of the bank's obligation to pay the net balance to the trustee in bankruptcy. The 1914 Act provided that the trustee in bankruptcy's title to the customer's assets related back, or took effect, from the date of the earliest act of bankruptcy proved to have been committed by him within three months before the presentation of the petition on which the bankruptcy was based. Unless an exception were made to this rule the bank would have to account to the trustee in bankruptcy for all amounts paid out of the customer's account after that date.

Further, s 284(1)–(3) of the Insolvency Act 1986 provides that any payment made by the customer before the date of the order but after the presentation of the bankruptcy petition is void unless it is made with the consent of the court or is subsequently ratified by it. Section 284 (4) then goes on to provide that the section will not apply if the payment is received by the payee in good faith, for value and without knowledge that a bankruptcy petition has been filed. Although s 284 will not grant a direct remedy against a bank, it does mean that if there is any possibility of the payment being declared void the bank will try and ensure that the proper procedure has been followed.

An issue for consideration is what is the position of a bank where a cheque drawn by its customer after the bankruptcy order has been made but before it is published in the *London Gazette*. In *Re Wigzell, ex p Hart* [1921] 2 KB 835 the court held the bank liable for the full amount of the credit balance standing in favour of the bankrupt customer's account on the day the petition was granted but which had by the order of the court, not been immediately published in the *London Gazette*. Some protection for a bankruptcy adjudication was given in s 284(5) of the Insolvency Act 1986 which provides that where a payment is made from an account at the insistence of the customer after the commencement of his bankruptcy, the bank may debit his account unless (a) the bank had earlier notice of the bankruptcy or (b) it is not reasonably practicable to recover the amount from the payee. The bank will not be able to rely on s 284(5) after the bankruptcy order has been advertised (*Re Byfield, ex p Hill Samuel & Co Ltd* [1982] 1 All ER 249).

The bank's position in respect to the payment of cheques where a company customer is wound up is similar to the bankruptcy of an individual. Section 127 of the Insolvency Act 1986 provides that any disposition of property, including any transfer of choses in action, made after the commencement of the winding up order is void. The date of the commencement of the winding up depends on whether the winding up is a voluntary one resulting from a resolution of the company to that effect, or is a compulsory winding up resulting from a creditor of the company or a member of it presenting a petition to the court to wind up the company. In *Re Gray's Inn Construction Co Ltd* [1980] 1 WLR 711 the extent of the bank's right to operate the customer's account after the commencement of the winding up was examined. The facts of the case were that the company had a current account with its bank. At the time that the winding up petition (3 August 1972) was presented, the account was overdrawn and the overdraft secured by the personal guarantee of the managing director. The petition was advertised on 10 August and the head office of the bank made aware of it on the 17 August. A compulsory winding up order was made on 9 October, the account having been continued unbroken until then. Between the presentation of the petition and the winding up order being made, substantial amounts were credited and then withdrawn from the account, leaving a small credit balance. The liquidator claimed either the amount of the credits paid into the account, or alternatively, the total amount of the debits as dispositions of the company's property under the former s 227 of the Companies Act 1948 under s 127 of the Insolvency Act 1986. It was agreed in the course of the proceedings that the loss should be restricted to that suffered as a result of the continued trading, approximately £5,000.

Templeman J held that the credits were not dispositions of the company's property within s 227, and exercising his discretion under the section held that the payments out were valid. The Court of Appeal, however, reversing the trial judge, held that the payment should not be validated as the 'dispositions' involved were effected with the purpose of discharging certain pre-liquidation debts in priority to claims of other creditors. Furthermore, the bank could not set-off an overdraft on the account against the amount of cheques collected after the commencement of the winding up. It expressed the view that, whenever possible, any amounts paid out in respect of pre-liquidation debts ought to be recovered from the payee.

Liquidation of the bank

The liquidation of the bank will terminate the banker and customer relationship. In *Re Russian Commercial and Industrial Bank* [1955] 1 Ch 148 the court expressed the view that the relationship is terminated when the legal personality of the body corporate ceases to exist. The credit balance held on behalf of the customer then becomes payable to him, or to his estate, immediately. The termination of the banker and customer relationship does not prevent a customer from recovering any unauthorized debits made against his account (*Limpgrane Ltd v Bank of Credit and Commerce SA* [1986] FLR 36). The customer will, however, be treated as an unsecured creditor of the bank and his right to recover amounts standing to the credit of the account effected by the liquidation of the bank.

The consequences of termination

The consequence of terminating the banker-customer relationship is that the customer is entitled to demand the immediate repayment of any credit balance due to him. As a general rule, the bank need not have regard to the claims of third parties who claim either the whole, or part, of the credit balance that stands in favour of the customer (*Tassell v Cooper* (1850) 9 CB 509). The courts may intervene to protect a third party either by way of a third party debt order or by granting a Freezing injunction.

Third party debt orders

A balance standing to the credit of the customer's account can be attached by way of a 'Third party debt order' under CPR Part 72, which came into effect in March 2002. Such orders replace the (previously known as) garnishee orders that were issued under the County Court Rules 1981 (CCR, Ord 30). Part 72 introduces the following main charges:

♦ the term 'garnishee' has been replaced by 'third party';
♦ 'order nisi' has been replaced by 'interim third party debt';
♦ 'order absolute' has been replaced by 'final order'.

Under CPR, Pt 72, the court has the power to order the third party to pay the amount of the debt due or accruing to the judgment debtor from the third party. Any surplus held by the bank can be paid in accordance with instructions from the judgment debtor. The book cannot later be made to account for moneys paid from that surplus in favour of the judgment creditor.

A bank or building society served with an interim third party debt order must carry out a search to identify all accounts held by the judgment debtor (CPR r 72.6 (1)). The bank or building society must disclose the following to the court and the creditor, within seven days of service of the order, in respect of each account maintain by the judgment debtor:

♦ the number of the account;
♦ whether or not the account has a credit balance;
♦ if the account is in credit:
  i) whether the balance of the account is sufficient to cover the amount specified in the order;
  ii) if not, the amount of credit balance at the date on which the order is served;
  iii) whether or not the bank or building society asserts right to any of the credit balance (CPR 72.6(2)).

If the judgment debtor does not hold an account with the bank of building society, or if it is unable to comply with the order for any reason, that fact must be notified to the court and creditor (CPR 72.6(3)).

The third party debtor order does not apply to accounts held in the name of the judgment debtor and another person (ie it does now extend to joint accounts) (72 PD.3). The order applies to a debt which is 'due or accruing due'.

All debts due or accruing due from any individual or corporation (excluding the Crown) to a judgment creditor can be attached but if a garnishee order is to be made it is essential that, at the time the order takes effect, there is a debt owing to the judgment debtor that the law recognizes to be a debt (*Webb v Stenton* (1883) 11 QBD 518). In *Joachimson v Swiss Bank Corpn* [1921] 3 KB 110 the court observed that the service of the garnishee notice on the bank operated as a demand and the debt became due and owing.

The position with regard to deposit accounts was more complicated because notice often has to be given in respect of these accounts or deposit may continue to be held until a fixed period. The law was clarified by the passing of s 38 of the Administration of Justice Act 1956 under which amounts standing to the credit of savings accounts, deposit accounts and fixed deposit accounts with banks may be attached. This provision was extended by s 40 of the Supreme Court Act 1981 (as amended by SI 2002/3649) to any deposit account with a bank or other deposit-taking institution, or to any 'withdrawable share account with any deposit-taking institution' and any condition requiring notice, or a personal application, or a requirement that a deposit or share account be produced, or any other prescribed condition be satisfied, will be disregarded.

Where an order nisi is made in respect of a credit balance expressed in a foreign currency, the bank that is served with the interim order must put a stop on such an amount of the foreign currency as is necessary to satisfy the judgment in sterling. To do this, the bank should set aside sufficient foreign currency to satisfy the judgment debt expressed in sterling at the rate of exchange prevailing at the time the garnishee order nisi was made. The bank should not convert the attached foreign currency into sterling until the order has been made absolute. When that has been done the bank should convert the attached currency into sterling at the then rate of exchange in order to meet the judgment debt; any surplus of sterling from the conversion, if the rate of exchange has moved in favour of the foreign currency, should be paid to the judgment debtor.

An interim order attaches the debt in the hands of the third party so that he cannot obtain a discharge by making payment to the judgment debtor. The interim order does not attach to amounts paid to the customer's account after the date on which the order is made and, in case of delay, when it is served on the bank.

Grounds for objection to the order being made absolute

The interim order gives the bank an opportunity to object to the order being made absolute. The most obvious reason for the court not to make an interim order absolute is that the debt has already been discharged. There are other objections, however, that a bank can raise to have the interim order discharged.

(i)   The bank's right to repayment will have priority over the amount of the interim order where the judgment creditor is indebted to the bank in circumstances that give the bank a right either to set-off or to combine the credit balance of the garnished account with a debit balance on another account maintained by the customer (*Tapp v Jones* (1875) LR 10 QB). This right would apply in respect of overdrafts which are repayable on demand and which the bank can readily set-off, but not loan agreements where the debt does not become payable until a future date.

(ii) A bank should object to the attachment order where the amount sought to be attached is standing to the credit of a trust account (*Plunkett v Barclays Bank Ltd* [1936] 2 KB 107).

(iii) An interim order will be discharged where the balance standing to the credit of the customer's account is held in a joint account. In *Hirschorn v Evans* [1938] 3 KB 801 the Court of Appeal held that a garnishee order could not attach a joint account of a husband and wife in respect of a debt owed by the husband only.

(iv) The bank is likely to object to an attachment order where the judgment debtor is described by a name different to that of the account sought to be attached (*Moore v Peachey* (1842) 8 TLR 406 and *Koch v Mineral Ore Syndicate* (1910) 54 SJ 600). In the latter case the order was, in fact, amended to comply with the name on the account but the bank was not liable for having paid cheques drawn on the account in the meantime.

(v) A bank may oppose the grant of an interim order where there is a possibility that payment of the debt to the judgment creditor will not be recognized as a discharge in other jurisdiction, with the effect that payment may have to be made twice (*Deutsche Schachtbau und Tiefbohgesellshaft v R'As as Khaima International Oil Co* [1990] 1 AC 259).

(vi) An interim order where the judgment debtor is insolvent and the third party debt order is used to give the judgment creditor precedence over the other creditors should not be made (*Whitbread Flowers v Thurston (Unreported)* (1979) CLY 22).

(vii) In *Alcom Ltd v Republic of Colombia* [1984] AC 580, the House of Lords held that the credit balance on an account cannot be attached if the account is held by a foreign state unless the account is used for commercial transactions. The account cannot be dissected and the different purposes for which it is used examined individually, as to enable an attachment order to be made.

(viii) Initially, where the credit balance in standing in favour of the judgment creditor has been assigned in favour of a third party the court will object to the third party debt order because of the conflict of priorities. In *Rekstin v Severo Sibirsko Gosudarstvennoe Akcionairnoe Obschestvo Komseverputij* [1933] 1 KB 47 (a case involving money transfer orders) the court held that once an amount due to the judgment creditor has been effectively assigned to a third party that part of the credit balance cannot be made subject to the garnishee order.

Thus, where the assignment has been completed before service of the interim order, the assignee's interest prevails over the judgment debtor.

The Freezing injunction

An unsecured creditor cannot, pending the outcome of an action brought by him, seek to freeze any assets belonging to the defendant. Until the introduction of the Mareva injunction (now known as the Freezing injunction), this therefore left the defendant free to transfer his assets in this country, abroad or to otherwise dispose of them pending the outcome of proceedings brought by the plaintiff. Consequently, a successful plaintiff might discover that the judgment obtained against the defendant remains unsatisfied because the debtor has transferred his assets out of the jurisdiction or has otherwise effectively dissipated them. The Mareva injunction (Freezing injunction) was therefore devised (*Nippon Yusen Kaisha v Karageorgis* [1975] 2 WLR 288; *Mareva Companania SA v International Bulk Carriers* [1980] 1 All ER 213) as a means of preventing the debtor from disposing of assets which were the likely subject of a court order. Lord Denning giving judgment in the *Mareva* case itself said that if it appears that a debt is due and owing, and there is a danger that the debtor may dispose of his assets so as to defeat the creditors expectation of satisfying his judgment by levying execution on assets in this country, the court has jurisdiction to grant an interlocutory judgment so as to prevent the disposing of the assets. Section 37 of the Supreme Court Act 1981 gives statutory recognition and extends the power of the High Court to grant an interlocutory injunction by providing that a Freezing injunction may be granted in respect of assets located within the jurisdiction regardless of whether or not the party is domiciled, resident, or present within the jurisdiction. The Freezing injunction is therefore available in disputes relating to both international and domestic transactions.

When granting a Freezing injunction the court should take care to ensure that the order does not interfere with third party rights. Thus, a Freezing injunction served on a bank does not attach to a joint account, except where all the account holders are made co-defendants or the order is so drafted that it applies to accounts to which the defendant is a party (*Z Ltd v A-Z and AA-LL* [1982] QB 558). Moreover, even where the account is maintained in the sole name of the defendant a third party may be able to establish a superior title, eg where the third party can show that amounts standing to the credit of the defendants account are trust account (*SCF Finance Co Ltd v Masri* [1985] 1 WLR 876).

The parties to a Freezing injunction

It has already been established that a plaintiff who is owed money and who brings an action for debt or for damages can apply for a Freezing injunction pending the outcome of the action. The effect of the order is to prevent the defendant from disposing of his assets or removing the assets outside the jurisdiction. The question that arose in *Chief Constable of Kent v V* [1983] QB 34 was whether, pending criminal prosecution for forgery and obtaining money by deception on forged instruments, the police could apply for an injunction to freeze amounts obtained by the accused. The court held that money obtained by forgery and paid into a bank account by the accused should be frozen, especially since the accused had been granted bail pending trial and would otherwise be free to draw on the account. Where money obtained dishonestly is mixed with funds obtained honestly by the accused, the Freezing injunction should be limited to the amount of the money obtained dishonestly. If, however, the stolen money can no longer be identified the court will, if necessary, make an order freezing the whole of the credit balance in the bank until the amount obtained dishonestly may be ascertained.

Some issues in respect of Freezing injunctions are as follows.

Who is the defendant and where does he hold the account?

If the Freezing injunction specifies the name of the customer whose account is sought to be attached and the branch where the account is kept, the bank will have no problem in identifying the account that is subject to the order. If, however, the plaintiff cannot identify the bank account (eg where a partnership account is held in a name other than that of the defendant or the partnership) the plaintiff may request the bank to conduct a search to determine whether the bank holds any account for or assets owned by the defendant. There is no doubt that a bank that has to search for the defendant's account is entitled to be reimbursed any expenses incurred, in addition to being paid for carrying out the search.

Pre-injunction transactions

Where the defendant has drawn cheques on his account before the injunction is communicated to the bank but the cheques are presented to the defendant's bank for payment after the bank has been served with notification of the Freezing injunction the question arises whether the payee or other holder of the cheque is entitled to be paid out of the account that has been attached. The defendant bank should therefore dishonour cheques presented to it after notification of the injunction, even though they were drawn before the order was made and notified to the bank. The bank must be cautious in giving reasons for the dishonour and ensure that they are not defamatory, eg imply that the drawer has insufficient funds to meet the cheque. If the defendant's bank is under a legal obligation to a third party to make a payment then the bank must honour its obligation. Thus, if a cheque is drawn before the Freezing injunction is granted, or before it is notified to the defendant's bank, and is backed by a cheque card, the bank must honour it on presentation because of the guarantee liability that the bank undertakes by means of the cheque card.

The banker's duty of confidence to its customer

The bank is bound by the duty of confidentiality except when ordered by a court (eg when the bank's duty to its customer is outweighed by its duty to the general public). Where, therefore, the plaintiff is uncertain about the extent of the credit balance of the defendant's account when the injunction is granted, the plaintiff must apply for an order of discovery at the time he applies for the injunction.

Moreover, a bank that has been served with a Freezing injunction is under no obligation to divulge whether the injunction has taken effect. Where the bank cannot give effect to the injunction, eg if the defendant does not have an account with the bank on whom the Freezing injunction is served or the account has a credit balance less that the plaintiff's claim, the bank is not obliged to give notice to the plaintiff of the absence or insufficiency of the defendant's account.

Jurisdictional problems

The purpose of a Freezing injunction is to prevent the defendant from removing his assets outside the jurisdiction or disposing of them so as to prevent any judgment in favour of the plaintiff being rendered ineffective. Even if the judgment of the English courts could be enforced abroad, the removal of the defendant's assets will inevitably result in delays and expense to the prejudice of the plaintiff.

An order of the English courts granting a Freezing injunction will not operate outside the jurisdiction. Thus, a Freezing injunction granted by the English courts will not have effect on overseas branches of UK banks conducting business abroad. The overseas branches of UK banks will have had to comply with the laws of the countries in which they carry on business, and the plaintiff would therefore have to obtain a Freezing injunction, or the equivalent, in that country (*R v Grossman* [1981] 73 Cr App Rep 302). Conversely, a Freezing injunction issued by an overseas court does not operate in the UK if the defendant has an account held by a branch of a bank in this country. The plaintiff must in that case obtain an injunction through the English courts.

Three

Legal issues affecting the business customer and bank

3.1 Customers of the corporate bank

A partnership is a contractual relationship. Partners therefore make a contract with each other and are generally free to agree to whatever terms they wish. In the absence of an agreement, s 24 of the Partnership Act 1890 implies certain terms into the partnership contract. Additionally, ss 28–30 set out fiduciary duties that partners owe to each other. Although fiduciary duties cannot be contracted out of, it is possible for the other partners to waive the breach.

The Partnership Act 1890, s 1(1), defines a partnership as a

> 'relation, which subsists between persons carrying on a business in common with a view of profit.'

The definition emphasizes that a partnership is merely a contractual relationship. A partnership is not a separate legal entity (unlike a company) with a legal existence of its own. Consequently, partners act on behalf of each other and partnership property and assets are held on trust for each other. The Limited Liability Partnerships Act 2000 enables a partnership registered with Companies House under that Act to obtain separate legal identity.

The Partnership Act 1890 requires the partnership to carry on a business together with a view to a profit. A business is deemed, for this purpose, to include every trade, profession or occupation, and even if the venture is confined to a single transaction (eg the purchase and resale of a consignment of goods) there may still arise a partnership (*Mann v D'Arcy* [1968] 2 All ER 172). A partnership does not exist when the persons involved merely undertake acts preparatory to the commencement of a business. In *Keith Spicer Ltd v Mansell* [1970] 1 All ER 462 the court held that promoters of a company were not carrying on business as a partnership when they ordered goods prior to the registration of the company. The acts were merely preparatory to the commencement of the company's business.

In order to become a partner, a person must carry on a business in common with other partners. In *Saywell v Pope* (1979) 53 TC 40 a partnership had been carried on by A and B without a written agreement being entered into. When a partnership agreement was drawn up, the wives of A and B were named as partners although they contributed nothing to the business. The two wives could not write cheques or draw on the firm's bank account, but they were warned of the risk of becoming partners. Neither the firm's bank, nor its creditors or customers, were told that the wives had become partners. In a dispute relating to tax liability, the court held that the wives were not partners, as they did nothing in that capacity. The question whether or not the wives were partners at the relevant time could only be determined by examining the facts of the case, and the partnership agreement is not conclusive. Therefore, an employee of a business will not become a partner merely because he receives a share of the business profits; something more is required eg participation in the decision-making.

It is not necessary that a profit be made before a partnership can exist but what is required is that the partners should intend to make a profit. This intention distinguishes a partnership from unincorporated associations, eg members clubs.

Presumption of a partnership

Whether or not a partnership exists will depend on whether the definition under s 1(1) of the Partnership Act 1890 has been satisfied. Section 2, however, establishes a number of presumptions that apply to help determine whether or not a partnership in fact exists.

♦ If property is held by persons as joint tenants or tenants in common, this does not in itself create a partnership in respect of property thus held. In *Davies v Davies* [1894] 1 Ch 393 property was left by a father's will to his two sons as tenants in common and it was employed in the course of a partnership business carried on by them. The property did not become partnership property or constitute the assets of a new partnership between them.

The sharing of gross profits does not itself create a partnership, whether or not the persons sharing such returns have a joint interest in the property from which the profits are derived (s 2(2)). Gross returns also may be referred to as gross takings and consist of all the money that the business has taken in over a specified period. Gross profits are different and consist of any surplus that remains after all liabilities have been discharged. In *Cox v Coulson* [1916] 2 KB 177 the defendant, who leased and managed a theatre, agreed to stage a play with the manager of a touring theatrical company. The defendant was to receive 60% of the gross takings whilst the manager of the touring theatre company was to receive 40%. During the performance, a member of the audience was injured and claimed damages from the defendant on the grounds that the defendant was in partnership with the manager of the touring company. The court held that there was no partnership and so the defendant was not liable. The mere sharing of the gross profits in itself did not impose a presumption of partnership.

♦ The receipt by a person of a share of the net profits of a business is prima facie evidence that he is a partner (s 2(3)), but the receipt of a payment, which is contingent on or varying with the profits of a business, does not of itself necessarily make him a partner in the business. The common law principle was established in *Cox v Hickman* [1860] 8 HL Cas 268 that established that the receipt of a share of partnership profits implied that the recipient was a partner in the absence of a contrary intention. Consequently, in deciding whether a partnership existed, the receipt of a share of profits was not conclusive evidence but merely one of the factors to be taken into account (*Davies v Davies* [1894] 1 Ch 393). Section 2(3) of the Partnership Act then provides that the recipient is not a partner: where he receives payment of a debt due to him by instalments out of the profits of the debtor's business; if an employee receives remuneration in the form of a share of profits; where a widow or child of a deceased partner receives an annuity out of partnership profits; where a loan is made and the lender is to receive a share of profits in place of interest or a variable rate of interest dependent on the profits from the partnership business. In these circumstances, the recipient is a creditor of the business and not a partner. Finally, the receipt of a share of the profits of the business in consideration for the sale of goodwill does not necessarily make the recipient a partner (*Pratt v Strick* [1932] 17 TC 457).

Under s 2(3) of the Partnership Act 1890 there is a prima facie evidence of a partnership and the court will attempt to ascertain the real intention of the partners and the person who is entitled to a share of the profits. In *Badley v Consolidated Bank* [1888] 38 Ch D 238 the lender was held not to be a partner although he was entitled to a share of the annual profits of the business.

The partnership agreement

Although a partnership can be created informally (and in some cases without the persons involved actually realizing that they have entered into a partnership), in most cases a formal partnership agreement will be drawn. The partnership agreement will deal with a number of issues that govern the relationship of the partners between themselves and also their relationship with the outside world. To the extent that the partnership agreement does not provide for certain matters, the Partnership Act implies certain terms. The partnership agreement should normally deal with the following matters.

The parties to the agreement/numbers of partners

The agreement should clearly identify the partners although the final decision as to whether or not a person is a partner will be made in the light of the circumstances and the evidence (*Saywell v Pope* [1979] STC 824). The fact that a person is not specifically identified as a partner will not prevent him from becoming liable as a partner or receiving the benefits of a partner.

As a general principle, a partnership firm may not consist of more than 20 partners. Professional partnerships, however, eg solicitors, stockbrokers and accountants, are allowed to have more than 20 partners. It is possible for a minor (person under 18 years of age) to become a partner, but the partnership agreement is voidable until the minor reaches the age of 18 and for a reasonable time thereafter. The minor cannot recover amounts paid as a premium to procure admission to the partnership unless there has been a total failure of consideration. If the minor does repudiate the agreement, he is no longer bound by debts incurred. If the minor does not avoid the agreement within a reasonable time of becoming 18, he will be bound by future debts of the firm but not any debts incurred whilst he was a minor. So, whether or not the minor avoids the agreement, he cannot be made liable for partnership debts incurred whilst he was a minor. Adult partners, however, are entitled to insist that partnership assets, including capital contributed by the minor, be applied in payment of the liabilities of the partnership.

The nature of the business

The nature and scope of the business must be clearly set out for a number of reasons. Thus, for example, the partners act as agents of the firm and of their fellow partners for the purposes of incurring obligations on behalf of the business, but not for other purposes. Moreover, the Partnership Act 1890 (s 30) imposes fiduciary duties on partners, the breach of which will make the responsible partner liable to his co-partners. The nature of the partnership business can only be varied by the unanimous consent of the partners (s 24(8)).

The name of the firm

Partners usually choose to be known by the collective surnames of all the partners, although they can choose any business name they may wish. There is no registry of partnership names (unlike a company) but partners must ensure that the name used by them complies with the requirements of the Business Names Act 1985 that applies to partnerships if they carry on business in a name other than the surname of all the partners. Even the use of their collective surnames and '& Co' will mean that the Business Names Act 1985 applies. Section 2 of the Act makes it a criminal offence to use certain names unless written approval of the Secretary of State for Trade and Industry is obtained, eg names that suggest a connection with the government or a local authority. Section 2(1)(b) prevents the inclusion of certain words or expressions as part of the partnership name, eg Royal, Police, Charity, Chartered, Dental etc. The reason for this restriction is that certain words are either associated with certain professions, certain types of business, a department of the government, charity, or an association with the royal family. Thus, the word 'bank' cannot be used in the course of a business unless the legislative requirements under the Financial Services and Markets Act 2000 are complied with.

A notice containing the names of each partner and an address at which they can be served with documents must be prominently displayed at any business premises to which customers or suppliers have access (s 4). Further, partnerships with 20 or fewer members must include the names of each partner and an address at which they can be served with documents on business letters, written orders for goods or services, invoices and receipts. Partnerships with more than 20 partners have to keep a list of all the partners' names and addresses at the firm's principal place of business, along with a statement on the firm's stationery stating where this document is kept.

Provided the Business Names Act is complied with, and as long as there is no intention to deceive the public, partners can trade under any name they like. If a name is likely to cause confusion with another business or likely to deceive the public, an action for the tort of passing off may be brought.

The Business Names Act 1985 does not prevent more than one firm from using the same or similar name nor does it prevent a firm from using a name similar to that of a registered company. To protect the goodwill and reputation of a firm the partners will have to rely on the common law tort of passing off. This is designed to provide a remedy either by way of damages, or by way an injunction, to prevent further injury to the goodwill of the business (*Ewing v Buttercup Margarine Co Ltd* [1917] 2 Ch 1).

Dates of commencement and dissolution

A formal partnership agreement will normally state the date on which the partnership is to commence. This is not conclusive evidence as to whether or not the partnership did in fact commence on that date (*Saywell v Pope* [1979] STC 824). The date on which the partnership commences is a matter of fact that will be determined on the basis of the evidence.

A formal partnership agreement may not give a date on which the partnership is to end. If a date is specified then the partnership can only be ended in advance of that date by a court order or by one of the matters specified in the Partnership Act. If no date for dissolution is fixed, the partnership is known as a 'partnership at will', and any one of the partners can dissolve the firm by giving notice (s 26(1)).

The capital of the firm and of the individual partners

Section 24(1) provides that

> 'all the partners are entitled to share equally in the capital and the profits of the business, and must contribute equally towards the losses, whether or capital or otherwise sustained by the firm.'

The presumption that partners will contribute equally to the capital, and be entitled to equal repayment of capital on dissolution, is commonly varied by agreement. If the effect of s 24(1) is to be ousted then the partnership agreement must clearly set out the intentions of the partners. The partnership agreement should also set out the circumstances under which property will become partnership property. This is discussed separately.

The management of the business

Section 24(5) states that

> 'every partner may take part in the management of the partnership business.'

Again, this subsection only applies if there is no contrary agreement, either expressly or impliedly, between the partners. It is possible to have a dormant or sleeping partner who has no right to manage the business, although such a partner will normally take advantage of the Limited Partnership Act 1907.

The partnership agreement should also set out the duties of the various partners.

Banking arrangements and the right to draw cheques

The partnership agreement should name the firm's bank and specify whether or not the individual partners have the right to draw cheques on the partnership account. Usually the signature of more than one partner will be required in order to safeguard against fraud or forgery. The partnership agreement does not bind the bank but it must determine the scope of the mandate given to it and obey that mandate.

The partnership agreement should also deal with issues relating to: the preparation of the firm's accounts; admission and compulsion of partners; death or retirement of partners. The partnership agreement should also deal with the process of resolving disputes between the partners and possibly contain an arbitration clause. A partnership agreement may have to be altered and the consent of all the partners is required.

The relationship of partners to persons dealing with them

Partners act as agents of the firm and of their fellow partners for the purposes of the partnership business. They can incur liability in contract and in tort for acts committed in the ordinary course of the firm's business.

Authority of the partners

A partner, as an agent of his co-partners, has general authority to bind the partnership by any acts done by him in the usual course of the partnership business (s 5). The power and the authority of a partner to bind the firm and the co-partners is derived from the fact that partnership business is conducted on behalf of the partners by some or all of their number. In addition to the actual or usual authority that a partner has conferred on him by the partnership agreement or by his fellow partners, he also has apparent, or ostensible, authority to do such acts as are normally within the scope of the business that the partnership carries on, and third parties who deal with him may treat the firm as bound by such acts unless they know that the act in question is outside the actual authority of the partner. The scope of the partner's authority to act on behalf of the partnership and to bind the co-partners was discussed in *Re Agriculturist Cattle Insurance Co (Baird's case)* (1870) LR 5 Ch App 725 where it was said that:

> 'as between the partners and the outside world, each partner is the unlimited agent of every other in every matter connected with the partnership business.'

For the co-partners to be bound, the act in question must not only be within the scope of the business carried on by the firm but it must be done in the usual manner in which an act of that type is done in a business of that kind. The firm will therefore be liable if the circumstances, time, place or manner in which the act is performed is normal to the kind of business which the partnership carries on. In *Higgins v Beauchamp* [1914] 3 KB 1192 where acceptance of an incomplete bill of exchange that lacked the drawer's signature was sufficiently unusual to place it outside the usual manner of carrying on the partnership business, and the holders of the bill could not sue the acceptor partnership on it. Nevertheless, an act that is outside the usual scope of the partnership business will bind the firm if the co-partners expressly authorize it. The scope of a partner's apparent authority is confined to such acts as are connected with the usual conduct of a business of the kind carried on by the partnership. It is a question of fact whether or not a partner's act falls within the scope of the partnership business. In *Mercantile Credit*

Co Ltd v Garrod [1962] 3 ALL ER 1103 the partners were in the business of letting garages and carrying out motorcar repairs. One of the partners, without the knowledge of the other, purported to sell a car to which the firm had no title to a hire purchase company. It was held that the other partner was accountable for the money received because the act of selling the car was sufficiently closely connected with the partnership business of running a garage as to be within the scope of the partnership business. A partner will be deemed to have apparent authority to bind the firm and his co-partners in the following circumstances.

♦ Every partner is deemed to hold such powers as are normally held by all partners (eg authority to sell any goods or chattels of the firm and to purchase goods normally used in the business, although they are subsequently misapplied by the partner who purports to purchase them on behalf of the firm). In *Mann v D'Arcy* [1968] 1 WLR 893 the court held that an arrangement entered into by one partner in a greengrocery wholesale partnership, that purported to commit the co-partners (and the partnership firm) to a joint venture with the plaintiff for the sale of a consignment of potatoes, was held to be a partnership arrangement and fully binding on the co-partners and the wholesale partnership firm.

♦ If a partner in a trading firm is deemed to have wider powers than a partner of a non-trading firm. A partner in a trading firm may borrow money on credit, may draw, issue or accept bills of exchange, and may mortgage or pledge partnership property.

Liability of the partnership firm and the co-partners

Section 6 of the Partnership Act 1890 provides that any act or instrument that relates to the firm's business may be done or executed in the firm's name or by any method that indicates an intention to bind the firm by an authorized person, whether a partner or not, and the act or instrument will be effective in binding the firm. If the partner enters into a transaction for his own personal benefit and not on behalf of the firm, the transaction will not bind the co-partners or the partnership firm if the other party is aware of the lack of authority. In *Beckham v Drake* [1843] 9 MNW 79 the court said that the question to be considered was whether the person who entered into the transaction was acting solely for his own benefit or on behalf of the partnership firm. The facts of the case were that two of the partners entered into a contract under which they agreed that the partnership would continue to employ X as foreman. It was held that although the third partner had not expressly agreed to the contract he was bound by it and could therefore be sued for breach.

The partnership firm will clearly be bound if a partner acts within his actual authority or his fellow partners ratify his actions. Where a partner pledges the credit of the firm for a purpose unconnected with the firm's ordinary course of business, the firm will not be bound unless the partner is in fact authorized to enter into a transaction by the co-partners. Section 6 does not affect the personal liability of the individual partner who will remain liable on the transaction unless and until it is ratified by his fellow partners. In *Bigmold v Waterhouse* [1813] 1 East 48 one of the partners granted a special favour to a consignor of goods whilst acting for the partnership, in return for a valid consideration as between him and the consignor but which was of no value to the partnership firm. The court held that the partnership firm was not bound by the concession granted although it was granted in the partnership name. Similarly, in *Kendall v Wood* [1871] LR 6 Ex 234 the defendant received £10,000 of partnership money from X, a partner, towards the discharge of a personal debt. On the dissolution of the partnership, the court held that the £10,000 could not be retained by the creditor as against the other partners, who had neither authorized the use of the money to pay off a private debt, nor led the creditor to believe that the indebted partner had the authority to dispose of the partnership property in this way.

Section 8 of the Partnership Act 1980 provides that any restriction on the power of the partners to bind the firm is effective and acts done in contravention of this restriction are not binding on the partnership firm if the third party had notice of the limitation. In *Cox v Hickman* [1860] 8 HL Cas 268 the court held that partners may, as between themselves, agree that some of them will only have a limited power to enter into contracts binding the firm but that such an arrangement between the partners will not affect the right of a third party who enters into a contract with a partner without notice of this limitation. Restriction on the power of the partners is normally two-fold.

Liability of partners for debts and obligations

A partner who enters into a contract that is binding on the partnership will bind his co-partners to joint and several liability in respect of obligations and wrongs entered into by the partner. Members of the partnership are not liable for acts done outside the apparent authority of a partner or unconnected with the ordinary business of the partnership. Occasionally, the partnership firm and the co-partners will not be liable even if the transaction is entered into in the ordinary course of the partnership business, if a third party deals with a partner as a principal (*British Homes Assurance Corpn Ltd v Paterson* [1902] 2 Ch D 404).

Any restriction on the authority of a partner to act for the partnership business must therefore expressly be set out in the partnership agreement. To ensure that the remaining co-partners are not liable in circumstances where the partner has exceeded his liability, the limitations on authority must be notified to third parties dealing with the partnership and the conduct of the remaining partners must be such so that they are not held liable for 'holding out'. Section 14 provides that a person who acts as a partner or allows others to represent that he is a partner is estopped from denying to persons relying on such a representation that he is not a partner. A person will be treated as a partner where eg he allows his name to be used in business correspondence or displayed over business premises. The defendant's name must be used with his knowledge of acquiescence. In *Tower Cabinet Co v Ingram* [1949] 2 KB 397 the use of the firm's notepaper by the remaining partners after one of the partners had retired was insufficient to impute liability on the retired partner. For liability to be imposed, it must be shown that the retired partner has, by spoken or written words or by his conduct, represented himself as a partner (*D & H Bunny Ltd v Atkins* [1961] VLR 31).

Liability of incoming and outgoing partners

Section 17 of the Partnership Act 1890 provides that a partner coming into a partnership firm is not liable for the pre-existing debts of the firm. A retiring partner remains liable for debts incurred before his retirement. A retiring partner will only be discharged from existing liabilities if a contract is made between him, the partners of the newly constituted firm and the creditors.

Liability of firms for wrongs

Partners may be jointly liable for wrongs done to a third party by one of their numbers either because the wrong was committed in the course of the partnership business (eg where one of the partners acts negligently whilst acting in the course of an ordinary partnership transaction) or because the wrong was authorized by the other partners. Section 10 of the Partnership Act 1890 provides that where a wrong is done in the course of the partnership business the co-partners are liable to the same extent as the partner who committed the wrongful or negligent act. In *Hamlyn v Houston & Co* [1903] 1 KB 81 a partner in a partnership business bribed a clerk in a rival firm to disclose confidential information concerning contracts and tenders submitted by his employers. The court held that obtaining information that might be useful to the partnership business was within the scope of the firm's business and that the method used to obtain that information, although unauthorized by the other partners, was sufficiently related to the conduct of the firm's business to make the other partners liable.

Section 11 deals with the misapplication of money or property received by the partnership firm and deals with two situations where the partners will be liable to the owner of the property:

♦ where one partner receives money or property belonging to a third party whilst acting within the scope of his authority and misapplies it;
♦ where the firm receives money or property belonging to a third party in the ordinary course of its business and one of the partners misapplies it.

In *Blyth v Fladgate* [1891] 1 Ch 337 a partner in a firm of solicitors made a loan on behalf of a client, the loan being secured by a mortgage on a house. The solicitor was negligent in that he did not check that the house was worth at least as much as the loan. The client lost money as a consequence and all of the partners were held liable because the solicitor had committed the tort while doing an act that was in the usual course of the firm's business. In *Arbuckle v Taylor* (1815) 3 Dow 160 a partner in a firm thought that an outsider had stolen money from the partnership firm. He brought a private prosecution that failed. The outsider then sued the firm for the tort of malicious prosecution and false imprisonment. The other partners were not liable for these torts because the act that gave rise to the criminal prosecution was not an act that was within the usual course of the firm's business.

The relationship of the partners with each other

Persons who enter into a partnership agreement are free to determine the scope of their powers and their relations with their co-partners by express agreement. Insofar as the partnership relationship is not governed by an express or implied agreement between the parties, certain statutory rules will govern the relationship. Further, because the relationship is one of good faith and trust, the partners owe to each other certain fiduciary duties.

Partnership property

Partnership property must be dealt with exclusively for the purposes of the partnership and in accordance with the partnership business. On the dissolution of the firm, every partner is entitled as against the others to have partnership property applied in payment of debts and liabilities incurred by the partnership firm and to have any surplus assets applied in payment of amounts due to the partners. Partnership property must be distinguished from the property belonging to the individual partners for the following reasons:

♦ if the property increases in value, this increase will belong to the firm rather than to any individual partner;
♦ partnership property should be used exclusively for the purposes of the partnership, as agreed in the partnership agreement;
♦ on dissolution, creditors are first paid out of partnership property.

Sections 20 and 21 of the Partnership Act 1890 provides that all property and rights brought into partnership stock, acquired on account of the firm, or acquired in the ordinary course of the partnership business are partnership property and must be applied by the partners exclusively for the purposes of the partnership business. Where partners own property as co-owners of an estate and the property it not itself partnership property, the property is held by them, in the absence of an express agreement, not as partners but as co-owners of the same respective estates as are held by them in the land at the date of ownership. Property purchased with money that belongs to the firm is bought on account of the partnership firm unless there is evidence to the contrary.

There is no limitation on what is capable of being partnership property and therefore land, leaseholds, goodwill, chattels and any other form of assets are all capable of being partnership property. The mere fact that property is used as partnership property does not necessarily mean it is partnership property. In *Davies v Davies* [1894] 1 Ch 393 a testator left his residuary estate, including a business to his two friends in equal shares as tenants in common. The friends did not enter into a partnership agreement but were held to be partners in the business that had been left to them by reason of their carrying on business as partners. The facts did not show that the land left to them as tenants in common was held as partnership property; instead the partnership merely had the use of such property. It is a question of fact whether any particular property is partnership property. An express agreement that property is to be partnership property will be conclusive but in the absence of an express agreement, the courts will look to see if an implied agreement can be inferred. In *Miles v Clarke* [1953] 1 All ER 779 the consumable stock in trade of a photography business was treated as partnership property, even though it had all been purchased by one of the partners whilst the remainder of the other property (the lease of premises from which the business was carried on, equipment and personal goodwill) was regarded as the property of the other partner who had brought it into the business. As the partners had made no express agreement, the court would only imply a term that property was partnership property if this was necessary on the grounds of business efficacy.

The relationship between the partners is one of 'utmost good faith' and s 28 provides that partners are under a duty to render true accounts and disclose confidential information on all matters affecting the partnership. In *Law v Law* [1905] 1 Ch 140 the court held that, in a transaction between co-partners for the sale by one to the other of a share in the partnership business, there is a duty resting on the purchaser who knows, and is aware that he knows, more about the partnership accounts than the vendor to put the vendor in possession of all material facts with reference to partnership assets and not to conceal what he alone knows. Unless such information has been furnished, the sale is voidable and may be set aside.

Accounting for profits

Every partner must account to the partnership for any benefit derived by him, without the consent of the other partners, from any transaction concerning the partnership or from any use by him of the partnership property name or business connection. In *Bentley v Craven* [1853] 18 Beav 75 a partner, who had on several occasions bought consignments of sugar very cheaply and then resold it to the partnership firm at the then current wholesale rates, was held to account for profit made. The court held that a partner in question had used a partnership asset and his position in the firm to make the profit from the transactions. In *Pathirana v Pathirana* [1967] 1 AC 233 two brothers, A and B, carried on a partnership business running a service station owned by Caltex. Relations between them deteriorated and A gave B three months notice to dissolve the firm. A informed Caltex that the firm was dissolved and asked Caltex to transfer the service station to his sole management. Caltex did this and A carried on business without accounting to B for his share of the capital and profits.

Competing with the firm

If a partner, without the consent of the other partners, carries on any business of the same kind and competing with the partnership firm, he must account to the partnership firm for all profits made by him (s 30). In this situation, a partner can be liable merely by competing with the partnership firm, whether or not he has used the firm's assets. In *Trimble v Goldberg* [1906] 95 LTR 163 one of the partners purchased shares on behalf of the partnership firm, but also took an option to buy other property belonging to the company. He then invited one of his co-partners to participate in the option scheme whilst excluding the remaining partner from this opportunity. The court held that the purchase of the option was not within the scope of the partnership's business. It was not competing with the firm or carrying on of a rival business and neither did he gain the information on which he acted in his capacity as a partner. He was therefore not accountable to the partner excluded from the business opportunity.

A partner cannot, unless his partners consent, commence a business competing with the partnership. In *Brown Janson & Co v Hutchinson (No 1)* [1895] 1 QB 737 it was held that one of the partners could restrain his co-partners from publishing, in an evening newspaper in which he had no interest, information obtained at the expense, and for the use, of a morning paper that was published by the partnership firm of which they were all partners. In *Aas v Benham* [1891] 2 Ch 244 a member of a firm of shipbrokers assisted in the formation of a company to build ships, using information derived by him from his membership of a stock broking firm. It was held that the information was used for purposes that were outside the scope of the ship broking business. Consequently, the partner using such information was not liable for a breach of duty not to compete in business with the partnership and not to obtain any personal advantage by the use of information available through the partnership. There are cases that are in conflict with the *Benham* case and the correctness of this decision may therefore be challenged (see *Boardman v Phipps* [1967] 2 AC 46; and *Regal (Hastings) Ltd v Gulliver* [1967] 2 AC 134).

Limited liability partnerships

The Limited Liability Partnerships Act 2000 created a new business medium intended to give organizational flexibility to partnerships and enable them to obtain the benefits of limited liability for their members.

The 2000 Act allows for secondary legislation to be made governing the application of company law, partnership law and insolvency law to the LLPs. Much of the applicable law is, therefore, contained in the Limited Liability Partnership Regulations that came into effect in April 2001. The regulations apply various parts of the Companies Act 1985, the Company Directors Disqualification Act 1986 and the Insolvency Act 1986 to LLPs, by listing the sections to be applied and setting out the relevant modifications. The modified texts of these Acts are therefore not set out fully and the regulations must be read in conjunction with the sections being modified.

A limited liability partnership (LLP) is a body corporate with a legal personality separate from that of its members. The veil of incorporation will therefore protect members against liability for the debts of the LLP. It will be possible to lift the veil of incorporation in the same circumstances as a company's veil can be lifted. LLP's have unlimited contractual capacity and therefore issues relating to ultra vires contracts will not apply. Indeed, the law relating to partnerships will not apply except insofar as specifically indicated in the 2000 Act. The LLP is therefore a new type of business organization having more similarity to registered companies than to partnerships. Members of LLP's are taxed as if they are carrying on an ordinary partnership business.

The Act provides that, in order to register an LLP, there must be two or more persons associated for carrying on a lawful business with a view to profit who must subscribe by their names to an incorporation document. This document must be delivered to the Registrar of Companies, along with a signed statement that the requirements of registration have been complied with. The Registrar must approve these documents. The incorporation document must state the name of the LLP, the jurisdiction of its registered office, the address of the registered office, the names and addresses of each member of the LLP on incorporation and state which of the members are to be designated members. There must be at least two designated members, who will have substantial administrative responsibilities, breach of which can lead to criminal conviction. A person who makes a false statement, or who makes the statement not believing in its truth, commits an offence. The name of the LLP must conclude with the words 'limited liability partnership', the Welsh equivalent, or abbreviation 'LLP'.

An LLP may change its name at any time but must notify the Registrar of Companies of any such change. The Registrar of Companies will issue the LLP with a certificate of incorporation that is conclusive evidence that the LLP is incorporated under the name specified in the incorporation document. Those signing the document will be the original members of the LLP. These rules closely resemble those relating to the incorporation of companies.

A person becomes a member of the LLP either by subscribing to the incorporation document or by agreement with the existing members. The relationship of members between themselves and the LLP is governed by agreement between themselves. In the absence of agreement, such rights are governed by the Limited

Liability Partnership Regulations 2001, SI 2001/1090. Every member of an LLP will be an agent of the LLP and for internal matters they fulfill the role of partners (s 4(4) makes it clear they are not to be regarded as employees unless they would have been treated as employees had the LLP been a partnership). An LLP will not be bound by an act done by a member if the third party knew that the member had no authority to undertake the act or did not believe him to be a member of the LLP. A member leaving the LLP will remain liable as a member unless persons dealing with the LLP know he has ceased to be a member or the Registrar of Companies has received notice that he is no longer a member. Where a member of an LLP commits a tort in the course of the business or with the authority of the LLP, the LLP will be liable. The member committing the tort may also be personally liable. Existing members may leave an LLP and new members join the LLP subject to agreement. If there is no agreement as to a member leaving, he may leave by giving reasonable notice to the other members. If a person ceases to be a member, the Registrar of Companies must be notified within 14 days. Changes of the names or addresses of members must be notified to the Registrar within 21 days. Where a member dies or becomes bankrupt or assigns his share in the LLP the personal representatives etc may not take part in the management of the LLP but can receive any amount to which the former member was entitled.

On the winding up of an LLP, members will not be liable to contribute to the debts of the LLP but anti-fraud measures are introduced by the legislation. The main winding-up and insolvency procedures applicable to companies are adapted to suit the needs of the LLPs. Sections 213 and 214 of the Insolvency Act 1986 apply to an LLP. Section 74 has been modified so that it allows for the enforcement of any agreement between the members, or between a member and the LLP, that a member should contribute to the assets of the LLP on a winding up in circumstances that have arisen up to an amount sufficient for paying off its debts and expenses, and for the consequent adjustment of the contributions of the other members as between themselves.

The new s 214A (made under 2001 Regulations) allows the court to declare, on application of the liquidator that a member is liable to contribute such amounts to the assets of the LLP as it thinks proper if certain conditions are satisfied:

(i)   within two years prior to the winding up the member withdrew any property of the LLP (including any profits);

(ii)   at the time of the withdrawal the member knew, or had reasonable grounds for believing, either that the LLP was unable to pay its debts or that it would become so as a result of the withdrawal;

(iii)   that at the time of the withdrawal the member knew, or ought to have known, that there was prospect the LLP avoiding going into insolvent liquidation.

3.2 The registration of companies

Types of companies

Companies registered under the Companies Act 1985 can be limited or unlimited and, if limited, limited either by shares or guarantee (s 1(1)(2)). A company limited by guarantee is the form of organization used for a non-profit-making group of people who have come together to further common purposes of a public, cultural, scientific or other intellectual or political kind. With a company limited by shares, people associate together so their money may be pulled and exploited to make a profit; in the case of a company limited by guarantee, the essential link is the sharing of a purpose and a wish to further that purpose. In such cases, money is raised by annual subscriptions and other appropriate sources (eg collections, appeals). Companies limited by guarantee are exempt from the requirements that they use the words 'limited' as part of their name, provided that the conditions laid down for this exemption are complied with (ss 30–31).

With an unlimited company, there is no limit to the liability of the shareholders for the debts of the company. In the case of a company limited by shares, the limit of the liability is set by the nominal value of the shares. In the case of a company limited by guarantee, the liability is limited by the amount (guarantee) stated to be the amount that all members will be required to contribute in the event of the company being wound up. A further distinction is that between public and private companies. The Companies Act 1985 established that any company registered is a private company unless the requirement for registration is as a public company of a field. Public companies must have a minimum of two members; private companies need only have one (s 1(1), (3a)). The distinction between public and private companies is significant in connection with the raising and maintenance of capital: only public companies may invite the public to subscribe to the shares. The articles of private companies usually restrict the sale of the company's shares, eg the shares must first be offered to other members of the company, or the shares can only be sold to persons of whom the directors approve.

Formation of registered companies

The promoters, who are required to file certain documents with the Registrar of Companies, undertake the formation process of a registered company. If the Registrar is satisfied with the documents, he will issue a certificate of incorporation. From the issue of this certificate, the company will come into existence as a body corporate and enjoy separate legal status. The documents, which must be filed with the Registrar of Companies, are:

♦ the memorandum of association;
♦ the articles of association;

♦ a statement giving the names of the company's first directors;
♦ a statement giving the name of the company's first secretary together with a statement that all statutory requirements in respect of registration have been complied with.

The Registrar must issue a certificate of incorporation if he is satisfied that all the requirements of process have been complied with and advertise the fact of the company's incorporation in the *London Gazette*. The Registrar can refuse to register a company if it is not formed for a lawful purpose.

The memorandum of association

The memorandum and articles of association are known as the constitutional documents of the company. The memorandum will set out the structure of the company and those who enter into business with the company have constructive notice of the company's memorandum. This is because the memorandum of the company, along with all documents, must be registered with the Registrar of Companies and be available for inspection. Section 2 of the Companies Act 1985 states that the memorandum of a company limited by shares must contain the following obligatory clauses.

The name clause

This states the name of the company. If the company is a private limited company then its name must end with the words 'Limited' or the abbreviation 'Ltd'. If the company is a public company then the name must conclude with the words 'Public limited company' or the abbreviation 'plc'. If the company is registered in Wales the appropriate Welsh equivalent to these words may be used instead. The name of the company can be altered by special resolution but ss 25 and 26 of the Comanies Act 1985 prohibit the use of certain names (eg the Registrar will refuse to register a name that is identical to the name of another company already on the register or if it is identical except for certain formal differences, eg the inclusion of the word 'the'. The Registrar will also refuse to register a name the use of which would, in the opinion of the Secretary of State, constitute a criminal offence or be offensive). Additionally, regulations made by the Secretary of State prohibit the use of certain words that suggest a connection with the government or with local authorities, and such names can only be used following permission from an appropriate body. The Company and Business Names Regulations 1981, SI 1981/1685, as amended, also include a list of words and expressions that can only be used if the Secretary of State gives permission.

Under s 8, the Secretary of State can order a company to change its name. Such an order can be made within 12 months of registration if the company name is too similar to one that is already on the register, or should have been on the register. If misleading information was given at the time of registration, the Registrar can order the company to change its name within five years of registration. If the name with which a company is registered gives a misleading indication of the nature of the company's activities and harm is likely to be caused to the public, the Registrar can order a change of name at any time (s 32).

In addition to the statutory restrictions to the choice of name, if a company registers a name that is too similar to the name of an established business, an action for the tort of passing off may be brought by the established business to prevent the newly-established company from trading under its registered name. If an action for passing off is successful, the court will grant an injunction to prevent the further use of that name and, if appropriate, damages for loss of business. An action in passing off will only succeed if the use of the name by the newly established business is likely to:

> 'mislead incautious purchasers or to deceive the unwary.'

In reaching a conclusion, the court will have regard to the nature of the market and the purchasers operating within that market. The essential question is whether injury to the business or goodwill of the plaintiff is reasonably foreseeable. In such circumstances, a claim may succeed even where the name is used bona fide. The courts will apply an objective test having regard to the evidence available (*William Grant Ltd v Glenn Catrine Bonded Warehouse Ltd* 1999 May 11, *The Times*).

All registered companies must publish their names legibly and conspicuously: outside their registered office and all places of business (s 348(1)); on all letters, invoices, notices, cheques, orders for goods and receipts (s 349); on the company's seal, if it is has a seal (s 350).

The registered office

This clause must state whether the company's registered office is in England and Wales, Wales or Scotland Companies Act 1985, s 2(1), (2). The place of registration fixes the nationality of the company. The company does not have to give the address of its registered office under this clause, which may be changed for business purposes.

The objects clause

The objects clause states the purposes for which the company is formed and prior to the abolition of the ultra vires rule in respect of third parties, establishes the contractual capacity of the company. It is possible for the company to register its objects as to carry on business as a general commercial company (s 3(a)).

Section 4 of the Companies Act 1985 allows a company's objects clause to be altered by special resolution. Shareholders who did not vote in favour of the resolution can file an objection with the court, but only if they hold 15% of the company's issued share capital or 15% of any class of share capital. The objection must be lodged within 21 days of the special resolution being passed and is ineffective until the court either confirms it (wholly or in part), or makes some other order in respect of it.

Limited liability clause

This will state whether the company is limited by shares or guarantee and, if the company is limited by shares, the liability of its members. If the members of the company unanimously consent, a private limited company may be re-registered as an unlimited company.

Share capital

A company must state the amount of share capital with which it proposes to be registered and the nominal value of each share into which that capital is to be divided. The amount of the share capital declared in this clause is known as the authorized share capital (or nominal capital or registered capital). The authorized share capital is the maximum number of shares, of a stated value, that the company directors are authorized to issue. Not all of this capital needs to be issued as shares in the case of a public limited company. The Registrar of Companies must be satisfied that its minimum nominal capital is £50,000, of which at least 25% is paid up (the company must therefore have £12,500 in paid up capital and a right to call on a further £37,500). If a company is to be limited by guarantee, then an equivalent clause must set out the amount that members agree to contribute in the event of the company being wound up. The memorandum may contain additional clauses in addition to the five compulsory clauses, that are required by statute.

The articles of association

The articles of association are the internal rules that bind the members and the company as it is signed and sealed by each other. The articles of association are subordinate to the memorandum and in cases of conflict the memorandum always prevails: to the extent of the conflict the articles are void (*Guinness v Land Corpn of Ireland* (1882) 22 Ch D 349) subject to the rule that, in cases of conflict, the memorandum always prevails. The memorandum and articles should be read contemporaneously to clear up any ambiguity or uncertainty (*Re Duncan Gilmour & Co* [1952] 2 All ER 871). The articles of association set out both rules and regulations that deal with the internal management of the company, eg powers of directors.

Alteration of the articles of association

The company may alter the articles of association by passing a special resolution under s 9 of the Companies Act 1985. In addition to this statutory requirement, the courts have imposed a requirement that when the members of the company exercise their right to alter the articles they must exercise this power bona fide for the benefit of the company as a whole, that is, for the benefit of the company in its capacity as a separate legal entity rather than for the personal interests of the shareholders. The courts have reviewed this requirement in a series of cases but have opted for the objective test that was explained in *Greenhalgh v Arderne Cinemas Ltd* [1951] 2 ALL ER 1120. The claimant had a minority shareholding in a company, the articles of which restricted transfers of shares to non-members if an existing member was willing to buy the shares at a fair price. The majority shareholders wished to sell their shares to an outsider and an extraordinary general meeting (EGM) was called to alter the relevant article to enable the shares to be sold to an outsider without first being offered to the minority shareholder. The procedural requirements being satisfied, the claimant brought an action challenging the validity of the special resolution on the basis that the interests of the minority shareholders had been sacrificed in order to protect the interests of the majority. The court held that the special resolution was valid and, in applying the bona fide for the benefit of the company requirement, said that the court must consider (objectively) the position of a hypothetical member of the company. Such a member may benefit from having the right to sell his shares to outsiders. The hypothetical shareholder is someone who may be a member of a company at any time, present or future, who does not necessarily have a particular number of shares or votes (and therefore not necessarily a particular interest in the company) and who is not affected by any particular distribution of shares or voting power.

If a company does not register its own articles, a model set of articles contained in Table A of the 1985 Company's Regulations (SI 1985/805) may be used. Table A articles can be used either for public or private companies but are not suitable for all companies. Most companies will use Table A as the basis for their own articles.

Additionally, the promoters of the company must send to the Registrar of Companys a statement giving the names of the company's first directors and of the company secretary, together with a statement that all the statutory requirements of registration have been complied with. Certain information, eg the full name of the company, the proposed address of the registered office, the names, previous names and addresses of the company secretary and director, the date of birth of the directors, business occupations and other directorships held, must be given in Companies House Form 10. The secretary and directors must sign their consent personally.

Once the Registrar of Companies issues a certificate of incorporation, the company becomes a body corporate. The certificate of incorporation is conclusive evidence as to the date of incorporation and that the requirements of the company's legislation are complied with. From the date of the issue of the certificate of incorporation, a private limited company can commence business. A public limited company will have to obtain a trading certificate (certificate of entitlement to do business) that is conclusive evidence that the company has satisfied the minimum capital requirements for a public limited company. Failure to obtain the trading certificate does not render any transaction entered into on behalf of the company void, but the directors will be personally liable for any loss resulting to the other party unless the certificate is obtained within 21 days.

The corporate veil

From the date of incorporation the company is a legal entity, distinct from its shareholders and directors. Consequently, the company can enter into contractual obligations in its own right. It will also be liable for torts or other wrongs committed in the ordinary course of its business by agents and employees. The principle that the company is a legal entity in its own right was reinforced by the House of Lords in *Salomon v Salomon and Co Ltd* [1892] AC 22 where the court held the:

> 'company is at law a different person altogether from the subscribers to the memorandum, the company is not an agent of the subscribers or trustee for them. Nor are the subscribers as members liable, in any shape or form, except to the extent and the manner provided by the Act.'

The *Salomon* case has had a far-reaching effect. Apart from protecting the shareholders and the officers of the company, the fact that the company enjoys separate legal status and its consequences are highlighted in a number of cases. Thus, in *Macaura v Northern Assurance Ltd* [1925] AC 619 it was held that a shareholder who had insured company property (timber he had sold to the company and to which title had passed to the company) in his own name, against loss by fire could not claim on the insurance policies. The court held that as a shareholder the plaintiff did not have an insurable interest in the timber because he did not own any part of it. This situation was not changed by the fact that he owned the majority of the shares in the company that owned the timber or the fact that the company owed him a lot of money. Similarly, in *Tunstall v Steigmann* [1962] All ER 417 the defendant ran a business from premises she owned. She also owned the shop next door but this was leased by her to the plaintiff. The defendant wished to end the lease (something she was entitled to do under the Landlord and Tenant Act 1954 if she intended to continue business from the premises) so that she could expand her business to the leased property. Prior to the hearing the defendant incorporated a company and transferred her business to it and argued that, as she owned all the shares in the company apart from two, she and the company should be treated as one, thereby giving her the right to claim the leased premises. The court applying the *Salomon* case held that the company is a distinct legal entity from its shareholders.

Although a company is regarded as a legal person it does not, and cannot, enjoy the characteristics of humans, eg it cannot vote at elections or sue for stress and aggravation (*Firesteel Products Ltd v Anaco Ltd* (1994) Times, 21 November).

In addition to the right of the company to own property, the recognition of separate legal status will have the following consequences.

♦ Because a company enjoys separate legal existence and is the creation of statute it will continue in existence until liquidated in accordance with statute. Therefore, the company can continue in existence indefinitely and has perpetual succession. The death of a shareholder or a change in the size of a shareholder does not affect the continued existence of the company (unlike a partnership where the death of a partner will dissolve the partnership).

♦ A company can own property, and this property will continue to be owned by the company regardless of who owns the shares or the size of the shareholding (*Macaura* case). This is important when a company needs to borrow money since the company can create a security over both present and future property it may own.

♦ A company has full contractual capacity and can sue and be sued for breach of contract. The power to enter into any such contract is delegated to agents (directors) and therefore the issue of authority of the directors becomes relevant.

♦ As a general rule, a defendant can only be liable for criminal acts if the guilty act (actus reus) can be established while having the guilty mind (mens rea). This has been a stumbling block in respect of the successful prosecution of companies where it is difficult to attribute the guilty mind. Courts are willing to hold a company guilty of crimes if they are prepared to regard the controllers of the company as the minds of the company (eg *Tesco Supermarkets v Nattrass* [1971] 2 All ER 127) where the court that a company can only act through living persons although not always as the person. In some cases the person is not acting as for the company but as the company and his mind, which directs the act, is the mind of the company. If he is guilty then the company is guilty.

Although due to the legislation (s 13) and as a result of the *Salomon* case, liability will be imposed on the legal entity for its acts or omissions, it is possible for the courts to lift the corporate veil. There are, therefore, both common law and statutory bases for lifting the corporate veil and looking at the identity of the shareholders to impose liability.

Where the company is formed for a fraudulent purpose or in order to evade legal obligations

The courts will disregard the separate entity principle if the corporate entity is used to evade legal obligations, eg *Gilford Motor Co Ltd v Horne* [1933] Ch 935 where the defendant wishing to avoid the effect of a restrictive covenant not to solicit his former employer's business clients formed a company through which to undertake that activity. The court granted an injunction against the employee who acted in breach of the covenant and the company incorporated by him as a vehicle through which to act. The court concluded that the company was a device to mask the fact that the defendant was carrying on a business in respect of which the plaintiffs might object. In *Creasey v Breachwood Motors Ltd* (1992) BCC 638 the controllers of a company transferred company assets to another company that was controlled by them in order to defeat a claim by the plaintiff for wrongful dismissal. The court held that the plaintiff could pursue a direct action against the company to whom assets had been transferred. In *Ord v Belhaven Pubs* (1998) BCC 607, where in the course of a legal action the plaintiff sought to substitute the defendant company for the defendant's parent company, the Court of Appeal held that the plaintiff could not substitute the defendants to the action because the subsidiary company against whom the action was initially brought had, following restructuring, had insubstantial assets.

Where the company can be characterised as an enemy alien in time of war

If enemy aliens own the company, the court may ignore the corporate veil and have regard to the nationality of its shareholders. In times of war both natural and artificial persons who are citizens of the state with which the UK is at war are likely to find their rights and activities restricted. In *Daimler Ltd v Continental Tyre and Rubber Co Ltd* [1916] 2 AC 307 the court held that the plaintiff company could not sue in debt in the English courts because the company, although registered in England, had assumed the character of an enemy alien due to the character (German Nationality) of its shareholders.

Where groups of companies are regarded as a single company

As a general principle, the separate entity principle will apply between holding and subsidiary so that each separate entity enjoys the benefits of the Salomon case. In exceptional cases the courts may lift the corporate veil either on the grounds of agency or on the grounds of economic reality. In *DHN Foods Ltd v Tower Hamlets BC London* [1976] 3 All ER 462 DHN ran a business through two wholly owned subsidiaries. One of these subsidiaries owned the premises from which the business by DHN was undertaken but carried no business of its own. The local authority compulsorily purchased the premises owned by the subsidiary and DHN claimed damages for the disturbance. The court held that the group of companies could be treated as a single economic entity because they were virtually a partnership. Although the DHN case has been criticised it has not been overruled and is treated as a case decided on its own facts. In *Woolfson v Strathclyde Regional Council* (1978) SC (HL) 90 the House of Lords came to a different conclusion on very similar facts. The distinction between the cases is that in DHN, the holding company owned all the shares in the subsidiary and the directors between the companies were the same. In more recent cases the courts have been reluctant to lift the corporate veil so as to regard the holding and subsidiary companies as one single enterprise. In *Adams v Cape Industries plc* [1991] I All ER 929 the defendants and two associated companies owned companies in South Africa and the USA. The American company was successfully sued by claimants who had been injured by asbestos marketed in the USA by the American company. The claimants sought to enforce these judgments in the UK against the two defendants. The court held that the corporate veil could not be lifted. The defendant could not be treated as one economic unit even though the subsidiary was set up as a façade. The court expressed the view that the Salomon case must be applied whenever possible and the circumstances in which the corporate veil will be lifted are extremely limited.

In addition to the common law exceptions to the *Salomon* case there are a number of statutory exceptions that will allow the courts to look at the identity of the shareholders and to make them personally liable, eg s 24 of the Companies Act 1985 requires all companies other than private single member companies to have at least two members. If membership falls below two, and remains below two for more than six months, then the sole member can become personally liable for debts incurred during the period when membership remained below two. Although this situation is never likely to occur with a public company, it could arise with private limited company. Other statutes that will look behind the corporate veil include the Insolvency Act 1986 (s 214; see further Chapter 7).

The management of the company

The company, being an artificial legal entity, is required to act through its agents. That task is usually conferred on the directors who act as agents of the company. Although the shareholders have the power to appoint and remove directors it is the directors, who are appointed to manage the day-to-day business activity of the company. Section 741(1) of the Company Act 1985 provides that the use of the term 'director' includes any person occupying the position of director, whether he calls himself that or not. In relation to 'shadow directors' the term includes any person in accordance with whose directions or instructions the directors of the company are used to acting. The first directors of the company will be named in documents submitted to the Registrar of Companies, as part of the registration process. A public company must have at least two directors and a private company must have at least one director although the articles of association of such a company may impose a higher minimum requirement. Section 288(1) requires every company to maintain a register of directors and secretaries at its registered office. Members of the company are entitled to inspect this register. Additionally, any changes in the directors of the company, or in the particulars contained in the register of directors, must be notified to the Registrar of Companies within 14 days. For companies listed on the Stock Exchange the listing rules also provide that the register gives the following information about each director: details of management experience; unspent convictions; details of personal insolvencies or insolvencies of companies in which they acted as executive director; details of public criticism by statutory authorities; whether they have ever been disqualified from acting as a director.

Executive directors are responsible for the management of the company's business and are usually employed by the company on a full time basis. Non-executive directors are generally paid a fee for their services and may be brought into the company to provide a particular expertise or knowledge of an area of business.

Shadow directors are defined by Statute (Companies Act 1985, s 741(2)) to extend the provisions of the companies legislation that require the disclosure and regulation of certain types of transaction, by directors, to persons who are influential in the running of the company but without taking a position on the board. The statutory definition of shadow directors was considered in *Secretary of State for Trade and Industry v Deverell* [2000] 2 BCLC 133 within which the court took the view that the purpose of the legislation was to identify those, other than professional advisors, with real influence in the corporate affairs of the company. It is unnecessary that such influence should be exercised over the whole field of corporate activities. The court must objectively ascertain whether any particular communication from an alleged shadow director is to be classified as a direction or instruction. Professional advice given in that capacity does not come within this definition.

There is a possibility that a parent company may find itself liable as a shadow director of a subsidiary when the level of control it exercise is such that the directors of that subsidiary are accustomed to acting in accordance with their instructions or directions. It will be a question of fact whether this level of control exists or not.

In addition to statutory duties imposed on shadow directors, they are also liable to fiduciary duties and other duties imposed on directors (*Youkong Line Ltd v Rendsburg Investments* [1998] 2 BCLC 485).

The board of directors

Collectively, the board of directors have the full scope of authority that is conferred on the management of the company. Decisions of the board of directors are recorded through the minutes of the meetings. Once the Chairman signs the minutes they are prima facie evidence of the proceedings at the board meeting. A company's articles of association may allow the board of directors to delegate any of their powers either to one of their number or to a committee.

The company's articles may allow for the appointment of a managing director and may allow him to exercise certain powers without the need to consult the board of directors. A person who is not a validly appointed managing director may be held out as acting in that capacity with the result that the company is estopped from denying his authority (*Freeman & Lockyer v Buckhurst Park Properties Ltd* [1964] 2 QB 480). Generally, the articles of the company will give the board of directors all the necessary authority to bind the company. For persons dealing with the company, difficulties may arise not from the lack of capacity, but from a lack of authority perhaps on the part of the board, but more usually on the part of the individual director, with respect to a particular transaction. When a problem of authority arises, the company may choose to ratify the transaction so resolving the problem. The company may try to disown the obligation by alleging the director had no authority to enter into the transaction. It is intended to deal (1) with a situation where the board exceeds its authority and (2) where the individual director exceeds his authority. The latter is a matter of applying the rules of agency law.

Where the board exceeds it authority to enter into contracts

Limitations on the authority of the board (as opposed to the authority of individual directors) are dealt with under s 35A of the Companies Act 1985 which states that, in favour of the person dealing with a company in good faith, the power of the board of directors to bind the company, or authorize others to do so, is deemed free of any limitation under the company's constitution. The effect of s 35A is that limitations on the powers of the board of directors may be ignored. There is a presumption that a person dealing with the company has acted in good faith unless the contrary is proved (s 35A(2)(c)) and such a person is not regarded as acting in bad faith by reason only of his knowing that an act is beyond the powers of the directors under the company's constitution (s 35A(2)(b)). To establish bad faith, it would be necessary to show something in addition to knowledge such as malicious intent or collusion by the third party in a breach by the directors of their duties. The result of this provision is to increase significantly the security third parties have when dealing with a company by enabling such persons to ignore constitutional limitations on the power of the board of directors to act. To that extent, the board of directors is given greater freedom to enter into contracts on behalf of the company. In *Smith v Henniker-Major* [2002] BCC 768 the court explored the whole of s 35A to see if it could be applied to validate decisions made during an inquorate board meeting and concluded that a director could not rely on s 35A because he was not an outsider in whose favour the section was intended to apply to validate whatever would otherwise be ultra vires transactions.

Section 35A of the Companies Act 1985 tends to redress some imbalance between the board of directors and the shareholders by permitting shareholders to seek injunctive relief and by allowing the company to bring an action against directors who have acted in breach of their authority. Section 35A therefore provides that a member may bring proceedings to restrain the doing of an act that is beyond the powers of the directors, although no such proceedings may be brought once an act has been done in fulfilment of a legal obligation. In other words, an injunction cannot be obtained once a contract has been completed that, but for s 35A, would be ultra vires. Furthermore, the validity of the transaction does not affect any liability incurred by the directors, or any other person, by reason of the fact that the directors acted in excess of their powers (s 35(a)(5)). This raises the possibility of the company, despite being unable to set aside the transaction, suing the directors.

The application of s 35A is modified by s 322(a) which provides that, where the parties to the transaction include a director of the company or of its holding company, or a person connected with such a director or a company with whom such a director is associated, then the transaction is voidable at the insistence of the company. This could result in a situation where a transaction is valid where the company deals with a third party (s 35A(1)) and voidable where the company enters into a contract with a person who has a connection with the company (s 322(a)(2)).

Finally, the significance of the rule in *Royal British Bank v Turquand* [1856] 6 E & B 327 has been much reduced. The rule in the *Turquand* case provided that persons dealing with a company are not obliged to enquire as to whether internal procedural requirements in respect of a transaction have been complied with. Thus, the third party can assume that the necessary resolution or board meeting has been held before the company enters into the transaction.

Acts in excess of the authority of individual directors

In practice, problems relating to the capacity of the board of directors will rarely arise particularly with the application of s 35A. The authority of individual directors to act on behalf of the company may still be disputed. It is always possible for the board of directors to ratify unauthorized contracts entered into by a director or other officer. Alternatively, the company may attempt to avoid a transaction by disputing the authority of a director to commit the company to a transaction. Here the law of agency becomes relevant to determine whether the company is bound by the transaction entered into or whether the third party should seek to redress against the individual director for damages for breach of an implied warranty of authority.

In order to hold the company bound by the transaction, it is necessary to show that the individual director had either actual or apparent authority to enter into the transaction on behalf of the company. Actual authority may be expressed or implied. Express authority arises from an explicit conferment of authority on a director that may be recorded in the board meeting. Implied authority arises from the position which the individual holds (eg if a person is appointed managing director, he has implied authority to undertake those acts that fall within the usual scope of that office). In *Hely-Hutchinson v Brayhead Ltd* [1968] I QB 549 the chairman of the company also acted as its managing director, entered into contracts on the company's behalf at his own initiative and subsequently reported them to the board. The board acquiesced to this practice but on a particular occasion the board refused to honour certain undertakings entered into by the director, as *de facto* managing director. The Court of Appeal held that the director did not have express authority to enter into the transactions in question and neither as chairman of the company did he have implied authority to enter into such transactions. As de facto managing director, he had the necessary implied authority to buy into the company whose board, by its conduct, had been acquiescent in his acting as managing director and committing the company to contracts without the necessary sanction of the board of directors.

Additionally, the director may be deemed to have apparent (or ostensible) authority with the result that the company is deemed to have held out the person to have certain authority to bind the company. In *Freeman and Lockyer v Buckhurst Park Properties (Mangal) Ltd* [1964] 2 QB 480 the court found that, whilst the company's director had never been properly appointed managing director (and therefore had no actual authority), his actions were within his apparent authority and the board of directors had been aware of his conduct and therefore acquiescent in it.

For the rules of apparent authority to apply, the agent must have been held out by someone with actual authority to carry out the transaction. The acts of the principal must constitute a representation that the agent had a particular authority and the agents conduct must be reasonably so understood by the other party to the transaction. The commonest form of 'holding out' is permitting the agent to act in the conduct of the principal's business (eg the company represents by its conduct that a person is the managing director of secretary of the company).

Despite the rules of agency law and the extension of the powers of the board of directors under s 35A of the Companies Act 1985 individual directors are still required to observe limitations of authority imposed on them by the constitutional documents (s 35) and a failure to observe these restrictions will allow the company internally to seek redress against the director concerned.

Duties of directors

Whilst directors must be given the freedom to manage the business and exploit business opportunity, there must also be some means of control over the directors in the exercise of their powers. The laws response has been to categorise directors as fiduciaries and to apply strict fiduciary principles to ensure that directors meet certain minimum standards of behaviour. These fiduciary obligations are merely one aspect of the means of controlling director's conduct: others include the Insolvency Act 1986. The result of a director being held liable for breach of fiduciary duties being that a director who participates in such a breach is jointly and severally liable to account for any profit made and to make good any losses suffered by the company on a stricter basis that the common law obligation to pay damages. Further, the relief available will extend to propriety remedy ensuring priority over any claim by other creditors in the defendant's insolvency or bankruptcy. Directors can therefore be described as trustees of the company's assets. In *Aberdeen Railway Co v Blaikie Bros* (1854) 1 Macq 461 the court said that:

> '... agents have duties ... fiduciary nature ... and it is a rule of universal application, that no-one, having such duties to discharge, shall be allowed to enter into engagements in which he has, or can have, a personal interest, conflicting, or which possibly may conflict, with the interests of those whom he is bound to protect.'

The fiduciary duties imposed on directors therefore are as follows.

♦ The duty to exercise their powers bona fide for the benefit of the company as a whole and not for any collateral purpose. The test to be applied is to be subjective and in *Regentcrest plc v Cohen* [2001] 2 BCLC 80 the court said that the question is not whether, viewed objectively by the court, the particular act or omission is in the interests of the company, but rather the question is whether the director honestly believes that his act or omission was in the interests of the company. The issue is one of the state of the mind of the director. In *Regentcrest plc* the directors of a property development company waived a claw-back claim (valued at £1.5 million) that the company had under an agreement with the vendors of certain property. The vendors (A and B) were members of the board of the company and the claw-back payment was waived at a meeting that took place 12 days before a creditor presented a petition for the winding up of a company. In return for the waiver, A and B undertook to work for the company without remuneration for a period of years. A and B took no part in the proceedings and neither did they vote in respect of the resolution to waive the claw-back. Applying the subjective approach, the court held that the board had acted bona fide. The decisive consideration for the waiver was the need to maintain a united board, and not to create a situation in which two of the directors were being sued by the company that was in difficult negotiations with its creditors at the time. In *Extrasure Travel Insurance Co Ltd v Scattergood* [2002] All ER (D) 307 the court held that the directors of the company had not acted in the interests of the company when they caused the company to transfer monies to another company in the group, to enable that company to pay a pressing creditor, without any honest belief that the transfer was in the interest of the transferor company. Adopting *Regentcrest*, the court said that a director's duty is to do what he honestly believes to be in the company's best interests. The fact that his alleged belief was unreasonable may provide evidence that it was not, in fact, honestly held but, if having considered all the evidence, it appears that the director did honestly believe that he was acting in the best interests of the company, then he is not in breach of his fiduciary duty merely because the belief appears to be unreasonable to the court. In addition to the requirement that the director must act bona fide for the benefit of the company as a whole, the courts have imposed a requirement that such conduct must not be for any collateral purpose. In *Howard Smith Ltd v Ampol Petroleum Ltd* [1974] AC 821 the court explained that, in determining whether the directors have exercised their powers bona fide, the court will further enquire into the purposes for which the power was exercised. The court is required to look at the situation objectively and determine whether the purpose for which the powers were exercised were substantially in the interests of the company. The court will therefore: identify the nature and extent of the power in question; identify the range of purposes for which the power might properly be exercised; identify the substantial purpose for which it was actually exercised in the particular case. Provided that the substantial purpose for the exercise of the powers is a proper purpose then the directors would be deemed to have acted bona fide in the interests of the company and not for any collateral purpose. In *Criterion Properties plc v Stratford UK Properties plc* [2003] BCC 50 the managing director persuaded the company to enter into an agreement with a substantial shareholder in the company that amounted to a poison pill, a device designed to ensure that any would-be bidder for the company would be deterred from proceeding. The effect of the agreement was to require the company to buy out the shareholder at a high price and compel a change of control of the company including the removal from the board of the managing director who had entered the company into this agreement. The managing director was dismissed and the company sought a declaration that the buy-out arrangement entered into was for an improper purpose. The Court of Appeal held that the agreement went far beyond anything that could be justified as a proper exercise of the powers of the directors in the interests of the company. The agreement could not be seen as motivated by a desire to advance the company's interests but to damage those interests so as to deter a bidder. It is a long established principle of equity that a fiduciary, eg a director, is precluded from entering into a transaction in which he has, or can have, a personal interest conflicting, or that may possibly conflict with the interests of those whom he is bound to protect (*Aberdeen Railway Co* case). Any resulting contracts with the company are voidable and may be set aside at the insistence of the company without any enquiry as to the fairness of the transaction, and the company may hold the director accountable for any profit that he has made from the transaction. The principle applies not only where there is a conflict between the duties that a director owes to the company and his personal interests but also where his duties to the company conflict with a duty that he owes to another. In *Aberdeen Railway*

Co and Blaikie Bros [1854] 1 Macq 461 the court held that a company was entitled to set aside a transaction for the purpose of buying equipment entered into between it and a partnership when it was discovered that the chairman of the board of directors was also the managing partner of the partnership. The courts have taken the view that claimants do not have to establish actual conflict of interest but that a mere potential for that conflict to arise will be sufficient for the transaction to be challenged (*Boardman v Phipps* [1967] 2 AC 46).

Directors owe fiduciary duties to their company as a whole, that is, to the members collectively and not to members individually. Therefore, it is the company, which can enforce breaches of fiduciary duties.

Article 85 of Table A contemplates that a director may make a contract with the company but that he must disclose any material interest that he has in the contract to the directors. No special formalities are required. Section 317 requires a director who has any interest in a contract that he makes with the company to declare that interest at a meeting of the directors.

Section 320 of the Companies Act 1985 makes it illegal for a company to enter into a substantial property transaction with a director unless the transaction is first approved by a resolution of the company in general meeting.

Directors may additionally owe other duties to the company arising as a result of the common law or statute.

Duty to exercise reasonable skill and care

In *Re City Equitable Fire Insurance Co Ltd* [1925] Ch 407 the court said that:

♦ directors need only show the amount of skill and care that could be expected from someone with their own personal levels of knowledge and skill;

♦ a director is not expected to give continuous attention to the company's affairs;

♦ a director is entitled to trust that an official to whom duties have been delegated is exercising those duties properly.

In *D'Jan of London Ltd* [1994] 1 BCLC 561 the court said that the common law standard expected of the director is that of a reasonably diligent person who has both the general knowledge, skill and experience that could be objectively expected of such a director and the skill, knowledge and experience that the director in question has. The dual objective/subjective standard is that set out in s 214 of the Insolvency Act 1986 in respect of liability for wrongful trading. There are similar dicta in *Norman v Theodore Goddard* [1991] BCLC 1028.

Flexibility in the application of the test as defined in s 214 is maintained by the obligation to have regard to the functions carried out by the director in question in relation to the company. In *Re Barings plc (No 5), Secretary of State for Trade and*

Industry v Baker (No 5) [1999] 1 BCLC the court stressed that the competence of the director must be assessed in the context of, and by reference to, the role in the management of the company that was in fact assigned to him or that he in fact assumed and by reference to his duties and responsibilities in that role.

If the director is an executive director, his conduct must be considered against what could be expected of a reasonably diligent person carrying out his duties and responsibilities as an executive director in that company. Similarly, the duties and responsibilities of a non-executive director will be judged by what could be expected of a reasonably diligent person carrying out his functions as a non-executive director of the company (eg a reasonably diligent director would not sign blank cheques) *Dorchester Finance Co v Stebbing* [1989] BCLC 498 or sign a simple insurance policy form without checking the accuracy of its content (*D'Jan of London Ltd* [1994] 1 BCLC 561).

Creditors

At common law, the directors of an insolvent company must have regard to the interests of the company's creditors but the obligation to have regard to and to safeguard the interests of the creditors only arises in the event of insolvency *Brady v Brady* [1988] 2 WLR 1308.

Comparison of the different forms of business structure

♦ A person going into business must choose the sort of business organization through which the necessary activity will be carried through. The choice of business status is extremely important and people involved in setting up the business venture should not only consider the advantages and disadvantages of trading through a particular business medium, but also the obligations and duties that will flow from establishing such an entity.

♦ A sole trader is personally liable for the debts of the business to the full extent of his personal estate. Partnerships, although not a separate legal entity, confer the advantage that partners will be jointly liable for the debts of the partnership business. Co-partners will also be able to bring either much needed capital or business skills to the venture, thereby enhancing the abilities that are necessarily restricted when business is carried on by a sole trader. The partnership firm will only be liable if the partner acts in the ordinary course of the partnership business, unless apparent or ostensible authority can be imposed.

♦ The partnership agreement is likely to set out how profits/losses are to be shared between the partners, but all partners are jointly and severally liable to outsiders for the partnership debts. If any of the partners are unable to pay their share of the partnership debts, the other partners assume unlimited liability. The Limited Liability Partnerships Act 2000 allows partnerships to be operated behind the veil of incorporation thereby conferring the advantages of limited liability on partners. This is, perhaps, the principle advantage of trading as a company. The extent to which limited liability is a true advantage depends on the circumstances of each individual business. The corporate veil can be pierced in certain circumstances to make members of the company personally liable.

♦ The rights of the partners to manage the affairs of the partnership are usually set out in the partnership agreement and this may be a reason for continuing business in that form. Partners are involved in the day-to-day decision-making and management of the partnership business. Shareholders, regardless of the size of their shareholder, do not have a right to manage the company's business. The right of management is vested in the board of directors. Small companies, where the members are all directors, may carry on business as what the law considers a quasi-partnership may confer some of the benefits of limited liability.

♦ A partnership will be created either for a fixed period of time or at will. Any partner can withdraw from a partnership at will by giving reasonable notice. It is possible for a partner to assign his share in the firm. The assignee will receive the share of the profits to which the partner would have been entitled but will have no right to manage the partnership's affairs. This lack of the right to manage might considerably reduce the value of the share that is assigned.

♦ Members of companies may have a right to transfer their shares to whomsoever they wish. The articles of association will normally determine this, although the articles of some companies may give directors the power to refuse to register any transfer of shares, or make such a transfer subject to conditions, eg right of first refusal.

♦ If sole traders wish to borrow money then they will need to provide security for the loan. Generally, they will either need to find a guarantor or give security against their own property. Partners are usually in the same position as sole traders except that, since there are more of them, they may find it easier to find guarantors or may have more property available over which security can be given. Companies have additional options available. They can sell shares to people who wish to invest in the company or raise capital by giving a floating charge over the company's assets.

♦ A partnership can be created without any formality but, although partners may have entered into a deed of partnership drawn up by a lawyer, that may not always be the case. A company on the other hand has to comply with certain formalities relating to registration that require documents to be filed with the Registrar of Companies. Although it is not difficult to form a company, some people may find the task daunting. Once a company has been created, it must hold at least one annual general meeting per year. Partners do not have to adhere to any formalities in respect of meetings.

3.3 Legal rules affecting business customers

Special types of customer

The operation of the bank account does not usually cause any problems but problems may arise if an individual has opened the account in some other capacity, eg the credit balance is held under a trust account or the account is a partnership account etc. In connection with special accounts, the bank must safeguard its position and ensure that (a) the person giving the mandate has the authority to act in that capacity, and (b) that the payment mandate is issued in favour of the person entitled to the money. If the bank fails to act properly with regard to either of these obligations, it may find itself liable to the true owner of the funds either because the mandate was defective and the bank has acted without authority or payment has been made to someone other than the true owner.

It is, therefore, intended to examine the types of special business accounts a bank may hold and some of the consequences of opening such accounts.

Partnership accounts

A partnership account resembles a joint account in that it will be opened in the name of more than one person. Unlike a registered company, a partnership does not enjoy separate legal status and the account is in effect a joint account of the specified partners. By s 5 of the Partnership Act 1890 each partner acts as the agent of his co-partners and the partnership business. Thus, a partner can open an account on behalf of the partnership in the partnership name but he cannot open a partnership account in his own name. In *Alliance Bank v Kearsley* (1871) LR 6 CP 433 Montague Smith J said that an account opened by a man in his own name is prima facie his private account. The other partners were therefore not liable to reimburse the bank in respect of losses incurred by the partner on the account although the account was used exclusively for partnership purposes.

The authority of partners to draw instruments

Where a partnership agreement has been drawn up it will usually state that an account is to be opened and operated either jointly by all of the partners or by some of their number. The bank should therefore consult the partnership agreement and request that the partners execute an authority in favour of the bank. The outcome of *Forster v Mackreth* (1867) LR 2 Ex163 is that a partner's ability to bind the firm and his co-partners will depend on what is considered to be in the usual course of the partnership business. Not only must the partner act within the scope of the authority conferred on him but the bank must conform to the strict terms of the mandate given to it with regard to the operation of the account.

A partner in a trading partnership also has implied authority to draw, accept and indorse bills of exchange or other negotiable instruments on behalf of the business (*Harrison v Jackson* (1797) 7 Term 207 at 210; *Williamson v Johnson* (1823) 1 B & C 146). Moreover a partner has implied authority to borrow money for the purposes of the partnership if the business is one that cannot be carried on in the usual way without such power (*Bank of Australasia v Breillat* (1847) 6 Moo PCC 152 at 194 where a partner was held entitled to overdraw on a bank account; *Fisher v Tayler* (1843) 2 Hare 218).

A partner will not be deemed to have authority to open a bank account in his own name for partnership purposes. In *Ringham v Hackett* (1980) 124 SJ 201 Megaw LJ held that a partner who dishonestly wrote his signature in manuscript below the printed name of his firm nevertheless bound the partnership. The *Ringham* case was followed in *Central Motors (Birmingham) Ltd v PA and SN Wadsworth* [1983] 133 NLW 555 where an account was opened in the partnership name, with both partners being required to sign the cheques drawn on the account. One of the co-partners drew a cheque for the purchase of a car without the consent of the co-partner. The court rejected the attempt to distinguish the *Ringham* case and held that s 5 of the Partnership Act 1890, together with ss 23(2) and 91(1) of the Bills of Exchange Act 1882 were sufficient to impose liability on the co-partner. Further, in *United Bank of Kuwait v Hammound* [1988] 1 WLR 1051 the Court of Appeal held that an undertaking given as security for a loan was within the ordinary course of business where there was an underlying transaction of a solicitorial nature. For the purposes of establishing ostensible authority the question of whether or not an undertaking was given in the usual course of a solicitor's business was to be considered on the basis of the transaction as it appeared objectively, irrespective of its true nature.

It is imperative that a partner acts within the course of the express or implied authority conferred on him. Additionally, the bank must conform to the mandate given, and that includes a judgment on the part of the bank as to the validity of the mandate given by the partner. In *Forster v Mackreth* (1867) LR 2 Ex 163 a partner indorsed some bills of exchange on behalf of the firm. He also drew a number of post-dated cheques in the partnership name. The Court of Exchequer held that it was not in the ordinary course of the partnership business to deal in bills of exchange and therefore indorsing such bills was outside the scope of the partner's authority. Further, drawing post-dated cheques was also outside the scope of the business and outside the scope of the authority conferred on the partner. Martin B reached this decision on the basis that:

> 'we cannot in substance distinguish this [post-dated] cheque from a bill of exchange.'

Recent cases, however, treat post-dated cheques as both valid and regular: *Guildford Trust Ltd v Goss* (1927) 136 LT 725.

The powers conferred by the Partnership Act 1890 upon a partner may be varied by agreement between the partners. In practice most partnership agreements will deal with the issue of the authority of a partner to operate a bank account and if the bank is given specific instructions, it should require all partners to sign the mandate given.

Death of a partner

Unless a partnership agreement expressly provides to the contrary, the death of a partner dissolves the firm. There is no rule of survivorship in the operation of the partnership account. Section 38 of the Partnership Act 1890 provides that the surviving partners have the power to continue to act for the partnership firm for the purposes of winding up the affairs of the partnership. For the purposes of winding up the affairs of the partnership, a surviving partner has, in law, the authority to complete unfinished transactions including the authority to sell the whole or part of the partnership property in order to pay off partnership debts *Barton v North Staffordshire Railway Co* (1888) 38 Ch D 458 and to draw upon the partnership bank account *Backhouse v Charlton* (1878) 8 Ch D 444. In *Backhouse v Charlton,* Malins VC took the view that a partner who draws on the partnership account after the death of a partner can assume that the surviving partner acts within his authority when drawing on the account. In that case it was held that the bank was not required to make any enquiry concerning the payment of the cheques drawn after the death of the deceased partner. Indeed the bank was bound to honour any of the cheques in question. In *Re Bourne* [1906] 2 Ch 427 on the death of one of the partners (Grove) the remaining partner, Bourne, continued the business in the partnership name until his death. At the time of Grove's death, the partnership account was overdrawn by £6,476. Bourne deposited with the bank, as security, title deeds over certain partnership assets in order to secure a further overdraft. At the time of Bourne's death the bank account was overdrawn by £4,463. Bourne's estate being insolvent, the question that arose was whether the bank or Grove's executors had priority to the proceeds of sale of the property charged in favour of the bank. The court held that the bank had priority to the proceeds of sale and Grove's executors appealed. The Court of Appeal held for the bank and said that the surviving partner had the power to give a good title to purchasers and mortgagees. Romer LJ said that:

> 'the account with them [the bank] was a partnership account. It was continued under the partnership name and apparently for the purposes of the partnership, and it appears to me impossible to say that it is not or may not be reasonable for a surviving partner to continue the partnership account for the purpose of winding up the estate.'

The bankruptcy of a partner

The bankruptcy of a partner dissolves the firm in the absence of a provision to the contrary in the partnership articles. The bankrupt partner then has no authority to bind the partnership (ss 33 and 38 of the Partnership Act 1890). Moreover, a bank has no lien on a partner's private account for an overdraft on the partnership account unless either the partnership agreement so states or the terms of the overdraft supplied by the bank so provide. In *Watts v Christie* (1849) 11 Beav 546 a partnership account was overdrawn although one of the partners maintained a private account with the same bank that was in credit. The bank failed and the partner holding the credit balance assigned to the partnership the amount of the credit due to him from the bank, in order to facilitate a set-off of the credit balance against the partnership's debit balance. If such a set-off were permitted, the partnership firm would recover the net credit balance resulting from the assignment and would not be obliged to pay the amount due under the overdrawn partnership account prior to the assignment to the bank's trustee in bankruptcy. Lord Langdale held that the purported assignment was ineffective. At law, a separate debt cannot be set off against a joint debt; neither can it be set off in equity or in bankruptcy (see *Ex parte Christie* 10 Ves 105 and *Addis v Knight* (1817) 2 Mer 117).

Company accounts

A company registered under the Companies Act 1985 (as amended) enjoys separate legal status from its members (*Salomon v Salomon & Co Ltd* [1897] AC 22). Consequently, the company can enter in contractual obligations in its own right and give a valid discharge for any indebtedness incurred on its behalf. Because the company is an artificial legal entity it must act through properly appointed agents. In the case of a company, these are likely to be persons appointed to the board of management. Until recently, a bank dealing with a registered company would have to satisfy itself that a transaction was not ultra vires the company. The Prentice Report recommended that a company should have the same capacity to enter into contracts as natural persons and a third party dealing with the company should not be deemed to have constructive notice of the memorandum and articles. The report also recommended that it should be possible for a company to ratify a contract in excess of a director's authority even where the third party had actual knowledge of the want of authority. The purpose of these rules is to validate transactions entered into by a company which but for s 35A of the Companies Act 1985 would be ultra vires or beyond the capacity of the company's objects. At the same time, personal liability will continue to be imposed on company directors for loss caused by them to their company by entering into ultra vires transactions. The section preserves the rights of individual members of the company to seek injunctive relief to prevent the company and its directors from entering into ultra vires transactions.

The directors remain under a duty to 'observe any limitations on their powers flowing from the company's memorandum'. If, therefore, directors cause their company loss by entering into transactions that are beyond their capacity, then they may be held in breach of their fiduciary duties and liable to compensate the company. Any transaction in excess of the director's capacity may be ratified by a special resolution of the shareholders.

Problems affecting banks

The two main issues that may affect a bank that maintains an account for a registered company are:

(i) lending to a company that is its customer;

(ii) the drawing and payment of negotiable instruments and the authority of the directors.

Lending to a company

The combined effect of the new ss 35A and 3A (which allows a company to register with a general objects clause allowing it to undertake general commercial activities) of the Companies Act 1985 is to allow a company to have the full contractual capacity of natural persons. The issue of whether a trading company can borrow certainly presents no problems.

A power to borrow will not be implied on a non-trading company whose sole function is to own property for its shareholders. Non-trading companies do not usually require the power to borrow and, despite the new s 35A, banks should scrutinize the company's memorandum and articles although the bank is no longer deemed to have constructive notice of any limitations of authority contained in such documents.

Form of company contracts

Companies registered under the Companies Act 1985 have always been able to execute contracts in the same way as individuals. This has been reinforced by the fact that a company need no longer have a seal. If a contract made by an individual has to be by deed (a legal conveyance, mortgage or lease of land), then a company must also make it by deed. This does not prevent verbal contracts being enforced against a company when the plaintiff has performed his obligations. Again, if the contract is one that must be in writing, it may be made on behalf of the company in writing and signed by a person it has authorized. This, however, applies not only to contracts that the law requires to be made in writing (eg hire purchase and consumer credit agreements) but also to contracts that are merely evidenced by a written memorandum and signed (eg contracts of guarantee). In this case it is not necessary that the memorandum should be prepared as part of the transaction or that the person authorized to sign it should be the agent who negotiated the contract (*Jones v Victoria Graving Dock Co* (1877) 2 QBD 314).

Current account operations

Transactions that are most likely to involve a bank in the current account operations of the company (customer) are the discounting or negotiation of bills of exchange or the payment of cheques drawn on behalf of the company. The purpose of discounting or negotiating a bill of exchange is to enable the bank's customer to obtain funds against an instrument that will mature at a future date. To that extent the bank may provide credit for the customer. Alternatively, the bank may be involved in honouring cheques on behalf of the customer against any credit balance on the customer's account or if the amount of the cheques is within an agreed overdraft limit. In both these instances the bank will act as an agent in carrying out the customer's instructions. The bank is therefore under an obligation to ensure that it acts within the mandate conferred by the customer.

Director's actual liability

Under the general law, directors can act on behalf of a company only at board meetings at which their collective decisions are expressed by resolutions. They have no power to act individually as agents of the company. Further, the board may not delegate any of its powers to one or more members of the board unless the articles expressly permit (*Re County Palatine Loan & Discount Co, Cartmell's Case* (1874) 9 Ch App 691). In practice the articles of the company will contain the widest powers of delegation both to individual directors (Table A, Art 72) and to other agents chosen by the board (Table A, Art 71). The articles of most companies empower the board of directors to appoint one or more of their number to be a managing director and to delegate to him any powers either concurrently with, or to the exclusion of, the board (Table A, Art 72). A managing director is vested with apparent authority to carry on the company's business in the usual way and to do all acts necessary for that purpose. Thus he may sign cheques and bills of exchange on behalf of the company (*Dey v Pullinger Engineering Co* [1921] 1 KB 77), even in favour of himself (*Bank of New South Wales v Goulburn Valley Butter Co Pty Ltd* [1902] AC 543, [1900–3] All ER Rep 935, PC), borrow money on the company's account and give security over the company's property for its repayment (*Biggerstaff v Rawatt's Wharf Ltd* [1896] 2 Ch 93), receive payment of debts owed to the company even by cheque made payable to him personally (*Clay Hill Brick and Tile Co Ltd v Rawlings* [1938] 4 All ER 100), guarantee loans made to the company's subsidiaries and agree to indemnify such persons who have given such guarantees themselves (*Hely-Hutchinson v Brayhead Ltd* [1968] 1 QB 549). The apparent authority of a managing director is confined to commercial matters (*George Whitechurch Ltd v Cavanagh* [1902] AC 117). An ordinary non-managing director or secretary has no power to act as an agent of the company by virtue of their office. If, therefore, a person negotiated a contract with a secretary or such director, the law at one time held that such a person acted at his own risk. Under the changes introduced by the Companies Act 1989, it is no longer possible for a company to raise the director's lack of authority.

Personal liability of the signatory

A bill of exchange, cheque or promissory note may be drawn, made, accepted or indorsed on behalf of the company by any person authorized to sign in its name, or by signing his name and adding words that indicate that he signs on behalf of the company (Companies Act 1985, s 37). The words used must clearly indicate that the instrument is signed as an agent and in order to release the signatory from being made personally liable on the instrument. It may not be enough to place the words 'agent' or 'director' after the signature since this merely indicates the office held by that person and does not necessarily indicate that it was signed in that capacity (*Parker v Winlaw* (1857) 7 E & B 942 and *Landes v Marcaus* (1909) 25 TLR 478). In *Chapman v Smethurst* [1909] 1 KB 927 placing the word 'director' after the signature was held to make the instrument a promissory note issued by the company. More recently, in *Bondina Ltd v Rollaway Shower Blinds Ltd* [1986] 1 All ER 564 it was held that a cheque signed by a director of a company, without any indication of the capacity in which he signed the instrument, was a cheque drawn on the company because by placing his signature on it he was adopting all the words on the cheque form, including the name of the company. It is impossible to be dogmatic about the words that will suffice to negate personal liability since the court is entitled to look at the document as a whole. Where the drawer of the instrument is a company, it may be possible for a holder to establish personal liability of the signatory under s 349(4) of the Companies Act 1985 (formerly s 108(4) of the Companies Act 1948).

The word 'holder' has been construed to mean the person to whom the order is addressed and who is to benefit by it. Personal liability attaches not only to the person who signs the irregular document but also to the person who authorizes the irregular document. In *Durham Fancy Goods Ltd v Michael Jackson (Fancy Goods) Ltd* [1968] 2 All ER 987 the plaintiffs had drawn a bill on the defendants that wrongly named them as 'M Jackson (Fancy Goods) Ltd' and prepared a form for acceptance in the same style. The director and company signed the acceptance without noticing the misdescription. The bill was dishonoured and it was held that the director was personally liable on the bill but that the company was estopped from enforcing the bill since it was responsible for the error. In *Maxform SpA v Mariani and Goodville Ltd* [1979] 2 Lloyd's Rep 54 a company director of Goodville Ltd was held personally liable on the bills drawn in its registered business name, Italdesign, without the mention on the bills of the name Goodville Ltd. The court held that the word name in the 1948 Act could only refer to the company's corporate registered name. In *British Airways Board v Parish* [1979] 2 Lloyd's Rep 143 and *Calzaturificio Fiorella SpA v Walton* [1979] CLY 23 the directors of two companies were held personally liable when the word 'Ltd' had been omitted from the company names, but in *Banque de l'Indochine et de Suez v Euroseas Group Finance Co Ltd* [1981] 3 All ER 198 it was held that s 108 of the Companies Act 1948 did not render the company director liable because the abbreviation 'Co' for 'Company' was well established. In *Barber & Nicholls v R & G Associates (London) Ltd* [1985] CLY 129 it was held that s 108 would not apply to impose personal liability on several dishonoured cheques because the bank had omitted the word 'London' from the company's printed name on the cheque forms.

Limited liability partnerships

Like a company, an LLP as a body corporate will be able to make its own contracts eg (i) in writing by seal; (ii) by any person acting under express, or implied authority. The latter therefore imports agency law into LLP law and the question will arise whether those acting on behalf of the LLP were acting within the authority conferred on them. In establishing the role of members as agents for this purpose, the rules that bind the members are derived from the Partnership Act 1890 (s 5). Section 6 of the Limited Liability Partnership Act 2000 provides that each member is an agent of the LLP. Section 6(2) then provides that the LLP is not bound by the unauthorized acts of a member where the third party is either aware of the lack of authority or does not know or believe the member to be a member of the LLP. In other respects ss 35A, 36A, s37-39 and 41 of the Companies Act 1985 apply to the LLP as to bills of exchange, execution of deeds abroad, and authentication of documents.

Banks dealing with an LLP should obtain the registration document that serves the purpose of the memorandum, and obtain written mandate in respect of a LLP.

Unincorporated associations' accounts

Unincorporated associations are mainly clubs, literary societies and charitable institutions. The objects of such bodies are non-commercial and they normally obtain their funds through subscriptions and donations. Such associations will, however, need bank accounts to pay cheques or receive payments. A bank that opens an account for an unincorporated association needs to be aware that it does not enjoy independent legal personality. Such an association, therefore, cannot sue or be sued in its own name. A legal action will have to be brought against the committee that acts on behalf of its membership.

The question then is who is liable for the debts of the association. Usually the liability of members is limited to the amount of the subscription or their membership fee. The action is instituted against the committee as to recover the amount claimed from the funds of the association but the members of the committee may also be personally liable. In *Coutts & Co v Irish Exhibition in London*

(1891) 7 TLR 313 an association was formed for the purpose of organising an Irish arts exhibition. Initially, the body was unincorporated and functioned through a committee. The bank granted an overdraft against the association's current account on the personal assurance of the committee members. Shortly after, the association was incorporated but then wound up because of the failure of the purpose for which it was incorporated. The bank brought an action to recover the amount of the overdraft from the committee members. The court held that the account had not been officially transferred to the corporation's name and the bank had not released the committee members from their liability to reimburse the amount involved.

The committee is not entitled to go beyond the powers conferred on it by the constitution and acting within the scope of its authority, the committee has the power to delegate. In *Bradley Egg Farm Ltd v Clifford* [1943] 2 All ER 378 it was held that the committee members were bound by the acts of a duly appointed agent. In *Fleming v Hector* (1836) 2 M & W 172 the court held that the committee of an unincorporated club was entitled to delegate its power to draw and indorse bills of exchange to an agent. When dealing with an unincorporated association, a bank should ensure that the instructions it receives are clear and unambiguous. It should obtain a copy of the association's constitution authorising an account to be opened (or a resolution to that effect) and the scope of the authority to draw and operate the account. The bank needs to be cautious when allowing overdraft facilities or granting a loan. Ordinary members of the association are not liable for the debts incurred by the association unless they have expressed their individual consent to the transaction. Therefore, the bank's ability to recover amounts owed to the bank from members of the committee depends on their personal financial standing.

Four

Lending to a corporate customer

4.1 Making the decision to lend

Before making a loan facility available, the lender will have to satisfy himself of the viability of the project so as to make a sound business decision. For example, a banker will want to know what exactly the loan is to be used for. There are two main reasons for this, namely:

(i)   he must assure himself first that the purpose is legal;

(ii) that the intended use is reasonably likely to produce a profitable result. Banks are, in general reluctant to provide 'standby' facilities except for the most reliable customers. Purely speculative projects will be avoided but it is not unreasonable for a bank to undertake 'a fair trade risk'. It should, however, be remembered that the extent of such a risk is likely to be narrower for a bank than for an entrepreneur.

The lending bank will also wish to know the source of repayment, so as to ensure that repayment proposals are clear, well-planned and within the borrower's ability. If the lending is not self-liquidating, ie if the project financed does not generate sufficient funds to repay the borrowing within a reasonable time, then the lending bank must be satisfied that there are alternative sources of repayment. The bank will have regard to the duration of the risk.

Where the bank is lending on a long-term basis it must be aware of the possible effect of changing economic and political circumstances. This is especially true when lending on the international market.

The bank will want to make a profit on its lending and its calculations must be based on the cost of funds to it (ie the interest it pays to depositors) and the overheads of business. The specific costs of documentation and arranging a particular loan are likely to be covered by the arrangement fee, but the bank will rely on the interest differential to provide the major part of the profit. The actual interest charged will be determined by many factors, including the bank's policy. Generally, the appropriate rates of interest will be determined by a bank's head office, although individual branch managers may be given some amount of discretion.

Forms of bank finance

Overdraft

An overdraft is a traditional method of bank finance and represents a line of credit made available by a bank to its customer through the normal use of the customer's current account. Although an overdraft is considered to be a short-term facility, a lot of businesses operate on a continuous overdraft. Therefore, an overdraft facility is not, in reality, always short-term in terms of usage. Interest is calculated on a daily basis but is debited to the account only periodically. As the amount of the overdraft is likely to fluctuate on a daily basis, the method of charging interest daily on the amount overdrawn is significant.

Legal nature of the overdraft

In normal circumstances, when the customer has a credit balance on his account, it is the bank which is in the role of the debtor to its customer (*Foley v Hill* (1848) 2 HLC 28) and it has 'contracted, having received that money, to repay to the principal, when demanded, a sum equivalent to that paid into his hand'. When the current account is overdrawn, the roles of the parties are reversed, and the customer becomes a debtor of the bank for the amount overdrawn. The main features of an overdraft are as follows.

♦ An overdraft facility may be granted to a customer as a result of an express agreement entered into with the bank. In such a situation, the bank is likely to agree to the customer being authorized to draw against his account up to a specified ceiling. As amounts are paid into the credit of the customer they are set off against the amount overdrawn, thereby giving the customer a larger balance on the overdraft against which amounts may be drawn. As further sums are drawn against the account, so the amount of the overdraft facility available will be reduced.

♦ Alternatively, an overdraft facility may be implied to the banker an customer relationship from the circumstances, eg where a customer draws a cheque for a sum that exceeds the credit balance on the account, that act of the customer is treated as a request for an overdraft facility and, if the cheque is honoured, the bank has extended an overdraft facility.

♦ In *Cuthbert v Robarts* [1907] 2 Ch 226 the court held that the drawing of a cheque by a customer for a sum in excess of the amount standing to the credit of the current account is really a request for a loan and, if the cheque is honoured, the customer has borrowed money from the bank.

♦ If, however, a bank agrees to allow the customer to overdraw in return for a consideration provided by the customer, then the customer is legally entitled to overdraw on the account up to any agreed overdraft limit. The bank will be liable in damages to the customer if it refuses to allow the customer to overdraw, or if it either erroneously or otherwise dishonours cheques drawn by the customer within an agreed overdraft limit. The giving of a security by the customer to its bank has been held to be adequate consideration for the bank's commitment to extend an overdraft to that customer (*Fleming v Bank of New Zealand* [1900] AC 577). In such a situation the bank is effectively estopped from denying that the customer was entitled as against the bank to overdraw up to a specified amount.

Withdrawal of the overdraft facility

An overdraft is repayable on demand unless the bank has otherwise agreed. There is only one judicial decision that appears to impose an obligation on the bank to give its customer a reasonable length of notice, prior to calling for repayment of an overdraft, before issuing a writ to recover the amount owing (*Brighty v Norton* (1862) 3 B&S 305). The preponderance of judicial opinion, however, is that a bank may demand immediate repayment of an overdraft at any time, and it owes no duty to the customer to ensure that the demand is made in sufficient time before it becomes effective, so that the customer has a reasonable opportunity to raise money elsewhere if necessary. The bank cannot, however, treat the customer as being in default until it has given the customer sufficient time to obtain the money to repay the overdraft from a bank in the locality of his residence or business address. In *Williams and Glyn's Bank v Barnes* [1981] Com LR 205 the bank granted its customer an overdraft facility in order to finance some transactions of a company of which the customer was the chairman and majority shareholder. When the company's financial position deteriorated further, the bank demanded immediate repayment of the amount outstanding on the overdraft. The court held that, in the absence of an express agreement providing for the duration of the overdraft facility or for the date of repayment, the task of the court must be to consider whether, according to the ordinary rules for the implication of terms into commercial contracts, any term for the duration of the facility or the date of

ﹾ be implied. If no such term is to be implied then the money lent
ty is 'no more than money lent and is, therefore, repayable on
urts have held the following.

- ﹾne mere knowledge of the bank that a customer intends to spend all, or
part, of the money in a business venture that will take a long time to come
to fruition cannot itself give rise to an implied term requiring a period of
notice for repayment calculated by reference to the probable duration of
that business venture. In *Bank of Baroda v Panessar* [1987] 2 WLR 208 Walton
J observed that a debtor who was required to pay money on demand was
only entitled to such length of notice as was necessary to implement the
mechanics of payment needed to discharge the debt. In view of the modern
methods of communication and transfer of money available, the time
needed may be exceptionally short.

- ◆ The bank's right to immediate repayment of the overdraft should not be
exercised so as to unduly prejudice the interests of the customer. In
Joachimson v Swiss Bank Corpn [1921] 3 KB 110 it was said that, in the
absence of an express agreement, reasonable time should be given to a
customer to repay the overdraft.

- ◆ Again in *Rouse v Bradford Banking Co* [1894] AC 586 a partnership was
reorganized and subsequently allowed to increase an existing overdraft
granted to the original firm. The House of Lords rejected the argument that
the new partnership had the right to expect to have the overdraft available
for a specified period. The Lords added that, although an overdraft
arrangement may not in itself grant the customer an indefinite time in which
he would be able to utilize the facility, neither of the parties would
contemplate a withdrawal of the facility without notice shortly after its
extension. Similarly, in *Cripps (RA) & Sons Ltd v Wickenden* [1973] 1 WLR 944
Goff J held that, although an overdraft was repayable on demand, the
customer must be given a reasonable notice before the facility is withdrawn.
The bank's right to claim immediate repayment of the overdraft may be
waived either by express or implied agreement.

- ◆ The court may decide that, as a matter of necessity and to give efficacy to
the contract, a term may be implied requiring the bank to give notice over
a reasonable period of time before the right to repayment arises. In *Williams
and Glyn's Bank v Barnes* [1981] Com LR 205) Gibson J held, on the facts,
that the documentation in the *Barnes* case established that the lending bank
had agreed that the overdraft was not repayable on demand and the facility
could not be cancelled without notice. The bank was required to give such
notice as would permit the customer an opportunity to explore alternative
sources of borrowing, or of selling part of its undertaking.

An express clause that an overdraft is repayable on demand is not necessarily
effective. In *Titford Property Co Ltd v Cannon Street Acceptances Ltd* (22 May 1975,
unreported) a facility letter was drawn up that granted the customer an overdraft

for a 12-month period, but which included a clause providing for repayment at call. When the bank demanded repayment prior to the expiry of the 12-month period, the customer brought an action against the bank claiming that the overdraft was not repayable on demand. Goff J held that, where a bank allows an overdraft facility for a fixed time, then any clause requiring repayment of the same facility on demand is completely repugnant to the purpose of the facility and should be read as subordinate to the main clause, or alternatively, completely ignored.

The decision in *Titford Property Co Ltd* was considered by Gibson J in *Williams and Glyn's Bank v Barnes* where the judge expressed the view that, if the judgment in the *Titford* case is to be regarded as stating that in a contest for primacy between a term loan and a clause for repayment on demand then provisions for the term loan must always prevail, he should not feel able to follow it. Gibson J expressed the opinion that if the bank could not reasonably have supposed that the borrower would treat the clause for repayment on demand seriously, and that the borrower could not sensibly be expected to have supposed that the bank did mean the term to be effective, the law both permits and requires the court to disregard the term. The approach adopted by Gibson J enables the court to reach its own conclusions and enforce the real intentions of the parties; for these reasons it must be submitted as correct.

Bank's right to withdraw an overdraft facility before the overdraft is utilized

Whether the bank can give notice to withdraw the overdraft facility where the customer has given consideration will depend on the terms of the contract.

♦ If it is a term of the contract that the overdraft will be available for a fixed period, eg for three months, it would appear that the bank is bound to provide the overdraft facility within the stipulated period and up to any agreed limit.

♦ In the case where the bank is under no contractual obligation to provide the overdraft facility but has merely represented to its customer that the facility is or will be available, the position is not entirely clear. It is submitted that the bank will have committed itself to allow the facility by its representations to the customer (*Jorden v Money* (1854) 5 HLC 185; *Argy Trading Co v Lapid Developments* [1977] 1 WLR 444).

♦ The question that arises is whether the bank can refuse to honour cheques or drafts, within the limit of the agreed overdraft, before any notice of withdrawal has been given to the customer. Here again the position differs according to whether or not the bank has a contractual obligation to grant the overdraft, but it is submitted that the customer must be given a reasonable opportunity to set his affairs in order (ie to arrange alternative financing facilities) (*Fleming v Bank of New Zealand* [1900] AC 577).

Interest on overdrafts

Interest will be calculated on overdrafts either at the agreed rate, or if there is no agreement, at the bank's currently published lending rate. This is fixed by reference to the bank's minimum lending rate (that tends to be uniform for all commercial banks) plus a number of percentage points over the minimum, depending on the risk to the bank and the credit worthiness of the customer.

♦ Overdraft interest is charged daily to the customer's account although not debited against the account until the end of the current quarterly or half-yearly period. Consequently, in calculating overdraft interest, account is not taken of amounts credited to the customer's account until the business day following that on which the bank receives the credit item. Where an account is continuously overdrawn a substantial part of the debit balance may actually represent interest.

♦ The charging of interest is a matter of banking practice. It can be recovered on the basis of the implied contract or on the basis of a course of dealings or mercantile usage. The court may award interest under s 3 of the Law Reform (Miscellaneous Provisions) Act 1934, although the Act does not authorize charging compound interest. In *National Bank of Greece SA v Pinios Shipping Co* [1990] 2 Lloyd's Rep 225 the House of Lords held that the usage under which banks are entitled to charge compound interest prevails generally as 'between bankers and customers who borrow from them and do not pay interest as it accrues'.

In *Minories Finance Ltd v Daryanani* (13 April 1989, unreported) the repayment of certain loans, granted by a bank in London to a Nigerian company, was blocked by an embargo imposed by the Nigerian government. The bank served a demand in London on the guarantors. On the question of compound interest the Court of Appeal held that, as the facility letter did not include an express provision entitling the bank to charge compound interest, the question of the bank's right to charge compound interest was a triable issue and leave to defend was granted. It should be remembered that in the *Daryanani* case the issue arose only in respect of interest charged prior to the date on which the bank made its demand.

Term loans

It is commonly considered as more prudent to finance the purchase of fixed assets or long-term projects by a longer-term loan rather than an overdraft.

During the early 1970s the banks expanded contractual term lending, with loans of up to five or seven years being available. Longer-term finance was made available through the merchant banks, many of which are, in reality, owned by the clearing banks. The loans provided by merchant banks are usually repayable over a period exceeding ten years, usually either at a fixed rate of interest or at a variable rate related to the corresponding current yields in the long-term gilt-edged market. It is normal for these loans to be secured on the existing fixed assets of the business.

Term loan agreement

Term loans are almost invariably made under a written agreement that sets out in detail the terms of lending. A typical loan agreement is likely to contain specific provisions relating to repayment, conditions, representations and warranties, creditor protection, undertakings and events of default. It is intended to discuss only the more common features of term loans.

The advance

The term loan agreement will invariably state the maximum amount of the loan. It will specify the method by which the loan is to be advanced, ie either by a single drawing of the whole amount at the option of the borrower or by successive installments over a period of months or even years. Where the purpose of the loan is to provide finance for a specified project it is usual for the loan to be advanced in installments, each installment being advanced only on submission and approval of appropriate documentary evidence that the previous stages of the project have been satisfactorily completed. In the case of large loans (particularly syndicated loans), the borrowing company may be required to give notice to the lending bank or the agent bank before it can draw the amount of the next installment on the next drawing date.

The loan agreement will provide that a charge will be levied on the undrawn balance of the maximum amount of the loan (a commitment fee). This fee is charged periodically at the time when interest payments fall due and it terminates when the maximum amount agreed has been advanced to the borrower. Where the loan is to be made in successive installments, a charge will be made only if the amount drawn by the borrower is less than the maximum available under the installment.

Duration of the loan

The agreement itself will specify the duration of the loan. The loan agreement is legally binding and the insertion of a term specifying the duration of the loan precludes any subsequent claim by the lending bank that the loan can be withdrawn at any time. Furthermore, any demand for repayment made before the stipulated expiry term is ineffective unless there is default on the part of the borrower that will entitle the bank under the terms of the loan agreement to call for immediate repayment, eg a failure to maintain the agreed payments of either capital or interest.

In the absence of a provision relating to the duration of the loan agreement, the loan will be repayable on the bank giving the borrower a reasonable length of notice demanding repayment (*Buckingham & Co v London and Midland Bank Ltd* (1895) 12 TLR 70), but it would appear that the borrower would be entitled to repay such a loan at any time without giving any notice in advance.

Repayment

The commencement and duration of the repayment period are a matter of negotiation. The agreed repayment terms are reciprocally binding on the borrower and the lending bank or banks. Consequently, the bank cannot require the borrower to repay the loan earlier than the date or dates agreed under the original agreement. The borrower cannot save interest by repaying the loan before the agreed date or dates, although it may make an early repayment if it also pays interest in advance calculated up to the agreed repayment dates.

A term loan agreement may give an option to the borrower to repay the whole or part of the outstanding balance of the loan earlier than the date or dates agreed. In this way, the borrower saves interest. It is usual, however, for the loan agreement to specify the earliest date on which prepayment may be made. Additionally, the loan agreement may also specify that the borrower must give the lending bank (or agent bank in the case of a syndicated loan) a specified notice before it can make prepayment and must pay interest on the amount prepaid for that period.

Where the loan is advanced for a specified purpose and the loan agreement does not deal with the issue of repayment, then the bank cannot withdraw the loan facility or claim repayment before the purpose is achieved (*Williams and Glyn's Bank v Barnes* [1981] Com LR 205), unless, of course, an event of default occurs that gives the bank an automatic right to immediate repayment.

Conversion into non-recourse loan

With some self-liquidating advances, the loan agreement may contain an option for the borrower to convert the outstanding balance of a loan into a non-recourse loan. A non-recourse loan is one under which a higher rate of interest is payable than under the initial loan, and the principal of the loan is repayable over a longer period than the initial loan period and only out of the profits or proceeds of the project financed. The importance of a non-recourse loan to the borrowing company is that repayment of the loan is made solely out of the generated profits from the financed projects. Consequently, any personal liability on the part of the borrowing company that could result in the company's insolvency is avoided. Those other assets are therefore available for the company to sell, lease or otherwise dispose of free from any charge or security created and they are also available to be used as security for further borrowing by the company.

The lending banks do not take an equity participation in the project or development and the bank is still a creditor of the borrower. It may recover any indebtedness (the outstanding balance of the loan with interest) in connection with the term loan out of the earnings or returns of the completed project. If the income of the project is not sufficient to discharge the outstanding principal sum and interest, the lending bank will have the power by the loan agreement to appoint a receiver to take over the management of the project or to sell the company's assets comprised in it.

Interest

Interest on term loans made by banks is charged at rates that vary with the market rates during the currency of the loan. Consequently, the risk of interest rates rising during the currency of the loan is borne by the borrower.

Consumer Credit aspects of the overdraft and term loan

The Consumer Credit Act 1974 applies certain protective measures to 'regulated credit agreements' and 'regulated hire agreements'. The debtor or hirer has to be a consumer whilst the financier, or credit provider may be 'any other person'. On the whole, banks and building societies enter into credit agreements.

The Consumer Credit Act 1974 applies to protect consumers (a term that extends to individuals, partnerships and unincorporated associations) in respect of transactions not exceeding £25,000.

♦ A bank overdraft falls within the definition of a regulated consumer credit agreement for unrestricted-use running account credit, even if it extended without prior arrangement with the customer. Examples of an unrestricted-use credit agreement include the provision of an overdraft facility, cheque cards, and a loan of money the use of which is at the free disposition of the borrower (even though the purpose of the loan may be known to the creditor).

As the Consumer Credit Act 1974 does not apply to corporations, it is not proposed to deal with the Act here.

Bank finance for specific purposes

The discussion, so far, has examined ways in which bank finance is available in general. Apart from these kinds of arrangements, banks, or their specialized subsidiaries, may agree to provide finance for a specific purpose or for a class of business dealings. These specific kinds of transactions may range from the issue of letters of credit in connection with import and export transactions to the sale of trade debts of companies. The remaining part of this chapter explores some methods by which banks may provide finance for specific purposes.

4.2 Lending for specific purposes

Facility letters and loan agreements

As a result of negotiations between a bank and borrowing customer, a document may be drawn up that sets out the nature of the contemplated loan and some or all of the terms to which it will be subject. Various terms are used to describe these documents, eg offer documents, heads of agreement, or commitment letters. The extent to which these documents, if any, are legally enforceable may become important if the borrowing customer refuses to pay, or a bank refuses to repay, a fee referred to in the document, or where one of the parties refuses to complete the more formal documentation contemplated.

♦ The legal character of a commitment letter depends on its individual nature. A commitment letter 'subject to contract' will automatically be regarded as not binding. In exceptional circumstances, such a commitment letter may subsequently be converted into a contract and there may be representations giving rise to a collateral contract, or some form of estoppel that prevents the parties from denying the effect of the transactions envisaged. While the phrase 'documentation satisfactory to us [the bank]' is used, it is for the bank to determine whether the final documentation is satisfactory and therefore a subjective test will be applied. As long as the bank acts honestly, the commitment letter will not be treated as uncertain. Where words such as 'subject to usual documentation' are used, that will not necessarily make the commitment letter too indefinite for the court and it may be able to determine the terms by an investigation of the circumstances. Otherwise, the test is whether the commitment letter was intended to be binding, or whether a binding letter is consistent with the reasonable expectations of the parties. Courts will have regard to all the circumstances and not just to the letter itself. The following may, therefore, be relevant.

♦ The manner in which the document is described may be some indication, eg a document expressed as an 'agreement' and containing a sentence that it is intended to be provisional until a legal agreement is drawn up may indicate an intention to be bound. In some financial circumstances, the term 'commitment' itself does not indicate a binding commitment but only definite interest (*Governor and Company of the Bank of England v Three I plc* [1993] BCLC 968 at 1022–27).

♦ Whether the commitment letter contains a reasonably complete statement of the proposed terms is a strong indication as to whether or not it is intended to be binding. Documents that do not contain all the terms that ordinarily occur in such agreements may still, in the light of the surrounding circumstances, be intended to be binding. A commitment letter may contain so few of the terms that would be expected in the formal documentation that it cannot be said that the parties intended to be bound. Omission of the interest rate, the currency, or the terms of repayment may prove to be significant omissions in the absence of customer commercial usage. In some instances, however, even if the parties appear to have agreed the terms, other circumstances may negate an intention to be bound.

♦ The courts may have regard to the steps preceeding, and subsequent to, the completion of the commitment letter. Protracted discussions about the proposed contents of the letter, a degree of formality, a belief by the parties that it will be binding, and the subsequent conduct (eg payment of the commitment fee pursuant to the letter) are some indications that the parties intended to be bound by it).

Even if the commitment letter is not binding, it does not mean that expenses and fees referred to within it are not payable. The fees may be payable for considering whether or not to grant a proposed loan or for the issue of the commitment letter itself. The intention of the parties will be significant.

The loan facility

Although the terms of different loan arrangements will vary they tend to contain certain core provisions.

♦ Generally a term loan can be drawn down during a limited period after the agreement is signed (sometimes called the commitment period). If it can be drawn down in tranches, the minimum amount of each payment may be specified. Notice may have to be given before the amount is drawn against first to enable a bank to make arrangements to have funds available. At the end of the commitment period the obligation to lend lapses. The borrower will not, generally, be obliged to draw on a facility.

♦ Insofar as the bank is concerned, the question may arise whether it is obliged to lend once a notice of drawdown is given, particularly if there is a sudden change in the condition of the borrower or in the general economic climate. Commercial loan agreements, therefore, usually contain conditions precedent to the availability of the loan: representations, warranties and covenants made and given by the borrower. Extensive events of default may also be agreed. The conditions precedent must be satisfied before the borrower can drawdown the funds. They usually require the borrower to supply the lender with specified documentation, eg the constitutional document of a corporate borrower, a resolution of its board approving the facility, and, in the case of cross-border loans, legal opinions of relevant foreign lawyers on its validity. Another common condition precedent is that the borrower must confirm that there have been no events of default and the representations and warranties remain accurate. The function of the covenants in a loan agreement will be to give the lender some control over the borrower and restrict the borrower in the conduct of its business so as to ensure the borrower's credit rating does not decline. Precisely which covenants appear in a loan agreement depends on a variety of factors, eg the size and duration of the loan, the financial position of the borrower, the negotiating strength of the borrower, and the presence of competition from other banks. Failure to comply with a covenant is usually an event of default, which entitles the lender to terminate the loan. The conditions in the loan agreement confirming security, interest, and repayments vary to a considerable extent. The arrangement for security depends on whether the borrower is a public corporation, a private company, an unincorporated trader, or a person borrowing for private purposes.

A great deal depends on the object of the loan. It is intended to look at some of the main types of clauses found in the loan agreement eg purpose clauses, illegality and vires.

♦ The purpose of the loan will shape the agreement concluded with the lending bank. It will determine whether the loan is consistent with the bank's lending policy and commercial logic. The purpose of the loan will determine the provisions the loan documentation must contain in order to protect the bank's position. The facility agreement may contain a purpose clause the volition of which may render the borrower in default and, in exceptional circumstances, subject the moneys to a *Quistclose* trust, giving the bank an advantage in the event of the borrower's insolvency (*Barclays Bank Ltd v Quistclose Investments Ltd* [1970] AC 567). In exceptional circumstances, others holding or paying away the borrowed moneys or knowing of the purpose clause may be held in breach of trust or liable for dishonestly assisting a breach of trust (*Twinsectra Ltd v Yardley* [2002] 2 All ER 377). A purpose clause, in practice, may be so vague as to make it impossible to say whether it has been breached, eg where the clause provides the funds must be 'used towards the borrower's working capital requirements'. Banks that wish to exercise any effective control over the borrower's use of the funds may need to build in other mechanisms (eg project certificates about the successful completion of each stage can be demanded before the next stage is funded).

♦ If a bank knows that a facility is illegal (eg in breach of exchange control regulations), the English courts will treat it as void and disallow any action seeking recovery of any amounts advanced. An agreement that is initially lawful but subsequently becomes illegal is regarded differently and the bank may be able to recover amounts advanced, although the courts in the other jurisdiction, in enforcing any judgment, may block any remedy. In international loan agreements, banks may insist on an illegality clause, eg where it becomes unlawful for them to continue with the loan (where governments impose a freeze on dealings in the borrower's country), the borrower must immediately repay. Borrowers may, in their turn, seek a variation of this clause to oblige a bank so affected to use reasonable endeavors to seek a substitute bank to continue with the loan.

♦ Banks must also check on the capacity of the organization to which they lend. Registered companies now have full contractual capacity and issues relating to vires are no longer a problem. Legislation may still restrict the contractual capacity of organizations to enter into transactions, including loan transactions. This was emphasized in transactions involving local authority swaps that under the relevant legislation were held ultra vires (*Hazell v Hammersmith and Fulham LBC* [1992] 2 AC 1). It has been held that banks could recover sums advanced under what was subsequently discovered to be ultra vires transactions and restitutionary principles (*Westdeutsche Landesbank Girocentral v Islington LBC* [1996] AC 669; *Guinness Mahon & Co Ltd v Kensington and Chelsea LBC* [1999] QB 215).

Repayment and interest clause

The conditions in the loan agreement concerning interest and repayments will vary with each agreement. Any security taken will depend on whether the borrower is a public corporation, a private company, an unincorporated trader, or a private individual.

The interest rate charged will depend on the bank's assessment of the risk, the period for which the loan is extended, and on the security furnished. The rate of interest is usually variable and quoted at a given percentage above the bank's prime rate, or in the case of many commercial loans, at an agreed margin over the market rate. Even a loan with a variable interest rate may contain a provision for a fixed rate period. The loan agreement will usually specify the purpose of the loan and failure to use it for that specified purpose will constitute a repudiatory breach of the loan agreement (*Reid v National Westminster Bank plc* (22 October 1999, unreported)). It may then be possible for the lender to show that money lent for a specified period was held by the borrower on trust for the lender, eg *Barclays Bank Ltd v Quistclose Investments Ltd* [1970] AC 567 where the House of Lords held that money lent for a specified purpose was held by the borrower subject to a primary purpose trust, and, in the event of failure of that purpose, on a secondary resulting trust in favour of the lender. In *Twinsectra Ltd v Yardley* [2000] Lloyd's Rep 438 the Court of Appeal allowed a lender to invoke the primary purpose trust when the borrower misapplied the loan. The court emphasized that, for a *Quistclose* type trust to arise, there must not only be a declaration of a specified purpose but also some additional indication that the borrower is not to have the full beneficial interest in the fund (eg a requirement that the borrower keep the loan monies separate from his other assets).

Payment of a term loan will usually be on a specified date or dates and usually by installments during the lifetime of the loan. This provides the bank with a greater degree of assurance that it will receive repayment than with loans under which the whole amount is repayable at the end of the life of the loan. Under English law, there is normally no need to give notice where a sum of money is payable on a particular day. The agreement may expressly oblige the bank to make a demand before the borrower can be said to be in default. Lending agreements usually contain a clause giving the lender the option of accelerating the repayment of the loan (and any other sums due) and terminating its commitment to make further advances, if a default event occurs (the Loan Market Association has recommended loans of syndicated facility agreements).

The purpose of the events of default is to try and reduce the risks to the lender if certain circumstances occur, eg the borrower's failure to repay the principal or interest when due, or his bankruptcy or, in the case of a corporate borrower, its being taken over by a receiver or being wound up. The occurrence of any of the events listed events of default may not automatically constitute default under the terms of the loan agreement, eg the borrower may be allowed a grace period to rectify the position or a materiality test may have to be satisfied before the lender can call in the loan. An important event of default in a commercial loan agreement is the cross-default clause. Such a clause provides that if the borrower defaults on any other indebtedness to the same or another lender, then there is deemed to be a default under the particular loan agreement. In this way, the lender will be able to protect his position if the borrower has defaulted under the terms of another loan agreement and that lender has started enforcement proceedings or renegotiation discussions.

In the case of corporate borrowers, there is no statutory control on the exercise by the lender of his discretion to invoke his remedies under the events of default clause. A consumer borrower may be able to rely on the Unfair Terms in Consumer Contracts Regulations 1999, SI 1999/2083, that may invalidate terms deemed to be 'unfair'. In *Director General of Fair Trading v First National Bank plc* [2000] QB 672 the bank's standard loan agreement contained a term which provided that, should the borrower default on his repayments, interest would continue to be payable at the contractual rate until any judgment obtained by the bank was discharged. The court held that the term was subject to the test of fairness set out in the regulations and did not fall within the exemption from the test that applies to clearly drafted 'core' terms.

Although the law does not impose a good faith or fair dealing requirement in the negotiation and performance of contracts, a corporate or consumer borrower may be able to rely on a range of common law doctrines used by the courts to monitor contractual bargains, eg the borrower cannot expect equity to give relief against forfeiture where the lender relies on an events of default clause (*T C Trustees Ltd v J S Darwen (Successors) Ltd* [1969] 2 B 295 (301/2)). Moreover, a clause providing for acceleration of repayment of the loan on an event of default taking place does not constitute a penalty and will not be declared void on that ground (*Protector Endowment Loan and an Annuity Company v Grice* [1880] 5 QBD 592; *Oresundsvarvet Aktiebolag v Marcos Diamantis Lenos* [1988] 2 Lloyd's Rep 122). If, additionally, the clause provides that interest is payable immediately for the full unexpired period of a loan, it is likely to constitute a penalty (the *Lenos* case). A clause which provides for a small ratable increase in interest, eg 1%, charged prospectively from default until repayment, is unlikely to be struck down as a penalty (*Lordsvale Finance plc v Bank of Zambia* [1996] QB 752).

Conditions precedent, representations and warranties, covenants

Conditions precedent

A commercial loan facility will usually contain conditions precedent to the availability of the loan. The conditions precedent must be satisfied before the borrower can draw down the funds and they usually require the borrower to supply the lender with specified documentation, eg the company's constitutional documents, a resolution of its board approving the facility, or in the case of a cross-border transaction, legal opinions from foreign lawyers on the validity of the transaction. The bank will have a wide discretion to determine which documents must be produced as condition precedents. It may also impose a condition precedent to each drawing under the facility that the representations and warranties are correct, and that no default is outstanding or will result.

The issues that arise in relation to the conditions precedent are as follows.

♦ Whether such clauses are conditions precedent to the agreement coming into effect, or whether they are conditions precedent to the bank's performance under the facility. The approach that has been adopted is that there is a binding contract once the parties have agreed to the terms but that, until the conditions precedent are satisfied, the bank need not make the funds available.

The effect of this approach is that the bank can claim the fees and expenses set out in the agreement and in that respect, the agreement has become effective. Alternatively, the bank may have to claim for a quantum meruit (that is to say, payment for how much the bank's trouble has been worth) for services performed.

♦ Whether the bank needs to co-operate in respect of the conditions precedent will depend on the nature of the clause. Some conditions precedent may depend on the actions of a third party, eg where a regulatory body needs to approve the facility and the borrower needs to obtain that approval, whilst satisfying the others will be solely in the hands of the borrower. There may be conditions precedent that unless the bank initiates action, the borrower may be unable to fulfill. In such circumstances, the bank needs to be careful so that its conduct is not deemed by the borrower to have waived compliance of such a condition precedent. If the condition precedent can be construed as imposing on the bank a duty to act, the bank's failure may not only render it liable in damages but also prevent it from claiming that the condition has not been satisfied.

Representations and warranties

There is some overlap between conditions precedent and representations and warranties in a facility agreement. The concern, the main existing facts and these act as a checklist in respect of which the bank must have information. Representations and warranties usually fall into two basic categories:

♦ those relating to legal aspects of the agreement, eg the legal status, powers and authority of the borrower and validity of the documents;

♦ those relating to commercial aspects covering the credit standing and financial condition of the borrowr. Additionally, the borrower will be required to make representations on other matters, eg that its accounts are accurate and have suffered no material adverse change since they were drawn up and that there are no legal proceedings pending that may have a material adverse affect on him. Where there is a syndicate of banks, there will also be representations about the accuracy of the information memorandum sent to potential members.

Representations and warranties are usually drafted on an 'evergreen' basis, which means that they are deemed to be repeated on each draw down of funds by the borrower and/or at other specified intervals. The loan agreement will usually specify that it is an event of default to make a representation or warranty that is incorrect in any material respect.

It has been said that representations and warranties perform an investigative role (*International Loans, Bonds And Securities Regulations*, P Wood (London) Sweet & Maxwell, 1995). Representations may relate not only to the borrower but also to its parent company guarantee and to subsidiaries. Borrowers therefore need to consider whether they can, with any accuracy, make representations about other companies in the group, particularly if they are based overseas.

Covenants

Covenants are undertakings given by the borrower as to what it will, or will not do, in the future eg it will regularly provide specified financial and other information to the bank; it will maintain certain financial ratios (eg Gearing, Minimal Tangible Net worth); it will ensure appropriate regulatory consent continues to be maintained; it will not dispose of its assets, change its business, or enter into an amalgamation, merger or reconstruction. The latter covenants are designed to preserve the corporate structure and its income producing assets for the lender bank. Other important covenants are the pari passu (ie 'equal footing') and negative pledge clauses, designed to achieve an equal ranking for the indebtedness incurred under the loan facility, by the bank. Which covenants are utilized in a loan facility depends on the nature and size, the position of the borrower and its financial needs, the purpose of the loan, the existence of other indebtedness in competition from other banks.

4.3 Protecting the bank's interest in contract

Breach by the borrower

Whether there has been a breach of the representations and warranties and the covenants is dependent on their interpretation. The representations and warranties and the covenants will be part of the default clause, so that their breach will enable the bank to cancel any outstanding commitments and accelerate repayment. Specific performance will generally not be available and an injunction, even if otherwise available, will only be practical if the lender learned of the threatened breach in time to take preventative action.

A bank can bring an action for damages although it may not add much to a claim for the loan itself. If the particular representation and warranty or covenant goes to the root of the contract, or if its breach constitutes a serious failure in performance, the bank will also have a right to terminate the agreement and thus be released from any further obligation under it. Failure to act may constitute a waiver of the breach and may be treated as a variation of the agreement.

The negative pledge and *pari passu* clauses

In its basic form, the negative pledge is simply a promise by a borrower that it will not grant security to a third party. The basic negative pledge provides that as long as any principal or interest is outstanding under the loan agreement, the borrower will not create or permit any mortgage, charge, pledge, lien or other encumbrance on its assets or revenues. In another form, there may be a promise on the part of the borrower to grant equal and ratable security in the same asset to the bank, or matching security in other assets, if it does grant security to a third party (the equivalent security negative pledge). Some negative pledge clauses go further and provide that the bank shares in any security the borrower grants in breach of the clause, or that security is automatically conferred in the same asset, should breach occur (the automatic security negative pledge). The following are the main features of the negative pledge.

♦ The negative pledge is a contractual restriction and is not considered as alternative or equivalent to security. It should not be treated like a floating charge charging all the assets of the borrower as security for a loan. The negative pledge, unlike a floating charge, does not control other liabilities that may rank equally against the assets.

♦ The prime function of the negative pledge clause is to prohibit the allocation of assets to a single secured creditor leaving an unsecured creditor merely with rights against the balance and thereby, in affect, subordinating the unsecured creditor. Credit analysis of a buyer generally proceeds on the basis that the assets will be divided pari passu amongst creditors on dissolution and any allocation of assets to one creditor would erode this basic assumption. To establish equality between creditors of the same class is a paramount function of the negative pledge.

♦ The negative pledge clause needs to extend to security given by the borrower's subsidiaries. A charge created by a subsidiary does not itself erode assets available to a bank lending to a parent, since the assets over which the security is given are not those of the parent and the value of the subsidiaries shares in the hands of the parent are the same whether or not the assets of the subsidiary are charged. The application of the restriction to a subsidiary is intended to prevent such transaction, as the grant of group secured guarantees in respect of the unsecured debt of the parent, and evasive transactions, eg the down-streaming of assets from parent to subsidiary that are subsequently used as security for a loan to the subsidiary.

An absolute negative pledge may be over restrictive and impose a straight-jacket on a borrower's normal commercial operations. A number of possible relaxations may therefore give the borrower some flexibility in his day-to-day business.

♦ The terms of the loan may therefore allow the borrower to create security if the bank is given equal and ratable security either on the same assets or on different but comparable assets.

♦ The negative pledge may free certain security interests (such as loans arising by operation of law, security interests existing at the time of the loan agreement and notified to the bank, security on after-acquired property existing at the time of acquisition and substitution for permitted security interests). The negative pledge may also free certain assets, eg permit purchase money mortgages and pledges on goods in the ordinary course of export and import trade. The negative pledge may also free certain indebtedness or restrict its scope to indebtedness of the same type as that arising under the loan agreement (eg borrowings and guarantees of borrowings). Similarly, there may be a 'basket' exception that permits the borrower to secure indebtedness up to a specified figure or up to a percentage of tangible net worth.

Remedies for breach of the negative pledge

Like other covenants in a loan agreement, breach of the negative pledge clause will trigger the default clause. It will also give rise to an action for damages if loss is caused by the breach. The default remedy may be impractical whilst an action for damages may be costly and time consuming. The bank may therefore have a number of alternative remedies as follows.

♦ A bank that acquires advance knowledge of possible default by the borrower may be able to obtain an injunction to prevent this happening, although the normal rule is that an injunction will only be granted where damages are an inadequate remedy. In exceptional cases, and in order to preserve the assets of the borrower pending final judgment or liquidation, the court may appoint a receiver on application by the bank to take control of the assets from the borrower.

♦ The equivalent security negative charge is an undertaking by the borrower to give equal and ratable security in the assets over which the third party has taken security, or to give matching security in other assets. The question that arises is whether a bank can obtain specific performance of this type of promise. Specific performance is a discretionary remedy and the courts should ask whether damages would be an adequate alternative. There are cases where specific performance has been granted on a promise to execute security when money has actually been advanced. In such circumstances, it does not matter whether the security was over real or personal property. Specific performance cannot operate retrospectively where the 'equal and ratable' clause is used. The bank may therefore lose priority to a third party's security interest, if this has already been taken.

♦ An equivalent security clause does not purport to give security on breach and the bank simply has a contractual undertaking that the borrower will give equivalent security in the case of an automatic security clause. The assumption is that, although the bank remains unsecured until breach, the occurrence of that contingency automatically triggers security in favour of the bank and that security has priority over the third party. An agreement for automatic security is conditional and the bank will never get security if the negative pledge clause is observed. The automatic security may fail for want of registration. Such registration may be required immediately if the clause is construed to create an immediate equitable charge, or alternatively, registration may be required when the clause is crystallized on the creation of other security. There is no requirement to register immediately under the Companies Act 1985 (s 395) if the agreement is to give security on some future event occurring (*Re Gregory Love & Co, Frances v Gregory Love & Co* [1916] 1 Ch 203).

The advantage of the negative pledge clause is that it may improve the remedies of a lender if such a clause is breached since specific performance of an agreement to give security is potentially available at the discretion of the courts (*Hermann v Hodges* (1873) LR 16 Eq 18). In *Kaplin v Chase National Bank* 156 Misc 471 the covenant stated that the company would not create any lien on, or pledge of, the stock of its subsidiaries without ratably securing the debentures. The trustee bank lent money to the company and received stock of its subsidiaries as collateral, without ratably securing the debentures. The court ordered the trustee bank to treat the pledged collateral as though such a provision had been made and was effective.

Security taken knowingly in breach of the negative pledge

Where a third party takes security from a borrower in breach of a negative pledge in a loan agreement with a bank, and the third party knows that his security is taken in contravention of the negative pledge, a number of possible consequences flow.

♦ The third party may be liable in damages to the bank for the tort of intentionally procuring a breach of contract. The tort is committed where a third party knowingly, and without lawful justification, induces a contracting party to break his contract with the other party to the contract. A law has been developed primarily in relation to trade disputes but applies to contracts generally (eg *Lumley v Guy* (1853) 2 EB 216) inducing an opera singer not to perform the contract). In *De Mattos v Gibson* (1858) 4 De GJ 276 the court said that:

> '... where a man, by gift of purchase, acquires property from another, with knowledge of a previous contract, lawfully and for valuable consideration made by him with a third party, to use and employ the property for a particular purchase in a specified manner, the acquirer shall not, to the material damage of the third party, in opposition to the contract and inconsistently with it, use and employ the property in a manner not allowable to the giver or seller.'

Applying the *De Mattos* principle to a negative pledge clause, it may be argued that the third party could be restrained by an injunction from exercising rights under the security. The third party would, therefore, be treated as an unsecured creditor along with the bank that would then be in the same position as it would have been had the negative pledge clause not been breached. The third party must have actual knowledge of the negative pledge clause to be bound by this principle. Other cases, however, have suggested that actual knowledge of the contract or its precise terms being broken is not necessary where the tortuous party intended to bring about a breach, or was recklessly indifferent whether a breach occurred or not, and shut his eyes to the possibility of breach, or where it is reasonable to infer that the tortuous party knew that his interference would involve a breach of contract. In *DC Thompson & Co Ltd v Deakin* [1952] Ch 646, the court suggested that:

> 'common knowledge about the way business is conducted.'

might be sufficient. There is, however, no active duty to enquire about the existence of contracts between others (*Leitch & Co v Leydon* [1931] AC 90).

♦ The parties may be liable in the tort of conspiracy (*Lonrho v Fayed* [1991] 3 All ER 303).

♦ The third party may be deemed to be a constructive trustee of his security for the bank to the extent of the bank's interests. It is unlikely, however, that liability will be imposed in this way unless the negative pledge expressly stipulates that any security taken in contravention of the negative pledge is to be held in trust for the bank.

The pari passu clause

The pari passu clause is common in an unsecured term loan agreement. The main features of such a clause are as follows.

- ♦ The clause amounts to an undertaking that the borrower will ensure that its obligations under the loan will rank at least equally with all its other present and future unsecured obligations.

- ♦ The pari passu clause is usually a companion to the negative pledge in that it relates to unsecured indebtedness while the negative pledge controls secured indebtedness. Both clauses are appropriate to unsecured loans in the context of a corporate loan: a pari passu clause is to be construed as a commitment or a warranty that on an insolvent liquidation, or a forced distribution of assets, unsecured creditors will be entitled to pro rata payment and also that, on the occasion of judicial compromises or agreed debt settlement amongst the creditors generally arising from insolvency, the bank will not be discriminated against.

Five

Legal principles of security interests

5.1 Bankers' securities

When the bank takes security it does not become the absolute owner of the property, but it will have certain rights over the property until the debt is repaid.

Classification of securities

(1) Possessory securities are based on the acquisition by the creditor of the possession of the chattel that serves as security, eg with a lien, the borrower remains the owner of the property, although the creditor is in actual or constructive possession of the property. Securities, that are subject to a banker's lien are those that the bank acquires, in the ordinary course of business, eg cheques, bills of exchange or other instruments deposited with the bank for collection. Whether a particular instrument in the possession of the bank is acquired in the ordinary course of business will depend not only on the nature of the banking business, but also on the nature of the business relationship or course of dealings developed between the bank and its customer. Under a pledge, however, the pledgee is entitled to the exclusive possession of the property until the debt is discharged, and the pledgee, in certain circumstances, will have a power of sale although ownership in the property remains with the pledgor. Unlike a lien, it is not essential that the pledgor actually has ownership in the goods pledged, but he must pledge with

the consent of the owner. The pledgee may sell the property subject to the pledge without recourse to the courts, but must account to the pledgor for any surplus remaining after repaying the debt. Securities subject to the pledge are usually goods and chattels and fully negotiable securities.

(2)   Proprietary securities are those where the creditor has the right to seize the goods if the debtor defaults or becomes insolvent and to satisfy the debt from the proceeds of their sale. During the existence of a loan arrangement the property is left in the possession of the debtor. A mortgage of chattels and land are illustrations of a proprietary security; so too are fixed and floating charges over assets comprised in a business. In such a situation, the mortgagee may enter into possession but will more likely exercise other remedies, eg appointment of a receiver or sale. The sort of securities subject to a mortgage are likely to be title deeds, life policies, stocks and shares and other choses in action.

(3)   Personal securities, eg guarantees, are personal obligations undertaken by strangers to a transaction for the performance of the duties under it by one of the parties.

The nature of the guarantee

Guarantees are widely used in dealings with individuals, traders, partnerships and limited companies that have insufficient assets for real securities. Personal guarantees may be given by partners and directors to guarantee a loan extended to the business. The bank therefore needs to ensure that the guarantor understands fully the effect of the guarantee and the amount involved. Such persons will be fully liable for the extent of the guarantee outside any business debt commitments. Under a guarantee the guarantor undertakes to 'answer for the debt, default or miscarriage' of another person known as the 'principal debtor'. The borrowing customer remains primarily liable on the debt; the guarantor's liability only arising if the person primarily liable defaults (see *Moschi v LEP Air Services Ltd* [1973] AC 331). A familiar example of a guarantee contract is where a director guarantees a company's indebtedness to the bank. Nevertheless, a person who promises to pay another person's debt is not necessarily a guarantor and that obligation must be distinguished from, eg an indemnity.

There are a number of strict rules restricting the liability of the guarantor and giving him certain rights against the creditor and principal debtor. The Code of Banking Practice provides that in relation to guarantees and other types of third party security, banks and building societies must advise private individuals proposing to give a guarantee that:

(i)   by giving the guarantee or third party security, liability may be imposed on them instead of, or as well as, the other person (principal debtor); and

(ii)   that the guarantor should seek independent legal advice before entering into the guarantee or third-party security. Additionally, certain other formal conditions have to be satisfied if the guarantee is to be enforceable.

(1)   A guarantee is unenforceable by action unless the agreement or some memorandum or note is executed in writing and signed by the guarantor or his agent (Statute of Frauds 1677, s 4). The guarantor's signature is usually witnessed but this is not strictly necessary.

(2)   A contract of guarantee must be supported by consideration, unless it is under seal or is expressed to take effect as a deed. The consideration need not be stated in the document but it must be proven. Where consideration is for 'further advances' against an existing overdrawn account, then it must be shown that such further advances have been made (see *Provincial Bank of Ireland v Donnell* [1934] 36 DLR (3d) 130). If a guarantee refers to an existing account, opening a new account is not sufficient consideration (*National Bank of Nigeria v Awolesi* [1964] 1 WLR 1134).

(3)   Capacity to enter into a contract of guarantee is essential. Since the abolition of the ultra vires rule, the capacity of a limited company to give a guarantee has not been in doubt, and any director may bind the company to that contract unless the bank knows of the limitations on the director's powers.

Multi-party guarantees

Where two or more persons give a guarantee their liability may be joint, or several, or joint/several. In a joint guarantee, each co-guarantor is liable for the whole of the sum guaranteed and they should be sued together. If proceedings are taken against only one or some of the co-guarantors, the remaining co-guarantors not included in the action are not discharged from liability, and may subsequently be sued (Civil Liability (Contribution) Act 1978, s 3). On the death or bankruptcy of a joint co-guarantor the estate of the deceased is freed from liability under the guarantee and the bank must enforce the guarantee against the remaining co-guarantors. In a several guarantee, each of the co-guarantors may be made liable separately for the whole of the guaranteed amount. An unsatisfied judgment against one of the several guarantors will not prevent an action against the remaining. The death or bankruptcy of one of the several co-guarantors does not of itself release the estate from liability for advances made before the bank receives notice of the events.

Discharge of the guarantee

The guarantee should make provision entitling the bank to release, discharge or make any arrangements with any one or more of the guarantors without discharging the rest; thereby excluding the rule that the release of one or more of the guarantors releases the others (*Barclays Bank v Trevanion* (1933), *The Banker* p 98).

When there are co-guarantors, the bank should ensure that all the proposed co-guarantors execute the contract and no advance should be made to the principal debtor until all the co-guarantors sign the guarantee. If one or more of the co-guarantors fails, or refuses, to sign the guarantee, then those co-guarantors who have already signed the guarantee, and can show that they signed the document on the understanding of it being signed by all the relevant parties, will be discharged from liability (*National Provincial Bank of England v Brackenbury* (1906) 22 TLR 797).

Limited, specific and continuing guarantees

Most guarantees given to a bank are intended to cover a series of transactions (eg a fluctuating overdraft balance) spread over a period of time. The bank will generally seek a guarantee over the 'whole debt' and it should exercise care in making any amendment to the standard wording of a guarantee that seeks, particularly to restrict the extent of guarantee. Thus, a form of wording that limits the extent of the guarantee should be avoided if the bank is likely to make further advances. A single or specific guarantee will be exhausted by an advance that takes the total amount advanced up to the agreed limit, ie the guarantor will be liable for up to a specified amount that might thereafter be reduced by the operation of the rule in *Clayton's Case* (1816) 1 Mer 530 on a current account. To avoid the operation of that rule, any advances made under a specific guarantee should be made on a separate loan account. By contrast, a continuing guarantee will cover all debts on the same account and is not affected by any payments into the principal debtor's account, since it does not secure any particular advance to the principal customer but rather the final combined balance on all the principal debtor's accounts (*Re Sherry, London and County Banking Co v Terry* (1884) 25 Ch D 692).

Rights against the principal customer

The principal debtor may give an express right of indemnity, in which case the guarantor's rights will be governed by the indemnity. A guarantor has an implied right to an indemnity from the principal debtor if he gives a guarantee at the request of the principal debtor. Under the implied right of indemnity, the guarantor has, unless the guarantee provides, an immediate right against the principal debtor on each occasion he pays on the guarantee, although he has no right to accelerate that right by paying the guaranteed debt before it falls due (*Coppin v Gray* (1842) 1 Y&C Ch Cas 205).

Rights of co-guarantors

A co-guarantor has a 'right of contribution' against the other co-guarantors of the same debt, each guarantor being liable proportionately to the amount he has guaranteed. If one of the guarantors is insolvent, any deficiency must be borne by the other guarantors ratably. The right of contribution against the other co-guarantors exists whether they are bound severally, or jointly and severally (*Scholefield Goodman and Sons Ltd v Zyngier* [1985] 3 All ER 105).

There is no right of contribution if the co-guarantors are liable under separate contracts for equal portions of the same principal debt, eg where each guarantor has entered into a separate transaction with the bank (*Coope v Twynham* (1823) Turn & R 426). If the right of contribution does arise, then it applies whether or not the guarantor who has paid knew of the existence of the co-guarantors at the time he gave the guarantee (*Claythorne v Swinburne* (1807) 14 Ves 160).

Before making payment to the bank any co-guarantor can compel the other co-guarantors to contribute towards satisfying the common liability and apply to the court for a declaration of his right to contribution (*Womershausen v Gullick* [1893] 2 Ch 514). If a co-guarantor is sued by the bank for payment under the guarantee, he can assert his right of contribution by joining the other co-guarantors as defendants in the action, or by obtaining an order directing that, when he has paid his own share of the common liability, the co-guarantor should indemnify him from further liability.

Termination of the guarantee

Termination of the guarantee means only that the guarantor is excused from all further liability incurred by the debtor. The guarantor is not excused from liabilities that have already accrued (*Westminster Bank Ltd v Sassoon* (1926) Times, 27 November). Where the guarantor guarantees the debit balance of a bank customer's current account, the rule in *Clayton's Case* (1816) 1 Mer 530 will have the effect of gradually discharging the guarantor's liability if payments are made to the credit of the account, since the debts for which he became liable were 'fixed' at the time the guarantee was terminated. This may be prevented if the guarantee contains a term such as the 'guarantor's liability for the amount due from the debtor at the time when the guarantee is determined shall remain notwithstanding any subsequent payment into or out of the account by or on behalf of the debtor' (*Westminster Bank Ltd v Cond* (1940) 46 Com Cas 60). Alternatively, the bank may stop the principal customer's current account, and open another one for him. In practice, banks do include terms such as the one used in *Cond*, but also stop the account.

A guarantee may be determined in a number of circumstances.

Corporate guarantees

A company is a distinct legal entity from its shareholders and enjoys separate legal status. The separate entity principle applies even when the shareholders in a company from an artificial legal entity themselves. This rule applies to companies within a group with each subsidiary company enjoying separate legal status. Each company within the group is responsible for its own debts and obligations. Inter-corporate guarantees are, however, routine in commercial transactions. Such guarantees effectively negate the limited liability of shareholders for corporate debt. The guarantees enable a corporate group to secure borrowing as a single unit even though, under company law each member is a separate legal entity. These guarantees facilitate the availability of finance in situations where a particular corporate entity's assets or net worth alone would not support the grant of the credit facility. In some instances, the lender may not be willing to lend to a company unless an affiliate agrees to guarantee the loan. Consequently, the terms of the guarantee provide the lender with additional assets against which to secure the ultimate repayment of the loan. Further, the collective borrowing base may upgrade the group's credit, allowing the group to obtain a lower cost of financing than each group could independently obtain.

When a company gives a guarantee or grants some other security interest to secure an affiliate's debt two important questions need to be explored:

(1)   was the guarantor company insolvent when the guarantee was given?

(2)   did the guarantor receive less than adequate consideration?

Where the answer to both these questions is positive, then the guarantee or security is a fraudulent transfer and voidable.

When a surety, or guarantor, guarantees an obligation of its principal debtor, it acquires a blend of liabilities and assets in exchange. The guarantor incurs a contingent liability since it may become obligated to pay the principal debt at some stage in the future, if the principal debtor defaults. The guarantor receives benefits which may be classified as follows:

♦   business benefits;
♦   equitable rights of exoneration, reimbursement, subrogation, and contribution.

The distinction between business benefits and equitable rights is important because the business benefits a guarantor receives depend on the relationship of the guarantor to the principal debtor (ie whether the guarantor is the parent or subsidiary), while the equitable rights that a guarantor receives are independent of the guarantor to the principal debtor.

Business benefits

A business benefit is a benefit received by a guarantor as a result of giving the guarantee and regardless of whether the principal debtor defaults. Such benefits may be tangible or intangible and need not be assets in the traditional sense. An important benefit is that an affiliated group borrowing collectively will up grade its credit and obtain a lower cost of financing than if each corporation raised finance separately. Frequently, a guarantee given by one very strong member of an affiliated corporate group will lift the credit rating of the group as a whole. Although the weaker affiliates benefit, the strong affiliate's credit rating may be weakened because of its link with the weaker affiliates. Another business benefit that will result from the joint guarantee is what may be termed as the 'convenient factor'. When a corporate group borrows as a unit, all that a potential lender will analyse is the consolidated group financial statement, rather than each affiliate's financial statement. This will lower the borrowing costs since the group only needs to give the bank one set of audited consolidated statements rather than audited financial statements from each member of the group.

Guarantor's equitable rights

On executing a guarantee, a guarantor becomes entitled to certain equitable rights and remedies against the principal debtor and co-guarantors. If the principal debtor defaults and the guarantor's liability is fixed, these rights enable the guarantor to bring an action for equitable relief. When the guarantor company pays under the guarantee, it becomes entitled to certain monetary relief. The rights and remedies available to the guarantor are as follows:

- ♦ exoneration – this is a right to compel the principal debtor and the co-guarantors to pay;
- ♦ reimbursement – this is the guarantor's right to be repaid, by the principal debtor, any amounts it is required to pay on the principal debtor's behalf in its capacity as guarantor;
- ♦ subrogation – once the guarantor has paid the whole of the outstanding amount of the principal debt, subrogation entitles the guarantor to be substituted to the position of the creditor it has paid and to enjoy any rights/benefits the creditor had, including security interests and liens, etc;
- ♦ contribution – if there are multiple guarantors of the same obligation, the right of contribution entitles a paying guarantor to have the co-guarantors pay a proportionate share of the principal debt. The right of contribution exists between the co-guarantors and the creditor may still collect the whole amount of the debt from any of the co-guarantors.

The extent of the contribution may be determined by contract.

Downstream, cross-stream, and upstream guarantees

Guarantees by affiliate corporations may be classified as follows:

- ♦ a downstream guarantee is where the parent guarantees its subsidiary's obligations;
- ♦ a cross-stream guarantee is where one subsidiary guarantees another subsidiary's obligations. In such cases, a lender will often require that the non-borrowing affiliate guarantees the obligation of the borrowing entity;

♦ an upstream guarantee is where a subsidiary guarantees its parent's obligations.

A downstream guarantee does not cause any concern about fraudulent transfers because the parent, through its stock ownership of the subsidiary, receives the benefits of the loan proceeds reflected in the increased value of the stock. Upstream and cross-stream guarantees may be subject to litigation on liquidation as fraudulent transfers, on the basis of lack of consideration or that the consideration provided is significantly less than its value (in other words, the transaction is at an undervalue and contrary to s 238 of the Insolvency Act 1986). In *Phillips v Brewin Dolphin Bell Lawrie* [2001] 1 WLR 143 the House of Lords held that, in deciding the value of consideration received by the company in a transaction alleged to be at undervalue, regard must be had to events occurring at the time of the transaction and to those occurring after the transaction (*ex post facto events*). Subsequent events are the only evidence on which the valuer may rely.

Letters of comfort

Letters of comfort are taken where a third party is unwilling to enter into a guarantee. Lenders and 'comfort givers' generally approach the matter from opposite directions: the lender will seek something like (or better than) a guarantee that imposes a secondary liability on the other person, whilst the 'comfort giver' may only be willing to acknowledge the existence of a transaction, but is not willing to undertake any legal responsibility if anything goes wrong. A lender may, therefore, turn to comfort letters when a third party is not prepared to assume formal liability, whether contingent or not, for the borrower's indebtedness. The most common situations where comfort letters may be given are where eg a parent company is asked to give an undertaking in respect of the obligations of its subsidiaries, where a foreign government wishes to encourage inward investment or in connection with international construction contracts. A parent company may prefer to give a letter of comfort rather than a formal guarantee for any one of a number of reasons, eg the parent company does not want to be legally committed.

If the letter of comfort is to be legally enforceable as a legally binding contract, all the essential elements of a contract must be present. Whether a contract is sufficiently certain as to bind the parties must be determined by an objective test, although there is a presumption that in the case of commercial agreements that the parties intended to create legal relations (see *Rose and Frank Co v J R Crompton Bros Ltd* [1924] All ER 245).

A letter of comfort that does not provide that it is intended to be binding in honour will only, prima facie, give rise to legal relations between the parties. Depending on the nature of the wording used, the letter of comfort may (or may not) give the party seeking to rely on it substantive rights. The courts have had to look at the effect letters of comfort are intended to have in order to determine whether the plaintiff is provided with any substantive rights. In *Chemco Leasing Spa v Rediffusion plc* [1987] FTLR 201 the letter of comfort was held to confer substantive rights on the plaintiff, which could be legally enforced.

The legal status of letters of comfort was re-examined in *Kleinwort Benson Ltd v Malaysia Mining Corpn Bhd* [1988] 1 All ER 714 where the court concluded that if the comfort letter merely indicates an 'intention' or evidences the 'policy' of the donor, ie to ensure that the subsidiary is in a position to meet its liabilities to the bank, it is likely that the letter simply constitutes a moral obligation rather than a legal liability. This is especially so where the bank charges a higher rate of interest as compensation for not having a full guarantee.

5.2 Possessory securities

The very nature of goods may present a number of problems from the security point. Goods may be perishable, the price of commodities may fluctuate, storage charges may be expensive and goods manufactured for one purpose may be inappropriate for resale. It may be difficult for a bank to dispose of goods, if the buyer defaults, without the assistance of the customer. This section examines the rights acquired by a bank over goods or documents that are in its possession because of the default of its customer.

The banker's lien

A lien is a right to retain property belonging to a debtor until he has paid the debt due to the person retaining the property. A lien may arise as a result of a particular transaction connected with the property subject to the lien. A general lien arises not only out of the particular transaction but also out of the general dealings between the parties. For example, an issuing or confirming bank under a letter of credit is entitled to hold shipping documents that it receives from the beneficiary as security for the amount it has paid, or committed itself to pay, under the bills of exchange. The banker's lien arises by operation of law in consequence of the instructions given to the issuing bank to open the credit and the lien is independent of any other security the bank may take by express agreement.

The ordinary right of the bank under its lien is a right merely to retain possession of the shipping documents, but in the case of documents, the lien carries with it the right to sell the goods represented by them. As such it approximates more closely to a pledge than to a common law lien. In the case of other documents over which a bank has a lien there is no implied power of sale or realization. In *Brandao v Barnett* (1846) 12 Cl & Fin 787 the court said that banks have a general lien on all securities deposited with them by a customer unless there be an express contract, or circumstances that show an implied contract, inconsistent with lien. This was reinforced in *Halesowen Pressworks and Assemblies v Westminster Bank Ltd* [1972] AC 785 where the court accepted the view that bankers have a general lien on all documents deposited with them by their customers.

The essential factor in deciding whether or not the documents are subject to a lien is whether they came into the hands of the bank in the course of its business, as a banker. The bank has a general lien or right of retention over all kinds of documents belonging to a customer over whom it has possession and the bank can hold them until all the amounts owed to it in respect of loans and advances have been paid back to the bank. The lien extends to all documents under which money will be paid to the customer or by means of which money may be obtained, whether they are negotiable or not. Where documents relate to goods the lien extends to the goods themselves, so that if the customer fails to reimburse the bank it can sell the goods and so realize the advance it has made on the customer's behalf. The bank may exercise a lien over cheques payable to its customer (*Barclays Bank Ltd v Astley Industrial Trust Ltd* [1970] 2 QB 527; *BCCI v Dawson and Wright* [1987] FLR 342), bills of exchange, share certificates and investment securities generally. In *Sewell v Burdick* (1884) 10 App Cas 74 securities were held to include bills of lading and other documents representing goods in transit.

The pledge

A pledge will arise as a result only of express agreement of the parties and incidents of the pledge are likewise determined by agreement. One of the forms of security available to the bank is a legal pledge of the goods in question and this is created by delivery of the subject matter to the bank as creditor, thereby giving the bank a legal right of possession until his indebtedness to the bank is discharged. The essence of a pledge is that the security vested in the pledgee consists exclusively of the possession of the goods and not of any derivative proprietary interest in them. The pledge comes to an end if the goods are returned by the pledgee to the pledgor otherwise than as agent for the pledgee (*North Western Bank v Poynter* [1895] AC 56). Although the pledgee has no proprietary interest in the goods a pledge confers an implied right for the pledgee to realize the security by selling the goods.

At common law a pledge can be created by delivery of the actual or constructive possession of the goods pledged to the pledgee. If the goods are in the hands of the pledgor he can effect the pledge by actual delivery of the goods. In other cases he can give possession by some other sufficient act, eg handing over the keys of the warehouse where the goods are stored so as to vest control over them in the pledge. If, however, the goods are in the hands of a third party who holds them on behalf of the pledgor, a pledge may be effected by the pledgor instructing the third party to hold the goods for the account of the pledgee and by the third party attorning to the pledgee (ie acknowledging that the third party holds the goods on behalf of the pledgee and the latter has constructive possession).

The common law has been supplemented by legislation the purpose of which was to protect banks that made advances to mercantile agents. Under the legislation a pledge of any document of title to the goods, whether a bill of lading, rail or road consignment note, airway bill, dock or warehouse warrant or a delivery order, may be valid but only if the pledgor is a factor (Factors Act 1889, ss 2 and 3). In *Lloyds Bank Ltd v Bank of America National Trust and Savings Association* [1938] 2 KB 147 the court held that the statutory exception in respect of a pledge by a factor applies whether the factor acts as a mercantile agent for a third person or on his own account. A further statutory exception is found in what is now s 25(1) of the Sale of Goods Act 1979 which provides that a bank that makes an advance has a valid pledge if the buyer of goods has received the documents of title to them from the seller, and has pledged the goods or the documents of title to them before the seller's lien or right of stoppage in transit, for the price payable under the contract of sale, has expired. The statutory exceptions raise uncertainties and therefore are rarely relied on in practice.

Where a bank is owed money advanced to pay the price of goods, it will probably release the shipping documents to the buyer so that he can sell the goods and reimburse the bank. The question is whether, having released the documents to the buyer, its charge or security over the goods is in any way affected. In *North Western Bank v Poynter Son & Macdonald* [1895] AC 56 the court held that delivery of goods, either actual or constructive, to the debtor destroys the possibility of a pledge continuing or subsequently arising. The bank did not give up possession of the goods and its pledge continued when it surrendered the bill of lading to the pledgor, with the limited authority only of selling the goods as its agent, so that it was entitled to the proceeds of the sale in priority to general creditors of the pledgor. In *Re David Allester Ltd* [1922] 2 Ch 211 the court held that the bank was entitled to have the value of the goods realized by experts, in this case the pledgor. Consequently, handing over the bills of lading for the purpose of selling the goods did not deny the continuing rights of the pledgee, the bank. In *Official Assignee of Madras v Mercantile Bank of India* [1935] AC 53, the Privy Council held that the respondents had merely parted with the possession of the railway receipts to the insolvent merchants for a limited purpose, ie as agents for the respondents for the purposes of dealing with goods.

Letters of hypothecation, letters of trust and trust receipts

In order to overcome the difficulties of the pledge as a form of security over the documents, two other forms of security are usually resorted to by banks that finance a purchase of goods, namely the letter of hypothecation and the letter of trust or trust receipt. A letter of hypothecation creates an equitable charge over the goods which means that, if the applicant sells the goods, the proceeds of sale are subject to a first charge in favour of the bank. Consequently, if the applicant becomes bankrupt, or in the case of a company if it is wound up, the bank ranks as a secured creditor and is entitled to be paid first out of the proceeds of sale. The letter of trust or trust receipt has largely superseded the letter of hypothecation. The trust receipt evidences an agreement between the bank and the customer that the bank will hand the documents of title to the customer so that he can obtain delivery of the goods. In turn the customer holds the documents of title, the goods when they are received, and eventually, the proceeds of sale of the goods on behalf of the bank.

The letter of trust or trust receipt is either embodied in the application for the issue of a letter of credit by the bank, or is given separately by the applicant (buyer) when the shipping documents have been taken up by the issuing or confirming bank, and they are delivered to the buyer so that he may collect the goods on arrival. Under the letter of trust, the buyer undertakes to hold the proceeds of sale as a trustee for the bank absolutely and to pay the whole of the proceeds of sale to the bank, which will retain what is owed and return the balance to the applicant of the credit. If the applicant departs from the authority given to him to deal with the goods, he is guilty of a breach of trust. The trust relationship that arises is treated by the courts as creating a valid security interest in favour of the bank (see *Re David Allester Ltd* [1922] 2 Ch 211). The bank can also sue the customer for conversion of the shipping documents (*Midland Bank Ltd v Eastcheap Dried Fruit Co Ltd* [1962] 2 Lloyd's Rep 359).

Choses in action

Credit balances as security

A balance standing to the credit of a customer's account is repayable on the terms under which it was made. Whilst the account is in credit the credit balance constitutes a debt owed by the bank to its customer. As such, the debt is an asset and the customer may utilize it as a security either in respect of a transaction financed by a bank or other financial institution. Using a credit balance as a security may cause difficulties, eg the customer making withdrawals may reduce the credit balance or the credit balance may be made the subject of a third party debt order. Further, problems can arise if the customer becomes bankrupt or goes insolvent. Although, these problems can be overcome, using a credit balance as security is likely to result in restrictions in the account holder's right to use the account. The method of granting security over the credit balance will depend on whether the security is given to the bank with whom the account is maintained or with a third party.

Set-off and flawed asset arrangement

Where a security is created in favour of a bank with whom the credit balance is maintained the bank has a right to set-off any amounts owed to it by the creditor (customer). The right to set-off is a procedural right and does not confer on the party entitled to exercise it a proprietary right. Although the equitable right to set-off is invaluable to banks (eg where a bank is required to make payment under a bank guarantee, it can reimburse itself by exercising a set-off against the customer's credit balance), it is subject to several limitations. Thus, until such time as a bank can exercise the right of set-off, the customer can make withdrawals against the credit balance thereby reducing the amount available for set-off. Further, a right of set-off is subordinate to the right of a judgment creditor who has served a third party debt order before the set-off is exercised.

When the customer is adjudicated bankrupt or becomes insolvent the bank's right to set-off is governed by statute (Insolvency Act 1986, s 323). The statutory right of set-off cannot be contracted out of, in the sense that the parties cannot limit its operation by agreement (*Halesowen Pressworks and Assemblies Ltd v National Westminster Bank Ltd* [1972] AC 785). The statutory right to set-off is considerably wider than the right to set-off debits against credits that the bank can exercise under the general law. In particular, the bank is entitled to set-off liabilities payable at a future date, and unliquidated liabilities against the deposit. What was uncertain was whether a purely contingent liability could be set-off, eg under a counter-indemnity taken in connection with the issue of a performance bond that has not yet been called. Since *Re Charge Card Services Ltd* [1986] 3 WLR 697 the view appears to be that contingent debts are capable of being set off provided that they satisfy the other requirements laid down. A significant requirement is that of mutuality, ie the debts must be between the same parties in the same right, with the result that only a liability owed to the bank by the depositor in the same capacity may be set off against the credit.

Because of the limitation attached to the equitable and statutory rights of set-off, it has become the practice of banks to take a contractual right of set-off. This right may be subject to special agreement (letter of set-off) or may be created by means of specific clauses incorporated in the underlying financial agreement between the bank and its customer. The object of the clause is to enable the bank to set off against the credit balance any claims the bank has, whether such claims are existing, contingent, unconditional, liquidated or unliquidated. The purpose of the clause is to restrict the right of the customer to make withdrawals so long as the liability is contingent. The bank must ensure that the customer's need for liquidity in respect of his account is not hampered.

The 'flawed asset' arrangement is a variation to the set-off arrangement. The arrangement imposes a 'flaw' on the customer's asset, ie the arrangement restricts the customer's right to utilize the credit balance. In its simplest form, the arrangement consists of the deposit of money under an agreement by which the depositor agrees that the deposit is not to become repayable until certain liabilities have been satisfied, or if the liabilities are contingent, are no longer capable of arising. Thus, the bank is entitled to freeze the bank balance until such time as the customer's liability is discharged.

Charges over bank balances

A credit balance standing in the customer's bank account is a chose in action and may be made the subject of a charge or mortgage, effected by means of an assignment. Where a charge is created over cash deposited with a bank, the bank seeks to become secured and to rank in the depositor's insolvency as a secured creditor. In ordinary circumstances, a security interest in a debt can either be created by mortgage or charge. The only method by which a debt can be mortgaged is by an absolute assignment under s 136 of the Law of Property Act 1925. The assignment will be coupled with an express or implied equity of redemption in favour of the assignor (*Durham Bros v Robertson* [1898] 1 QB 765). It has been suggested that the Act requires a tripartite transaction and that a deposit cannot be mortgaged in favour of the bank with which it is held, since on assignment back to the debtor the debt would cease to exist (Goode, *Commercial Law*, p 721, *Legal Problems of Credit and Security*, p 86). An assignment by way of charge (ie an equitable assignment) is an adequate security. An equitable charge is created when the chargor and chargee agree that a given liability will be paid out of a chose in action belonging to the charger. Where such a security is given to a third party (eg supplier of goods on credit) it is essential to include provisions preventing the depletion of the security by withdrawals. Whether a security over a bank balance can be given to the bank which itself maintains the account was considered in *Re Charge Card Services Ltd* [1986] 3 WLR 697 where it was held that a charge in favour of a debtor of his own indebtedness to the chargor is conceptually impossible. In *Re Bank of Credit and Commerce International SA (No 8)* [1998] AC 214 judicial support for charge-backs can be found in the obiter of Lord Hoffmann. Doubts respecting the correctness of *Re Charge Card Services* also were expressed in *Welsh Development Agency v Export Finance Co* [1991] BCLC 936.

Where a security given over a bank is merely a contractual right of set-off then such an arrangement will not have to be registered under the Companies legislation. Where such an arrangement is treated as a charge then such a charge will need to be registered.

5.3 Proprietary securities

Land as security

A legal mortgage of land under the Law of Property Act 1925 may be created by:

(a) granting the mortgagee a lease in the legal estate (mortgage by demise for a term of years; or

(b) by a charge by deed expressed to be granted by way of legal mortgage. Unless a legal charge is employed a legal mortgage must vest a term of years in the mortgage and any attempt by the mortgagor to convey the whole of his legal estate in the land to the mortgagee operates automatically as a grant of a term of years, leaving a reversionary legal estate vested in the mortgagor (Law of Property Act 1925, s 85 (2)).

The term of years granted to the mortgagee is subject to a termination on the redemption of the mortgage. The mortgagor retains the legal estate subject to the term of years, and this enables him to create further legal mortgages that take effect either as legal charges or as demises for a term of years longer by at least one day than the preceding mortgage.

Where a legal mortgage in land is created by way of a legal charge the protection given to the mortgagee is identical to that given by a legal mortgage created by demise and the legal chargee has the same rights and remedies as a legal mortgagee.

The difference between a legal mortgage and a legal charge is that the legal charge does not contain a conveyance of a legal estate to the mortgagee, so that the mortgagor remains vested with his original legal estate instead of holding a reversionary interest. Instead of granting the chargee a legal estate, the mortgagor or chargor charges the land by way of legal mortgage with the payment of the principal interest and any other monies secured by the charge. Furthermore, there is no provision for redemption in a legal charge, which is simply determined on repayment of the amount secured by it. In all other respects the legal mortgage and the legal charge are precisely the same; the covenants entered into by the mortgagor and the powers of the chargee are identical.

The Law of Property Act 1925 provides that a first mortgagee of land has the same right to the possession of the documents of title as if his security included the whole legal estate of the mortgagor (s 5(1)). Failure to take possession of the title deeds may give priority to a subsequent mortgagee. The deposit of title deeds with the legal mortgagee protects the priority of his mortgage over any subsequent mortgages that may be created. A mortgage secured by a deposit of the title deeds can be created without all the deeds being deposited provided that those which are deposited include the instrument by which the legal estate was vested in the mortgagor.

Equitable mortgages

An equitable mortgage is simply an agreement to create a legal mortgage and it is treated in equity as the equivalent of a legal mortgage so far as possible. This means that (a) equity will compel the mortgagor to execute a legal mortgage by deed and (b) will give the same remedies to the mortgagee as are available to a legal mortgagee, except those which statute expressly reserves to legal mortgages, eg the statutory power of sale.

A legal or equitable mortgage or charge of a legal estate made after 1925 and not protected by a deposit of documents relating to that legal estate is registrable either as a puisne mortgage or as a general equitable charge. The Land Charges Act 1972 (Land Registration Act, ss 20(1) and 23(1)) provides that registrable mortgages are void as against a subsequent purchaser of land or of any interest in the land, whether legal or equitable, unless the mortgage is registered at the Land Charges Registry. In addition to this provision the Law of Property Act 1925, s 96 provides that every legal or equitable mortgage of a legal estate in land that is not protected by the deposit of documents will rank in priority according to its date of registration as a land charge under the Land Charges Act 1925. This provision conflicts with the Land Charges Act 1972 in that it makes the priority of a second mortgage over a prior unregistered mortgage, conditional on the second mortgage itself being registered.

Tacking

Prior to the Law of Property Act 1925, the rule was that, where a mortgagee advanced money on an equitable mortgage or charge without at the time of the advance having notice of a prior equitable mortgage, he could afterwards, by acquiring an existing legal mortgage that had priority over the equitable mortgage, claim the same priority for his own equitable mortgage or charge as that which attached to the legal mortgage, and in effect tack, or add, the amount advanced to him on his equitable mortgage or charge to the amount secured by the legal mortgage. This rule was extended so as to enable a first legal mortgagee to obtain priority if intervening mortgages were created, eg if A, the legal mortgagee at the time of making a further advance, had no notice that subsequent to his legal mortgage a second mortgage had been created in favour of B, A was allowed to tack his second loan to the advance secured by his first legal mortgage and to claim priority for both advances over intervening mortgages of which he was unaware. In order to prevent A tacking the second advance to the first, B would have to prove that A had actual or constructive notice of B's mortgage at the time of his second advance (*Hopkinson v Holt* (1861) 9 HLC 514) but if A had such notice, B's mortgage would rank before A's further advance even though A, the first mortgagee, had given a binding undertaking to make further advances on the same security (*West v Williams* [1899] 1 Ch 332).

The Law of Property Act 1925 abolished tacking except as expressly permitted (s 94 (1)) with the consequence that a later mortgagee cannot now gain priority over an intermediate mortgage by acquiring an earlier legal mortgage. The express exception serves a useful purpose when securing loans by banks to their customers since when banks take security for overdrafts it is generally contemplated that variations in the customer's balances will occur during the subsistence of the security and, when the overdraft facility is drawn on, the bank will in effect make further advances.

Section 94(2) of the Law of Property Act 1925 provides that, if the first mortgage was created expressly for securing a current account or further advances made by the mortgagee the registration of a subsequent mortgage or charge does not amount to notice of that charge to the first mortgagee. A first mortgage in this case may therefore tack further advances made after the registration of the later mortgage or charge provided that at the time of the further advance the later mortgagee had not brought the charge to his attention by some positive act other than registration (the rule in *Hopkinson* is thus confirmed). A mortgagee who takes a security to secure further advances must search the register for prior charges at the time of the original loan and is bound by any mortgages or charges then registered, but he is not required to search again when he makes further advances and can treat mortgages registered meanwhile as ineffective against him. This is, of course, an exception to the principle that registration is equivalent to actual notice and is of exceptional importance to banks to whom the taking of a mortgage for a customer's overdraft would be of little value if cheques drawn by the customer after the date of the mortgage could not be honoured without first making a search in the Land Charges Register. The exception applies to all mortgages where the contract contemplates further advances and not merely to mortgages securing current accounts.

If a subsequent mortgagee has given notice of his charge to the first mortgagee before a further advance is made, the first mortgagee cannot then tack further advances, and if the mortgage secures an overdraft the rule in *Clayton's Case* (1816) 1 Mer 529 will apply as regards subsequent payments into the account, so as to reduce the debit balance at the date the bank receives notice of the subsequent mortgage. If, therefore, there is a reduction of the overdraft by the bank after it has notice of the subsequent mortgage, there will be a corresponding reduction of the debit balance at that date for which the bank has priority, and if further advances are then made by the bank increasing the overdraft, the bank cannot tack them to the original loan and will be deferred to the amount owing to the subsequent mortgagee. In order to avoid the operation of the rule in *Clayton's Case,* in this situation the bank should close the mortgagor's overdrawn account as soon as it receives notice of a subsequent mortgage and any future payments in or drawings by the mortgagor should be credited or debited to a separate account. The leading case in which the bank suffered by its failure to close the original account on receipt of the second mortgage was *Deeley v Lloyds Bank Ltd* [1912] AC 756 where a customer of Lloyds Bank mortgaged his business premises to the bank in 1893 to secure his overdraft on current. In 1895 he created another mortgage in favour of a second mortgagee who gave notice of his mortgage to the bank. The bank failed to close the mortgagor's overdrawn account at that time or to open a separate account for further transactions. The mortgagor subsequently made payments into and out of the account, and under the rule in *Clayton's Case,* the subsequent payments into the account had the effect of reducing the balance owing to the bank on the first mortgage, which had priority over the second mortgage. The House of Lords accordingly held that the second mortgage took priority over any advances made by the bank after notice of the charge had been brought to the bank's attention.

Finally, s 94 of the Law of Property Act 1925 provides that, if by its contractual undertaking a bank or other mortgagee has placed himself under an obligation to make further advances, whether or not it has notice of an intermediate mortgage or charge, the first mortgagee has priority over that mortgagee or chargee for all advances made by it in fulfilment of its obligation. This rule reverses the decision of the court in *West v Williams* [1899] 1 Ch 132 where it was held that a mortgagee who is bound to make further advances on the security of a mortgage did not obtain priority for his later advances until they were actually made and, accordingly, he could not tack them to his original advance if he had notice of an intermediate mortgage when the further advance was made. By s 94(1)(c), however, a first mortgagee now obtains priority for his further advances if he is obliged to make them and neither registration nor actual notice of an intermediate mortgage will prevent him from tacking them to his original advance. Banks rarely commit themselves contractually to making further advances when overdraft facilities are granted and so s 94(1)(c) is likely to be of benefit to a bank only when it agrees to make a loan for a term of years on the security of a mortgage and the loan is to be made by installments.

Registered land

Increasingly, land is registered under the Land Registration Acts 1925-1962. Loans on the security of registered land may be made and protected in one of the following ways namely:

(a) by a legal mortgage or legal charge created by a deed completed by the substantive registration of the lender as the proprietor of the mortgage or charge in the charges register of the title (the registered charge);

(b) by a legal mortgage by deed protected by a mortgage caution on the proprietorship register of the title;

(c) by a legal or equitable mortgage protected by a notice on the charges register of the title or by a caution against dealings entered on the proprietorship register;

(d) by an equitable mortgage or lien created by a deposit of Land Certificate relating to the title and protected by a special notice of deposit entered on the charges register of the title.

As between themselves, registered charges affecting a legal estate in registered land rank according to the order in which they are entered in the charges register of the title and not according to the order in which they are created.

The provisions relating to the tacking of mortgages of unregistered land do not apply to registered charges of registered land (Law of Property Act 1925, s 94(3)) but s 94(1) does apply as regards other mortgages and charges of registered land between themselves. When a registered charge is made for securing further advances or a current account, the Chief Land Registrar will enter a notice to that effect on the charges register and before making a subsequent entry on the register that would affect the priority of the chargee for any further advance, the Registrar gives notice of the intended entry to the proprietor of the charge. The proprietor of a charge to secure further advances on a current account can tack advances subsequently made by him unless the advance is made after he should have received the date of a proposed entry in the register from the Registrar. If, for example, a registered charge is created in favour of a bank to secure an overdrawn account, the honouring of cheques that increase the overdraft constitutes a further advance for which the bank is entitled to priority unless it has received notice from the Land Registry of an intended entry protecting another mortgage or charge, or unless such a notice has been sent to it and it should have received the notice before the further advance is made.

If the proprietor of a registered charge is under an obligation noted on the register to make further advances, all subsequently registered charges and other mortgages and charges of the registered land are subject to the right of the bank to claim priority in respect of such further advances (Land Registration Act 1925, s 30(3)).

A legal or equitable mortgage or registered land by deed may be protected by mortgage caution. Section 106 of the Land Registration Act 1925 provides registered land may be mortgaged in any manner that would have been permissible had the land been unregistered, provided the instrument of mortgage describes the land either by reference to the register itself or so fully that the registrar is able to identify it without reference to any other document. The mortgage can be protected by entering a caution on the register (this is known as a mortgage caution) and the mortgagee then has all the powers and remedies of the proprietor of a registered charge, but cannot sell the registered land until the mortgage has been converted into a registered charge. The effect of a mortgage caution is that dealings by the registered proprietor of land cannot be registered until the Chief Land Registrar on the mortgagee has served notice.

A deposit of title deeds is a common method of securing a temporary loan and s 66 of the Land Registration Act 1925 provides that a mortgage by deposit of the land certificate may be made in one of two ways, namely:

(i)   the proprietor of the land first deposits the land certificate with the mortgagee and the latter gives notice of the deposit to the registrar;

(ii) before making the deposit the proprietor of the land gives notice to the registrar of his intention to make a deposit of the land certificate. The registrar will enter this notice in the register and then send the land certificate to the chargee named.

The power to create a lien by deposit of the land certificate is subject to any restriction on the register and the lien itself can only take effect subject to overriding interests and to any other rights and interests already protected on the register at the time of deposit. The entry of the notice of deposit in the registered Land Charges Register preserves priority for the holder of the lien against other persons. Consequently, an equitable charge that has been protected by a notice of deposit has priority over subsequent mortgages and charges. In *Re White Rose Cottage* [1965] Ch 940 a company, the proprietor of certain registered land executed a memorandum of deposit of the land certificate with a bank to secure advances and undertook to hold the property as trustee for the bank to preserve its security. Notice of deposit of the documents was duly registered. Subsequently, judgment creditors of the company obtained charging orders and lodged cautions with the land registry. The bank then applied to the land registry to enter a notice on the register of an equitable charge created by the memorandum. Notice of this was given to the judgment creditors who objected to the notice being entered except on condition that their two charging orders were given priority over the bank's charge. The bank, under a power of attorney, later executed a transfer of land and in the transfer, the bank released the land from moneys secured on it in favour of the purchaser. The court held that the bank's notice of deposit of the land certificate operated in the same way as an ordinary notice and the bank's security therefore took effect in priority to the subsequent charging orders. The judgment creditors were consequently not entitled to object to the registration by the bank of a notice in the ordinary form to protect its charge. Further, the transfer to the purchaser was to be construed as a sale by the company as mortgagor with the concurrence of the bank, and the transferee therefore took the same title as the company had, freed from the bank's mortgage but subject to the equitable charges conferred by the charging orders.

5.4 Securities created by companies

Fixed and floating charges

In the case of a trading company, trading stock and book debts often constitute the most valuable assets of the company. In *Holroyd v Marshall* (1862) 10 HL Cas 191 equity sanctioned the creation of a charge over future property, that automatically attaches to the subject property on acquisition. The case involved an equitable mortgage of machinery under which the mortgagor had liberty to substitute new machinery that would become subject to the charge. The court upheld the validity of the mortgage and held that the mortgage had priority over the claims of an execution creditor.

Equity also recognized the floating charges in *Re Panama, New Zealand and Australian Royal Mail Co* (1870) 5 Ch App 318 where it was held that the debenture holders had a charge upon all company's property, past and future, and that they stood in a position superior to that of the general creditors who could touch nothing until the debenture holders were paid. Since *Re Panama* there have been a number of judicial statements that have described the nature of the floating charge.

Comparison with specific charge

A security must be either floating or specific: the terms are mutually exclusive. The floating charge is the antithesis of a specific charge. Fixes and floating charges can be created over both present and future assets of the company. Upon the creation of a specific charge, the charge fastens upon the charged assets either immediately or, in the case of future property, upon the company acquiring an interest in the charged property. The consent of the creditor would therefore be required before the company can deal with the charged property. The distinguishing feature of a floating charge is that the debtor company is left with the freedom to deal with charged assets in the ordinary course of business, without the need to obtain the consent of the holder of the floating charge (*Re Panama* case).

Crystallization of floating charges

The term crystallization denotes the conversion of a floating charge into a specific charge. On crystallization the debtor company's freedom to manage the charged assets ceases, the floating charge no longer floats over the subject of the charge but fastens on the assets owned by the debtor company comprising in the charge at the date of crystallization and also on all such assets comprised in the charge that are subsequently acquired by the company (*NW Robbie & Co Ltd v Witney Warehouse Co Ltd* [1963] 3 All ER 613).

Charge on future property versus purchase-money charge

In a typical situation a company, in order to secure an overdraft, may create a floating charge in favour of the bank over all its present and future assets. Subsequently, the company may borrow money from, say X, to purchase a piece of land upon terms that X should have a charge on the property so purchased. The question arises as to whether the bank's floating charge or X's purchase-money charge has priority over the property. The law was uncertain as to how the priority of purchase-money mortgage against other competing interests, including interests under a floating charge over after-acquired property, is to be determined. The legal position has been clarified in *Abbey Building Society v Cann* [1990] 2 WLR 832 where the House of Lords held that the mortgagee had priority. It was held that, where a purchaser relied on a loan for the completion of his purchase, the transactions of acquiring the legal estate and granting the charge were one indivisible transaction, at least where there had been a prior agreement to grant the charge on the legal estate when obtained. The purchaser never acquired anything but an equity of redemption and there was no *'scintilla temporis'* during which the legal estate vested in him free from the charge. The legal estate was, from the outset, encumbered by the charge and could not be available to feed the estoppel free from it.

As a result of the decision in *Cann*, it is now clear that where money is advanced and relied on for the purchase of property against an agreement to charge the property as security, the mortgage has priority over an after-acquired property charge, whether fixed or floating.

Ranking of the floating charge

Floating charge versus interests created before crystallization

Subsequent specific charge

A specific charge, whether legal or equitable, has priority over an earlier floating charge. This is because the essence of the floating charge is that it is subject to the powers of the debtor company to dispose of the charged assets in the ordinary course of business, and the creation of specific mortgages and charges is within the ordinary course of business (*Re Colonial Trusts Corpn, ex parte Bradshaw* (1879) 15 Ch 465). In *Wheatley v Silkstone and Haigh Moor Coal Co* (1885) 29 Ch D 715 North J held that the holder of a floating charge had priority over general creditors only. A subsequent specific charge still has priority even if the specific mortgagee or chargee had notice of the earlier floating charge (*Re Hamilton's Windsor Ironworks* (1879) 12 Ch D 707).

Restrictive clauses

Most floating charges contain restrictive clauses, commonly known as negative pledge clauses, prohibiting the creation of any mortgage or charge ranking in priority to, or pari passu with, the floating charge. It is established that notice of the existence of a floating charge does not constitute constructive notice of the restrictive clause (*English and Scottish Mercantile Investment v Brunton* [1882] 2 QB 700). In *Re Standard Rotary Machines Co* (1906) 95 LT 829 it was held that notice of the floating charge itself did not constitute notice of the restrictive clause contained therein. A company issued debentures by way of a floating charge over all its undertaking and property. The floating charge contained a restrictive clause prohibiting the creation of any mortgage or charge ranking in priority to, or pari passu with, the charge. The company subsequently created a specific charge over some of its fully paid shares in favour of the plaintiff. The court had to decide whether the later specific charge had priority over the earlier floating charge. The floating charge was duly registered. It was held that, even assuming that the bank had notice of the floating charge, the bank did not have notice of the restrictive clause.

Subsequent floating charge

In *Re Benjamin Cope & Sons* [1914] 1 Ch 800 Sargeant J said although a floating charge can be displaced by a fixed charge it does not follow that an earlier floating charge can be displaced by a subsequent floating charge. Nevertheless, where a floating charge expressly allows the debtor company to create a further floating charge over a specific portion of the charged assets, the subsequent floating charge has priority over the first (*Re Automatic Bottle Makers* [1926] Ch 412).

Execution creditors

An execution creditor has priority over a holder of a floating charge if, and only if, the execution is completed before crystallization of the floating charge (*Robin v Smith* [1895] 2 Ch 118).

Execution against goods

As regards execution against goods, it is settled that the execution is not completed merely upon seizure of the goods. In *Re Standard Manufacturing Co* [1891] 1 Ch 627 and in *Re Opera Ltd* [1891] 3 Ch 260 the court held that the holder of the floating charge was entitled to priority over the execution of creditors.

Execution of debts

It was decided in *Robin v Smith* [1895] 2 Ch 118 that an execution creditor over debts has priority over the holder of a floating charge where the garnished (third party) debt has been paid to the garnishee (third party) before the floating charge crystallizes. In this case a garnishee order absolute was made against Smith ordering him to pay to the garnisher a debt owed by him to a company. Subsequently the plaintiff, holder of a floating charge, gave notice to the garnishee claiming that he was entitled to all debts of the company and required the garnishee not to pay others. The garnishee complied with the garnishee order and paid the debt to the garnisher. The plaintiff sued the garnishee, claiming that the latter had no right to pay to the garnisher after the receipt of the notice. The court held that the payment to the garnisher was good against the charge holder on the ground that the floating charge had not crystallized at the time the garnishee paid the debt. In *North v Yates* [1906] 1 KB 112 the question arose as to whether the execution creditor still had priority when the floating charge crystallized before the payment of the garnished debt. The court held that the garnishee order did not amount to a transfer of the debt; the garnisher did not thereby become a creditor of the garnishee. Therefore the right of the garnishee order nisi was subject to such rights and equities as already existed over the garnished debt. Since a receiver was appointed the holder of the floating had priority. In *Evans v Rival Granite Quarries Ltd* [1910] 2 KB 979, the court established that the mere existence of a floating charge did not defeat or prevent executions by judgment creditors.

Debtor asserting right of set-off

Debtors can claim a right of set-off if the cross-claim arises before crystallization, even if he has notice of the floating charge at the time the cross-claim arises. In *Biggerstaff v Rowatt's Wharf* [1897] AC 81 Kay LJ treated the debentures as incomplete assignments that did not become complete until such time as the receiver was appointed.

Floating charge versus interests created after crystallization

Once a floating charge crystallizes, it becomes a specific charge that fastens on to the charged assets, and the general rule is that it has priority over all subsequent competing interests. There are however exceptions to this rule.

Automatic crystallization and crystallization by notice

Although the court has sanctioned the validity of automatic crystallization clauses, the question of priority between floating charges that have been converted into a fixed charge under such a clause and a subsequent specific mortgagee or chargee remains open. In other words, the effect of crystallization on the debtor company must be separated from its effect on other encumbrancers.

It has been argued that the specific mortgagee has priority over the floating charge despite its crystallization; the reason being that, by creating a floating charge, the chargee has conferred authority on the debtor company to sell or charge the charged assets in the ordinary course of business. While automatic crystallization or crystallization by notice terminates the company's actual authority to deal with the charged assets, the company still has apparent authority to do so, and any dealing with the charged assets within the ordinary course of business of the company must bind the holder of the floating charge despite the fact of crystallization. Therefore, if the company creates a specific charge over the charged assets after crystallization and the chargee has no notice of the fact of crystallization, the specific charge must have priority over the floating charge.

The same principle does not apply to unsecured creditors, their rights are subject to any rights and equities as already existed over the company's assets; they are unaffected by the company's actual or apparent authority to deal with the assets subject to the floating charge. Hence as soon as the floating charge crystallizes before completion of execution, whether by automatic crystallization clause or not, the floating charge has priority over the execution creditors.

Fixed and floating charge over book debts

Ever since the floating charge was invented by Victorian lawyers, it has been customary for companies to create security over its book debts by way of floating charge, ie the chargor company is left free to dispose of the book debts and the proceeds of collection. On crystallization the floating charge fastens on all the existing and future book debts of the company (see: *NW Robbie & Co Ltd v Witney Warehouse Co Ltd* [1963] 3 All ER 613) and the receiver appointed by the holder of the floating charge will take control of the chargor company.

Lenders had sought to strengthen their security by creating fixed charges over book debts that have several advantages over the floating charge in terms of priority. Debts are peculiar because they cease to exist on payment by the debtor. Therefore in order to create a fixed charge over debts, it is not enough to restrict the chargor company's right to dispose of the charged debt; there must also be a restriction on the way the chargor company is free to collect its debts and dispose of the proceeds. What has been created is a floating charge and not a fixed charge, even if the charge is described as a 'fixed' or 'specific' charge by the instrument of charge.

In *Siebe Gorman & Co Ltd v Barclay's Bank Ltd* [1979] 2 Lloyd's Rep 142 the court decided that it was possible in law to create a fixed charge over book debts. There the debenture in question, in addition to restricting dealings with the charged debts, also required the chargor company to pay all proceeds of debts into the company's account with the chargee bank. Slade J held that a fixed charge had been created since on the construction of the debenture the bank would not have been obliged to allow the company to draw upon the account at a time when it still owed the bank money under the debenture. He concluded that, if the borrower company imposed sufficient controls on the disposal of the book debts prior to their collection and sufficient controls on the company's ability to use the collected amounts, then the charge on book debts could be fixed. Sufficient controls on disposal prior to collection essentially meant that the company was only permitted to receive payment of book debts and could not assign, factor, discount, sell, charge or otherwise deal with them. In *Re Keenan Bros Ltd* [1986] BCLC 242 Keenan Bros created, in favour of its bank, a charge over its present and future book debts. The instrument of charge referred to the charge as a 'fixed charge' and obliged Keenan Bros to pay all moneys it received in satisfaction of the book debts secured by the charges into a designated bank account with the chargee bank, with withdrawals only being possible with the prior written consent of the bank. The Supreme Court of Ireland held that the charge created in favour of the bank was a fixed and not a floating charge.

Both *Siebe Gorman* and *Re Keenan Bros* were distinguished in *Re Brightlife Ltd* [1987] 2 WLR 197. In that case Brightlife by a debenture created, inter alia, a 'first specific charge' over 'all book debts now or at any time during the continuance of this security due or owing to the company'. The debenture prohibited Brightlife to sell, factor or discount debts without prior written consent of the debenture-holder but there was no provision restricting dealings with the proceeds of debts collected. The issue before the court was whether a first fixed charge had been created by the debenture. Hoffmann J held that the debenture, though expressed to create a 'first specific charge' operated to create a floating charge. He distinguished *Siebe Gorman* on the ground that there the debenture was in favour of a bank and not only prohibited the company from selling or charging its book debts but required that they be paid into the company's account with that bank. Slade J decided that as a matter of construction the bank would not have been obliged to allow the company to draw upon the account at a time when it still owed the bank money under the debenture. Hoffmann J also distinguished *Re Keenan Bros* on the footing that there the company was obliged to pay the proceeds of all debts into a designated account with the bank and no withdrawals could be made without the prior consent of the bank.

Re New Bullas Trading Ltd [1994] 1 BCLC 449 appeared to offer a solution to this debate. In that case the charge created what was called a fixed charge on book debts and provided that money collected from the debtors was to be paid into an account at a named bank and then applied as directed by the chargee but, if no directions were given, the money was 'released' from the fixed charge. The court held that at the time the administrative receivers were appointed the uncollected debts were subject to a fixed charge; therefore subject to s 40 of the Insolvency Act 1986 (preferential debts must be paid out of assets subject to a floating charge in priority to the chargee's debt). In *Agnew v Inland Revenue Commissioners (Re Brumark Investments Ltd)* [2001] 2 AC 710 the Privy Council overruled *Re New Bullas*. The result of *Bullas* was that a charge on book debts that provided that they could not be assigned without the chargee's consent was a fixed charge, despite the fact that it allowed debts to be collected unless the chargee gave directions. The Privy Council expressed the view that assignments and collection were alternative ways of turning a debt into money and a charge contract that allowed either method of realization without the chargee's permission must be a floating charge, not a fixed charge.

Charge of debts in favour of a bank

In *Re Charge Card Services Ltd* [1986] 3 WLR 697 it was found impossible to have a charge in favour of a debtor of his own indebtedness. The court derived support from the House of Lords decision in *Halesowen Pressworks & Assemblies Ltd v Westminster Bank Ltd* [1972] AC 785 where the view was expressed that a bank could not have a lien on the credit balance in its customer's current account. The implication of *Re Charge Card Services* to the banker is that it cannot have a charge over the credit balance in its customer's account. It can merely set off against the credit balance any indebtedness due to it from the customer. In *Re Bank Credit and Commerce International SA (No 8)* [1998] AC 214 there is dicta that supports the bank having a proprietary interest binding assignees and a liquidator or trustee in bankruptcy.

Priorities equitable assignee (chargee) versus equitable assignee (chargee)

Priority between competing equitable assignees and chargees of book debts is governed by the rule in *Dearle v Hall* (1828) 3 Russ 1: priority goes to the first to give notice of his interest to the debtor unless he has notice of an earlier assignment at the time he acquires his interest. Notice of a prior assignment can be actual or constructive. Since a charge or mortgage of book debts by a company is registrable under the Companies Act and registration constitutes notice to a subsequent mortgagee or chargee (Companies Act 1985, s 416), normally a subsequent incumbrancer will be bound with constructive notice of a prior incumbrance. Registration is constructive notice only of matters appearing on the register at the time at which the subsequent incumbrancer acquires his interest, and constructive notice does not apply to subsequent purchasers of book debts. Thus, a subsequent incumbrancer who acquires his interest before the registration of a prior interest does not have constructive notice of it, neither does a factor, whether he acquires his interest before or after registration of the prior interest. Moreover, assignment by way of sale, ie factoring, needs not be registered under the Companies Act. Notice of a prior floating charge does not affect priority because the essence of the floating charge is that the chargor company is free to dispose of the charged assets in the ordinary course of business, which includes the creation of mortgages or charges and the selling of book debts to a factor. Where the floating charge contains a negative pledge clause that forbids the company from assigning the charged book debts, a subsequent chargee or factor who has notice of the charge does not thereby have notice of the restriction since registration constitutes constructive notice of the required particulars only.

Stocks and shares as security

The types of stocks and shares likely to be offered to a bank as security for a loan are 'registered' stocks and shares and 'fully negotiable' stocks and shares. Where stocks and shares are registered, the names of the owners are recorded on a register, and no change of legal ownership can occur until the name of the old owner is removed from the register and the new name inserted. Where stocks and shares are in bearer form, they are negotiable instruments and ownership vests generally in the bearer. The main types of registered stocks and shares are public authorities' loan bonds and stocks, and stocks and shares of companies.

Public authorities' loan

Governments, local authorities, and nationalised industries issue public body stock and other public bodies as security for loans made. The holder of a public authorities' loan stock is usually entitled to receive a fixed rate of interest and repayment of capital at a fixed date. Some public authorities' stocks are 'listed' on the stock exchange and these are better security for a loan made by a bank than stocks that are not listed. This is because listed stocks are readily marketable and it is possible to ascertain a market value for them at any given time. The Bank of England maintains the register of ownership for British government stocks, although several British government stocks are also registered on the National Savings Register or the registers of the Trustee Savings Banks. Ownership of Government Stock (Marketable Securities), British Savings Bonds and National Savings Income Bonds is rewarded on the National Savings Stock Register.

Stocks and shares of companies

Fully paid shares may be converted into stock and vice versa. Some types of company stocks and shares are safer security for a loan than others. The safest security for a loan is 'debenture stock' that represents a loan made to the company. The holder of the debenture stock has a right to receive interest from the company, usually at a fixed rate and is usually a secured creditor of the company. The nature of the security will depend on what assets are charged by the debenture trust deed.

Unsecured loan stock may also be given as security. The holder of unsecured loan stock is a creditor of the company and has a right to receive interest from the company. Preference shares may also be used as security for a loan, although the preference shareholder is not a creditor of the company, he does have a right to receive a dividend on his shareholding prior to the ordinary shareholders.

The registers of both public and private companies are kept either by the company itself or by an outsider, eg a bank or chartered accountant. The register will show the names and addresses of the stockholders and/or shareholders and the quantity of shares and stock held. Holders are given a stock or share certificate and may transfer their holding by executing a stock or share transfer form and delivering it, with the certificate, to the transferee.

Creation of a legal mortgage of registered stocks and shares

A bank will take a legal mortgage of registered stocks and shares by obtaining from the registered holder a properly executed form of transfer, together with the stock or share certificate, and then being registered as the new registered holder of the stocks and shares. Where the registered holder is not the registered mortgagor himself but the nominee, then the transfer form must be executed by the mortgagor's nominee and not by the mortgagor. The form of transfer cannot be registered unless the transferor signs a written transfer of the stock or shares.

When taking a legal mortgage of registered stocks and shares, the bank should give the mortgagor a 'facility letter' or formal 'loan agreement', describing the loan, the terms of repayment and the nature of the security. The bank should also take from the mortgagor a memorandum of deposit, containing details of the bank's powers in relation to the stocks and shares. The memorandum of deposit should either list the mortgaged stocks or shares from time to time deposited with the bank.

The memorandum of deposit should state which debts owed to the bank are secured by the mortgage. If the mortgage if given to secure a fluctuating debt, eg an overdraft, the memorandum should state that the mortgage is given as a continuing security for the balance on the debtor's account with the bank so that the rule in *Clayton's Case* (1816) 1 Mer 572 will not have the effect of reducing the debt that is secured. The memorandum should also state (if that is the case) that the mortgage is being taken in addition to any other securities given to secure the same debt, not in substitution for them. The memorandum normally includes provision for the bank to sell the mortgaged stocks and shares if the mortgagor defaults. In the absence of an express provision in the memorandum, the bank will have an implied right of sale if the mortgagor defaults (*Deverges v Sandeman Clark & Co* [1902] 1 Ch 579). Where no date for repayment is fixed, the courts have held that the bank can enforce the security on giving reasonable notice to the mortgagor. In *Deverges* a month's notice of the bank's intention to enforce the security was held to be reasonable.

A legal mortgagee of partly paid stocks and shares is liable for any 'calls' on such stocks and shares and the memorandum should provide for the mortgagor to indemnify the bank in respect of any calls.

Creation of an equitable mortgage of registered stocks and shares

A share certificate is prima facie (but not conclusive) evidence of title. The presumption arising from possession of that certificate can be rebutted. The company may be estopped from denying the facts as stated in the certificate, eg if the company issues a share certificate that describes shares as fully paid-up, a third party may rely on the company being estopped from denying that the shares are such. An equitable mortgage of registered stocks and shares is created when the mortgagor enters into a binding agreement to execute a proper form of transfer in favour of the bank or his nominees or where the bank (or his nominee) has not yet been registered as the new holder of the mortgaged stocks and shares. A mortgagor may create an equitable mortgage by depositing his stock and share certificates with the bank by way of security. In *Harrold v Plenty* [1901] 2 Ch 314 Cozens-Hardy J pointed out that such an act seems

> '... to amount to an equitable mortgage or, in other words, to an agreement to execute a transfer of the shares by way of mortgage.'

Deposit of the stock or share certificate will not amount to an equitable mortgage unless it can be shown that the deposit was by way of security. A bank may find it difficult to show that the deposit of the certificate was by way of security unless the mortgagor gives the bank a memorandum of deposit or a blank transfer form, with the intention that the mortgagee will, when necessary, fill the blank and perfect the security. The memorandum of deposit should contain essentially the same information as a memorandum of deposit deposited when a legal mortgage is created. Additionally, the memorandum should describe the circumstances in which the bank is permitted to complete the blank form of transfer in either its favour or that of a third party.

Whether a transfer may be written ('under hand') or by seal is governed by the requirements of the company's articles of association, but fully paid-up shares may be transferred under s 1 of the Stock Transfer Act 1963 by a signed instrument of transfer in the statutory form, notwithstanding anything contained in the company's memorandum or articles.

A blank transfer cannot be by deed. If a person seals and delivers a document that is left in blank, it is void for uncertainty and cannot be perfected by completion after execution (*Markham v Conaston* (1598) Cro Eliz 626; *Powell v London and Provincial Bank* [1893] 2 Ch 555).

A bank that has an equitable mortgage over British Government stock, or company stock or shares, can further protect itself by means of a 'stop notice'. The effect of the 'stop notice' is to prevent any dealings in securities or the payment of a dividend, without prior notice to the person serving the notice having an opportunity to assert his claim. A bank that serves such a notice on the company in respect of securities charged to it may obtain a restraining order or injunction to prevent the distribution or dealings in the securities.

Fully negotiable stocks and shares as securities

Fully negotiable securities taken in good faith and for value may be retained by the purchaser (including a mortgagee) against the true owner. In that respect they are an excellent security. Where a mortgagee takes them bona fide, for value and without notice of a defect in title, he can hold them against the true owner. Fully negotiable securities are charged by way of pledge rather than a mortgagor. Although the mere deposit of a fully negotiable security gives the bank a complete title, it is desirable to take a memorandum of deposit showing the purpose of the deposit.

A bank that takes the fully negotiable instrument from a customer as security will acquire a valid title if he takes in good faith and for value, and without notice of any defect in the pledgor's title. Whether a bank takes the securities in good faith is a question of fact and mere negligence in taking the securities will not necessarily deprive the bank of his rights, but negligence or carelessness when considered in connection with the surrounding circumstances, may be evidence of bad faith.

Life policies

The assignment, legal or equitable, of a life assurance policy is a very general form of security for an advance up to the surrender value of the policy. Provided premiums continue to be paid it is a security that increases in value. It is useful as a supplementary security because, in the event of the borrower's death, part or whole of the debt will be liquidated when the policy monies are paid over by the insurance company.

A contract for life assurance is a contract of the 'utmost good faith' and the assured must disclose all material facts within his knowledge affecting the life. Non-disclosure of a material fact may result in the policy being void. If the insurers are to avoid a policy on the grounds of non-disclosure, they must prove the fact to be material. A material fact is one that 'would influence the judgment of a prudent insurer in fixing the premium, or determining whether or not to take the risk and is a question of fact'. Examples of material facts are: failing to disclose convictions for dishonesty (material for house insurance) (*Woolcott v Sun Alliance and London Insurance Ltd* [1978] 1 WLR 493); failing to disclose that a number of other insurers had declined the risk of life assurance (*London Assurance v Mansell* (1879) 11 Ch D 363); failing to disclose doubts about the assured's mental health (that might have made him prone to suicide) (*Lindenau v Desborough* (1828) 8 B&C 586).

The assignment

The assignment is taken from the person entitled to the benefit that forms the security value, ie the person to whom the surrender value or monies are payable under the policy. This 'beneficiary' may or may not be the life assured. The beneficiary must be of full capacity or the assignment will be ineffective. A legal assignment must be in accordance with the Policies of Assurance Act 1867. The Act requires the assignment be witnessed and signed, although it need not be by deed. The insurer must be informed of the date and effect of the assignment.

The effect of a legal assignment of a life assurance policy is as follows.

(i) After receiving notice, the insurer is bound to pay the assignee only, and is discharged by earlier payment to another.

(ii) The insured is to be entitled to the defences of set-off or counterclaim existing between himself and the assured before notice.

(iii) The priorities between successive assignees are regulated by the order in which notice is received by the insurer (the rule in *Dearle v Hall* (1828) 3 Russ 1).

An equitable assignment may be made by an oral agreement, by memorandum (*Myers v United Guarantee and Life Assurance Co* (1855) 7 De GM&G 112) or by deposit of the policy with intent that it be security. A memorandum of deposit may be taken to explain the purpose of the deposit. Alternatively, the bank may take an irrevocable power of attorney, entitling it to sell in the name of the assignor.

Keyman insurance

This type of policy is used by businesses to ensure that they have the necessary operating capital and to find a replacement in the event of the death of a key person within the business. Investors in a business, where one or a small number of individual employees are key to the success of the venture, often demand that keyman insurance is taken out. With keyman insurance, the death or disability of the injured person usually leads to the corporation receiving the proceeds as the beneficiary of the insurance policy. The money is then available to the business attempting to overcome the loss of the services of the key employee, to distribute to the investors on the firm being dissolved.

Most small businesses do not need keyman insurance. It is usually purchased when an investor fears the loss of a key manager or employee. It is not meant to replace personal life insurance taken out by that person for the benefit of their family.

Such policies can be registered at Companies House but there is no statutory requirement to do so.

Six

Default events and remedies for breach of contract

6.1 Events of default

Remedies in absence of express events of default

Term loan agreements usually contain express events of default, eg non-payment and insolvency, on the occurrence of which the bank is given an express right to terminate the obligation to advance further loans and to call in all amounts outstanding by way of acceleration.

Where there are no express events of default, ordinary contractual remedies are available although adapted to the special circumstances of loan contracts. In particular, if the default is serious, the borrower may be taken to have impliedly repudiated the contract. Implied repudiation occurs where the party in default has so conducted himself as to lead the reasonable man to believe that he will not perform, or will be unable to perform, at the stipulated time eg *Household Machines Ltd v Cosmos Exporters Ltd* [1947] KB 217 (refusal to pay for goods).

The events of default range from non-payment of interest and principal, through breach of the representations, covenants and other obligations in the agreement, to events that anticipate default, eg events indicating insolvency.

The occurrence of the events set out in a default clause may not automatically constitute default since there may be requirements that notice be given to the borrower, grace periods, materiality tests, and other limitations brought into the clause. For example, a borrower with bargaining power may be able to have a clause drafted so that, to constitute default, payment must be overdue eg for 30 days. Alternatively, default may be defined so as not to occur unless a breach of the agreement is material or has an adverse affect on the ability of the borrower to repay (*Pan Foods v ANZ Banking Group* (2000) 74 ALJR 791). Further, a borrower may be able to negotiate that default will only be deemed to have occurred if the reasonable man would come to that conclusion. Otherwise, the courts will only impose the requirement that the bank act honestly in reaching its conclusions. Further, events of default may have to be continuing if the bank wants to exercise its remedies under the default clause.

Where a borrower fails to pay an amount payable by it when due, the bank has the following remedies.

♦ The bank can sue for the unpaid amount as a debt due. The common law does not award general damages for delay in payment of a debt beyond the date when it becomes legally due (*President of India v La Pintada Naviagacion* [1985] AC 104). In some cases, the bank may be able to exercise a set-off, eg against a deposit owed by it to the borrower.

♦ Further, the bank may call in the entire principal and cancel the contract if the breach amounts to an anticipatory repudiation of the contract by the borrower, eg where the time of payment is not of the essence (eg with sale of goods contracts) it may be that the principles of sale of goods contracts will afford guidance. Section 31(2) of the Sale of Goods Act 1979 states that it is a question in each case depending on the terms of the contract and the circumstances, whether the failure to pay a single installment of the purchase price is a repudiation giving the right to rescind or merely a severable breach giving rise to a claim for damages. If the default in payment is such as to destroy the innocent party's confidence in the defaulting party's credit worthiness, the breach may be treated as going to the root of a sale of goods contract (*Decro-Wall International SA v Practitioners in Marketing Ltd* [1971] 2 All ER 216).

♦ The bank may petition for the liquidation or administration of a borrower that is a company within the Companies Act if the non-payment amounts to an inability to pay debts under s 123 of the Insolvency Act 1986.

Where the borrower fails to comply with a term of the loan agreement other than an obligation to make payments, eg an undertaking to delivery financial information or a negative pledge, again the bank has a number of remedies:

♦ theoretically, the bank has an action for damages but an action for damages may not add anything to the claim for the loan itself;

♦ specific performance may be available but is a discretionary remedy;

♦ an injunction may be available to restrain a threatened breach of a contract;

♦ if the borrower's conduct is such as to evidence an intention of repudiating his obligations under the contract, the bank can accept the repudiation and terminate the contract;

- where the lender has entered into the contract as a result of a misrepresentation made by the borrower, the lender may, subject to limitations, rescind the contract. Additionally, or as an alternative, the borrower may have a claim for damages. The position depends on whether the misrepresentation is fraudulent, negligent or innocent;
- if the representation has become a term of the contract, a notional claim for damages is available if the breach is minor. Termination may be available if the breach is major in the context of the contract.

Where the borrower goes into liquidation then the bank has the following remedies:

- the bank can prove for its unpaid claim even though payable in the future;
- the bank may be able to treat the contract as repudiated. The commencement of a winding up under the Insolvency Act 1986 does not of itself put an end to the company's contracts or amount to a repudiation by the company. If the effect of the insolvent liquidation is to put it beyond the power of the company to perform or the liquidator declares the company's inability to perform its contracts, it will almost invariably follow that the lender can terminate the contract and cancel the obligation to make further loans.

In *Wallace v Universal Automatic Machines Co* [1894] 2 Ch 547 the court held that where a company goes into insolvent liquidation, a loan secured by a floating charge becomes payable even if there is no express statement to that effect.

Usual express events of default

Generally express events of default are inserted in term loan agreements. It is expressly provided that on the occurrence of any of these events, the lender may, by notice to the borrower, cancel its obligation to make further loans and accelerate payment of any outstanding loans. Events of default may be grouped into two categories:

- breaches of the law of contract itself eg non payment, failure to comply with a covenant or inaccuracy of a warranty;
- anticipatory events of default, ie events that make it probable that it is only a matter of time before the borrower is actually in default under a term of the agreement itself. Thus, for example, in an insolvency situation, the lender should not have to wait for an actual non-payment.

Examples of common events of default include default in payment of any installments of principal or any interest or other amount payable by the borrower when due. Acceleration on such event has been held not to be in the nature of a penalty (*City Land & Property (Holdings) Ltd v Dabrah* [1968] Ch 166). Failure to comply with another obligation under the loan contract may trigger an express default clause, as will the incorrectness of a representation or warranty in the agreement itself, or otherwise inducing the contract, or in any other documentation such as accounts furnished under the loan agreement. Material adverse changes in the financial condition or other circumstances, giving rise to the belief that the borrower may be unable or unwilling to perform, may affect a default clause. The questions, which need to be asked, are whether the:

(1)   adverse circumstances render an inability to perform certain, probable or merely possible;

(2)   bank can decide that the matter in its opinion amounts to a 'material adverse change'. such clauses are of significance in sovereign credits where they are designed to cover state insolvency, war, rebellion and other political or economic changes that may impede the ability or willingness of the borrower to comply.

Cost default clauses

A default on one loan agreement may be merely a prelude to a general default so that a cross default clause may be inserted to achieve a pari passu position for all creditors of the same class. Thus, for example, any default under another agreement with, eg Bank B, may be an event of default under an agreement with Bank A, even though Bank B has chosen not to call default. Any event, with the giving of notice, lapse of a grace period, determination of materiality, or fulfillment of any other condition, would constitute an event of default under the other agreement with Bank B, and may constitute an event of default with Bank A.

From the point of view of borrowers, the cross-default can trigger a domino effect if there is a default under any one of its term loan agreements. Few borrowers would be in a position immediately to honour their debts if all their borrowings became immediately payable. The cross-default clause usually crystallizes on:

(1)   non-payment; and

(2)   acceleration of other debts by reason of default.

Sometimes it also crystallizes on the mere occurrence of an event of default under another agreement (eg breach of covenant), which entitles the other lender to accelerate immediately or after a remedying notice period. Where the loan is guaranteed, the events of default should also relate to the guarantor. Without this cross-referencing, the lender would be unable to call in the loan and then proceed directly against the guarantor if the guarantor were, eg to default in a covenant in the guarantee or to go into liquidation.

Materiality clauses

Where it is provided that an event of default occurs only if the event, eg breach of warranty, or an adverse change in financial condition, is material in the opinion of the lender, then a reasonableness test may be applied. This test will not be applied if it is clear from the language of the term agreement that the lender is at liberty to decide the question without reference to reasonable cause in which case his decision can be challenged only on the ground of want of good faith. In *Diggle v Ogston Motor Co* (1915) 84 LJKB 2165 the duties of an employee were to be carried out 'to the satisfaction of the directors'. The court held that, although the directors had no reason to be dissatisfied, they were generally dissatisfied and this discretion should not be overridden. In *Docker v Hyams* [1969] 3 All ER 808 the court said that 'where a condition is that something is to be done to A's approval or to his satisfaction then he is the judge, and as long as he is honest, he need not be reasonable'.

Some loan contracts provide that a certificate of the lender as to certain matters, eg the rate of interest payable, the amount of funding losses on a default, or whether an event is material, is to be conclusive. In *Bache & Co (London) Ltd v Banque Verns et Commercial de Paris* (1973) 117 Sol Jo 483 a guarantee given by a bank stated that the creditor's notice of default by the debtor was to be 'conclusive evidence' of the bank's liability to the creditor. The court held that such a provision was binding and a notice could not be challenged unless it was on the face of it inaccurate or unless fraud could be established. There was nothing in public policy to prevent the claim from being enforced. In *P & M Kaye Ltd v Hosier & Dickinson Ltd* [1972] 1 All ER 121 an architect's final certificate was to be conclusive that certain work had been carried out properly. The court held that the provision did not have the effect of ousting the jurisdiction of the courts that retained ultimate control in seeing that the architect acted properly, honestly and in accordance with the contract, but the method of proof chosen by the parties was legitimate.

Acceleration and cancellation

Some loan agreements provide that the lender may, at any time, after the default accelerate the loans. The question that arises is whether the loan can be accelerated after the default has been cured. The test appears to be whether, as a matter of construction, the default is capable of being subsequently rectified.

♦ In *The Brimnes, Tenax SS Co Ltd v The Brimnes (Owners)* [1975] QB 929 the ship owner had a right in a charter party to withdraw the vessel if there was a failure to make 'punctual and regular payment' of the hire. The charterer paid the hire late but before the withdrawal of the vessel. The court held that although it could be said that a person who had paid late had remedied his failure to pay, it could not be said that he had remedied his failure to pay punctually so that the owners could withdraw the vessel notwithstanding a belated payment preceding the withdrawal unless the owner subsequently, by unequivocal act, waived the breach. In *Mardorf, Peach & Co Ltd v Attica Sea Carriers Corpn of Liberia, D Laconia* [1977] AC 850 it was held that, where the owners had a right to withdraw if payment was not made 'in advance', the right to withdraw was not cured by a late payment and could be exercised after the payment was received unless in the meantime the breach was waived. In both cases, the default could not be remedied.

In *Mardorf, Peach & Co Ltd* the court hinted at the possibility of equitable relief where it would be unconscionable of owners to take advantage of a failure to pay where the failure 'might be due to pure accident and might occasion no real detriment to the owners, whereas withdrawal might cause very heavy loss to the charterers'.

♦ Although no request or demand for performance of a contract is necessary in order to create a right of action for breach (first demand for payment of debt is not necessary: *Walton v Mascall* (1844) 13 MW 452, it was held in *Esso Petroleum Co Ltd v Alstonbridge Properties Ltd* [1975] 3 All ER 359 that a demand is necessary to accelerate a loan repayable by installments because the acceleration is an act that radically changes the nature of the debtor's obligation.

Where a contract contains a provision for its termination or acceleration by notice, then the notice must be given strictly in accordance with the terms of the contract (*Re Berker Support Craft Ltd's Agreements, Hartnell v Berker Support Craft Ltd* (1947) 177 LT 420).

♦ If the event of default occurs by reason of an act or omission of the bank then the bank cannot insist on the stipulation for acceleration becoming effective: a party cannot take advantage of his own wrong to terminate a contract (*New Zealand Shipping Co Ltd v Societe Des Ateliers Et Chantiers De France* [1919] AC 1).

General remedies available for breach of contract

The normal remedies available for a breach of contract may become available to a party where the terms of the loan agreement have been breached.

The general contractual doctrine of frustration applies to loan contracts, as it does to other contracts. Where performance of the contract becomes impossible, or possible only in a radically different way from that originally contemplated, then the contract may be frustrated and the law excuse further performance (*Davis Contractors Ltd v Fareham UDC* [1956] AC 696).

In respect of loan contracts, the frustrating circumstances may prevent the borrower from making payments or from performing another obligation, or may affect the performance of the lender's obligations, eg to make the loan available.

The frustrating events must not have arisen through fault of either party (*Denmark Productions Ltd v Boscobel Productions Ltd* [1969] 1 QB 699).

♦ A contract is not discharged merely because it turns out to be more difficult or onerous to perform than originally intended. The parties are not released from their obligations under the contract merely by reason of unexpected obstacle, eg the appreciation of currency so that the loan transaction becomes more expensive.

♦ A contract may nevertheless be discharged by frustration even though the parties could foresee, or could reasonably have foreseen, a frustrating event (*Ocean Tramp Tankers Corpn v B/O Sovfracht, D Eugenia* [1964] 2 QB 226). Where the parties have made provision for the foreseen event, the doctrine of frustration generally does not apply except in the case of frustration by illegality. In *Ertel Bieber & Co v Rio Tinto Co Ltd* [1918] AC 260 the contract was abrogated by the outbreak of war notwithstanding a clause providing for suspension. Such a clause was deemed to be against public policy.

The circumstances may be so devastating as to be outside the contemplated scope of an express provision. In such circumstances, the doctrine of frustration will apply and not the express provision. In *Fibrosa Spolka Akcyjna v Fairbairn Lawson Combe Barbour Ltd* [1943] AC 32 an express term provided for reasonable extension for the performance of the contractual obligations but was held not to refer to prolonged delay occasioned by World War II.

Where a contract is frustrated, then both parties are excused from further performance. The discharge is mutual, automatic and without any election of the parties. Even if the contract is discharged, an arbitration clause may remain in force to govern matters up to the date of frustration where the issue arises from the frustration itself (*Kruse v Questier & Co Ltd* [1953] 1 QB 669).

♦ The Law Reform (Frustrated Contracts) Act 1943 applies where a contract governed by English law has become impossible of performance or has been otherwise frustrated and the parties are discharged from further performance because of the events.

♦ The Act does not apply to contracts governed by foreign law.

♦ Where the Act does apply, all sums paid to a party before discharge in pursuance of the contract are recoverable from him as money received for the use of the party by whom the sums were paid, and all sums payable at the time of the frustrating event ceased to be payable (s 1(2)). The lender will, therefore, normally be entitled to recover loans already made and would cease to be under any continuing obligation to make further loans.

♦ Any expenses incurred by the party to whom the sums were paid or payable before the frustrating event, may be retained or recoverable, in whole or any part of the sum paid or payable, to an amount not exceeding the actual expenses incurred (s 1(2)).

- Where a party to a frustrated contract has obtained a valuable benefit before the discharge, other than payment of money falling within s 1(2), that other party may recover any sums the court considers just, having regard to the circumstances.

Any express provisions in the contract may not override the 1943 Act.

Illustrations of frustrating events

A change of law subsequent to the contract may render the contract or its performance illegal and impossible. In such circumstances, the courts may excuse performance of the contract. The illegality must be one that is recognized by the English courts as affecting the contract, eg the illegality arises under the proper law of the contract, or the illegality arises under the law of the place of performance and renders such performance illegal there.

Another common cause of frustration is the outbreak of war. At common law, where the continued performance of the contract after the outbreak of war would involve dealings with the enemy or detriment to the interests of the UK, any subsisting right to performance of the contract is abrogated. A right to the payment of a liquidated sum of money will not be abrogated or confiscated but merely suspended for the duration of the war. In normal circumstances, therefore, an English borrower's obligations to a bank that becomes an enemy alien will merely be suspended. An English bank's obligations to advance money to a borrower who is an alien enemy will be abrogated.

- In *Schering Ltd v Stockholm Enskilda Bank Aktiebolag* [1946] AC 219 a Swedish bank agreed to advance to a German company Reichsmarks to the value of £84,000 and the German company agreed to repay just over £50,000 over an eight-year period. An English company initially guaranteed the German company's obligations and subsequently agreed to pay the installments as primary obligor under a contract governed by English law. Due to the outbreak of war in 1939, the English company argued that its contract to pay further installments was abrogated since the contract benefited the German company to the detriment of English interests. The court held that, since the Swedish bank had already performed its obligations at the outbreak of the war, the contract was executed and the English company's obligations were unaffected by the war. The court held that a contract that is completely executed on one side, and under which nothing remains to be performed except payment to be made by the other of a liquidated sum, is unaffected by the outbreak of war and the payment obligation remains enforceable. The payment cannot, in fact, be made between enemies in time of war and so long as the war lasts, the payment is suspended. The enforcement, however, during the war may be impossible, but such rights will survive the war.

♦ In *Arrow Bank Ltd v Barclays Bank (Dominion, Colonial and Overseas)* [1954] AC
459, Arrow Bank had a deposit with the Jerusalem office of Barclays Bank.
When war broke out between Israel and the Palestinians in 1948, Israeli
legislation required Barclays to pay the deposit to a local custodian of
absentee property. Arrow Bank sued Barclays at its head office in London
for the repayment of the deposit and they maintained that, although a
deposit might be payable at the office where it is located, a prohibition at
the place is a good defense to the bank holding the deposit. Nevertheless,
the war wholly abrogated the deposit contract. The resulting cancellation of
the credit balance gave rise to a new right to recover from Barclays Bank in
London. The House of Lords held that the Arrow Bank claim failed. The
Arrow Bank claim was a liquidated claim and accordingly the Arrow Bank's
right to its payment was only suspended during the war, not abrogated. Since
the right to recover the deposit was closely situate in Israeli territory, it was
subject to Israeli legislation and was properly rested in the local custodian.

In *Bevan v Bevan* [1955] 2 QB 227 an executory contract providing for separation
and maintenance was not to be abrogated by the fact that the payee resided in
enemy territory, though payments should be made to the custodian of enemy
property during hostilities.

Insolvency brought about by external forces will not normally constitute a
frustrating event. A contract is not frustrated merely because performance
becomes more difficult. The issue has been discussed in *Russian Indemnity case* of
November 11, (1912) 11 UN Rep 421 where Turkey's defense to a default on a
peace treaty indemnity to Russia was rejected because the default resulted from
economic difficulties occasioned by insurrection and foreign war.

Term loan agreements sometimes contain a number of provisions intended to
provide for the legal relations between the parties if circumstances outside the
control of the parties affect the position of the parties. Express contractual
provisions can therefore displace the operation of the Law Reform (Frustrated
Contracts) Act 1943. Thus, an illegality clause may provide that, if by reason of a
change in law it becomes impossible for the bank to either perform its obligations
to make the loan, to maintain a loan (eg having it outstanding) or to fund the loan
in the matter contemplated by the contract, the bank may cancel its obligations and
call for an immediate repayment of any loans already made. Such a clause, in effect,
extends the operation of the doctrine of frustration applying in the case of
illegality. Thus, it covers illegalities that may not amount to a frustrating event (eg
illegality in funding in a particular market); it may deal with issues relating to
whether the obligation concerned is severable and it applies to changes in the law
that are binding on the bank (eg in its own jurisdiction) but which would not be
recognized under the proper law of the contract.

Assignments

Only rights on the loan agreements can be assigned and not obligations; the transfer of a bank's obligation, eg the obligation to lend money, would require the agreement of the borrower and would in effect amount to a novation agreement.

♦ The usual policy of banks, however, is to ensure that their assets are transferable and a bank may wish to have the power to transfer the benefit of a loan for a number of reasons, eg to allow the loan to be discounted with a central bank if the lending bank is in difficulties or if the central bank will advance funds to the commercial banking sector only against a transfer of loan assets, or in the event of a default, to transfer the loan to another bank that owes a deposit to the borrower to enable a set-off to be utilized for the benefit of both banks. Borrowers may have an interest in restricting such rights of transfer of the benefit of the loan, eg to reserve some control over the identity of the borrower's creditors. Some term loan agreements may expressly permit transfers of the lending office. The transfer of a loan from the books of one office of a bank to another office does not require a novation because it is not between separate legal entities.

An obligation under a contract can be transferred only with the consent of the party entitled to the benefit of the obligation. Thus, a bank cannot transfer its obligation to lend without the agreement of the borrower and such a transfer has to be by novation between the debtor, the transferor and the transferee whereby the debtor agrees to release the transferor from his obligations and the transferee agrees to assume those obligations. In effect, there is a new contract and parties to the original contract are being substituted. Novations may be implied from the conduct of the parties, eg where the person entitled to the benefit of the obligation by his conduct takes the transferee as the promisor and the original obligor as having been released (*Re Head v Head (No 2)* [1894] 2 Ch 236).

A bank wishing to assign a loan must first establish whether the loan is assignable. A loan may be made non-assignable in the following ways.

♦ By implication: thus for example, where the effect of the assignment of rights under a contract is to increase the burden on the debtor, then the contract is not assignable unless the contract expressly contemplates an assignment. Alternatively, the court may allow assignment but limit the assignee's right to recover to the extent that the assignor could have recovered.
Where the contract involves personal skill or confidence it is not assignable unless the contract expressly contemplates assignments. The benefit of the contract is only assignable in 'cases where it can make no difference to the person on whom the obligation lies to which of two persons he is to discharge it' (*Tolhurst v Associated Portland Cement Manufacturers* (1900) Ltd [1903] AC 414). This is to be decided on objective grounds.

♦ Where rights of action are non-assignable: it would be unusual for the assignment of a loan to be subject to the rule that a bare right of action (eg an action for fraud, defamation or assault) is not assignable. The test is whether the assignee's real object was to acquire an interest in the property or merely to acquire a right to bring an action, either a loan or jointly with the assignor (*County Hotel and Wine Co Ltd v London and North Western Railway Co* [1918] 2 KB 251). The rule may be brought into play if, eg the bank assigns not a debt claim under the loan agreement, but a right of damages for beach of covenant or a right to rescind the loan agreement for misrepresentation separately from the debt claim.

♦ Where a contract contains an express restriction on assignments, it would appear that an assignment contrary to the provision would be invalid. In *Helstan Securities Ltd v Hertfordshire County Council* [1978] 3 All ER 262 a building contract for roadworks with the County Council provided that the contractor was not to 'assign the contract or any part thereof or any benefit of interest therein or thereunder without the written consent' of the Council. The contractor assigned sums owing by the Council under the contract without the Council's consent. It was held that the debt due from the Council to the contractor was 'a benefit or interest' under the contract and accordingly the assignment was void. In *Re Griffin v Griffin* [1899] 1 Ch 408 a bank deposit receipt stated 'this receipt is not transferable, and will be required to be produced on each occasion of any withdrawal'. It was held that the fund in the bank could not be assigned since the prohibition merely prevented transfer of the document and not the fund. In *Re Turcan* [1888] 40 Ch D 5 a husband took out a life policy expressed to be 'not assignable in any case whatever'. It was held that even if the insured could not have assigned the policy there was nothing to stop him from making a declaration of trust of the policy money in favour of trustees of a marriage settlement. Thus, where there is a restriction on assignments, it may be possible to use the device of declaring a trust, or alternatively for the bank to take an assignment of proceeds.

Legal and equitable assignments

An action can be assigned both in equity and under the Law of Property Act 1925. To be a legal assignment, the assignment itself must be:

- ♦ in writing under the hand of the assignor;
- ♦ it must be absolute and not by way of a charge;
- ♦ it must relate to the whole of the debt (*Forester v Baker* [1910] 2 KB 636);
- ♦ it must be notified to the debtor.

Notice is deemed to have been given when it is received by the debtor (*Holt v Heatherfield Trust Ltd* [1942] 2 KB 2). There is no time limit, but the notice will be ineffectual if it is given after the action for the debt has commenced. Either the assignor or assignee may give the notice. In *Gatoil v Amstalt v Omennial Ltd, v Balder London* [1980] 2 Lloyd's Rep 489 a notice of assignment of a charter party provided that, until notice was given by the assignee, the charterer could continue to pay the charter hire direct to the owner. The court held that the proviso prevented the notice of assignment, from operating as a proper notice assignment under the Law of Property Act 1925 s 136. The dicta appear to assume that a notice cannot be effective if the debtor is permitted to continue paying the assignor.

An assignment that fails to meet any of these requirements may take effect in equity. The rules for an equitable assignment are more relaxed than those required to be satisfied for a legal assignment. All that is required is that the creditor should manifest a clear intention to make an irrevocable transfer of the debtor or obligation. The assignment will be effective as between the assignor and assignee even if notice is not given to the debtor, although the debtor will not be affected by the assignment until notice is given to him. An equitable assignment may take place in one of three ways.

♦ When the creditor either signs a written transfer and sends it to the assignee or makes a binding agreement for assignment that will be given effect in equity. Neither writing nor signature is required by equity, and an equitable assignment will be effective if it is made by conduct or orally. All that is required is an intention manifested to the intended assignee to make a present assignment (*William Brandt's Sons & Co v Dunlop Rubber Co Ltd* [1905] AC 454).

♦ When the creditor declares himself to be a trustee for the intended assignee. Such a trust may be express or implied from the agreement, eg where the assignor undertakes to account to the assignee for sums paid to him by the original creditor (*International Factors Ltd v Rodriguez* [1979] QB 351).

♦ When the creditor notifies the debtor directing him to make payment to the third party who is the intended assignee. In *Re Kent and Sussex Saw Mills Ltd* [1947] Ch 177 it was held that such a direction must be given in pursuance of a prior agreement between the creditor and third party, or be communicated to the third party subsequently (*Curran v New Park Cinemas Ltd* [1951] 1 All ER 295). A direction to the debtor that has not been assented to by the third party or subsequently notified to him is merely a revocable authority to pay, even if it is expressed as being irrevocable. The direction to the debtor must also make it clear that the right to receive payment has become vested in the assignee and that the creditor is no longer entitled to receive payment (*James Talcott Ltd v John Lewis & Co Ltd* [1940] 3 All ER 592).

Priorities

Priority between competing equitable assignees and charges is governed by the rule in *Dearle v Hall* (1828) 3 Russ 1 and priority goes to the first to give notice of his interest to the debtor, unless he has notice of an earlier assignment at the time he acquires his interest. Notice of a prior assignment can be actual or constructive as between competing equable assignees; if neither assignee has given notice to the debtor, assignments rank in the order in which they were created. An earlier assignee may rank after a subsequent assignee if the equity's are not equal (*Rice v Rice* (1854) 2 Drew 73).

Assignment of part of a debt

Assignments of parts of term loans are relatively common. The assignment may be effected by way of a sale of participations by the original lending bank or the partial assignment may be effected in connection with the implementation of certain forms of pro rata sharing clause.

Under English law, there is no objection to the assignment of part of a debt and it is possible to split up a debt into several portions. Any objection that splitting the debt subjects the debtor to a multiplicity of actions is met by the rule that, as the assignment is equitable, all parties interested in the debt must be joined in an action against the debtor by any assignee. It is not permissible to assign part of a judgment debt (*Foster v Baker* [1910] 2 KB 636). A partial assignment is an equitable assignment and not within s 136 of the Law of Property Act 1925.

Syndicated loans

The basis of syndicated loans is that two or more banks each agree to make separate loans to a borrower on common terms governed by a single agreement between all the parties. Large loans, where a single bank is unable or unwilling, to advance the loan lend themselves to syndication and both the amount and the purpose for which the money is being borrowed may determine the size of the lending syndicate.

The loan is initiated by the grant of a mandate to a single bank (managing or arranging bank).

♦ The main function of the arranging bank is to put together the loan.

♦ The arranging bank may also agree to underwrite the loan (agree that it will lend the whole amount if it cannot find other lenders to join the syndicate). The mandate is generally expressed as a non-legally binding commitment that is subject to contract, ie it operates as a commercial understanding between the parties until the formal loan documentation is completed. If the mandate is not expressed to be subject to contract, it may be commercially binding if its terms are sufficiently precise.

♦ The arranging bank will prepare an information memorandum about the borrower and the loan. The Information Memorandum generally contains:
  ● details of the loan, eg as to its maturity, interest rate, purpose etc;
  ● details of the history and business of the borrower;
  ● details of the management of the borrower;
  ● the borrower's financial statements.

225

Where the loan is to finance a project that relies for its repayment on that project, the information memorandum will often contain full costs and analysis of the cash flow of the project on various dated assumptions indicating how the loan may be serviced.

This will be used, together with supporting documentation, to market the loan to other banks. The loan documentation is generally negotiated first with the borrower and then provided to the proposed syndicate members. Execution of the loan agreement brings about direct contractual relations between the borrower and the banks that are members of the lending syndicate. Each bank in the syndicate will enter into a debtor/creditor relationship with the borrower. Member banks do not underwrite each other in a normal syndicated loan. All of the loans are made on precisely the same terms, contributions to loans are made by banks in proportion to their commitments and payments by the borrower are generally divided between the banks in the same proportion.

To ease the burdens of administration of the loan facility, one of the banks will be appointed agent of the syndicate for the purposes of carrying out administrative functions and rarely does this bank have significant management functions. The banks may agree to delegate limited decisions to majority control, eg certain waivers of non-payment obligations and the right to accelerate the loan on an event of default.

A syndicated loan must be distinguished from loan participation. In the latter, only one bank, the lead bank, enters into the loan agreement with the borrower. The lead bank then sells part of its interest in the loan to other banks (the participants). The transfer will be covered by a participation agreement.

Terms of a syndicated loan agreement

In 1999, the Loan Market Association, the Association of Corporate Treasurers, and major city law firms, introduced recommended forms of primary loan documentation. Such attempts to standardize documentation used in syndicated loans have generally been successful. Syndicated loan agreements generally provide that:

- each bank will make loans up to its specified commitment during the commitment period;
- each bank's obligations are several;
- each bank's rights are divided.

These provisions recognize the fact that each bank makes a separate loan to the borrower and failure by one bank to perform its obligations does not absolve the other banks from performance. In normal syndicated loans, the banks do not underwrite each other.

Each bank may separately enforce its own rights, unless the bank has agreed to refrain from so doing under the terms of the loan agreement, and it is common for the syndicate banks to agree to abide by the decision of a majority of the members. A syndicated loan will generally also contain a pro rata sharing clause, eg each bank agrees to share with the other banks amounts recovered from the borrower (eg by way of set-off, litigation, taking into account the proportion each has contributed).

Legal nature of a loan syndicate

Syndicate banks do not generally enter into a partnership agreement, ie they are not entering into a relationship in which net profits will be shared between the members of the syndicate.

The members of the syndicate therefore do not have fiduciary duties imposed on them except in exceptional circumstances. There is some support for imposing a fiduciary relationship between the arranging bank and other banks. A number of cases have explored this issue.

- ♦ In *UBAF Ltd v European American Banking Corpn* [1948] 1 QB 713 the defendants invited UBAS to participate in two loans that the defendants intended to make to two companies which were part of a shipping group loaned to them. UBAS claimed that the defendants represented to it that the loans were 'attractive financing for two companies in a sound and profitable group'. Relying on these representations, UBAS participated in the loan and when the borrowers defaulted, UBAS started proceedings against the defendants alleging, inter alia, deceit and misrepresentation under s 2(1) of the Misrepresentation Act 1967, and negligence. Although the court did not consider the specific question of the arranging bank's relationship with the participants Ackner LJ stated that the defendant received money on behalf of UBAS and the other participants.

It must be remembered that this view was merely obiter in an interlocutory appeal on a jurisdictional point where the court did not hear full argument on the fiduciary issue.

- ♦ In contrast, in *Natwest Australia Bank Ltd v Trans Continental Corpn Ltd* [1993] ATPR (Digest) 46-109 the Supreme Court of Victoria was willing to impose a duty of care, the breach of which resulted in the arranging bank being held liable to the participant for its negligence. The facts of the case were that the arranging bank prepared and distributed an information memorandum to perspective participants but did not disclose that the borrower had given a third party guarantee supporting company obligations, including one in favour of the arranging bank itself. The most recent accounts of the borrower failed to disclose these contingent liabilities. When the borrower went into liquidation, a participant claimed the arranging bank had been negligent in failing to disclose the existence of these earlier contingent liabilities. The participant had enquired specifically about such liabilities and claimed it would not have participated in the loan had the liabilities been disclosed. The court held that, given the nature of the relationship between the arranging bank and the participant banks, and the specific enquiries that had been made of the participant, the arranging bank was under a duty to disclose the existence of the guarantees.

◆ Further, in *Suimtomo Bank Ltd v Banque Bruxelles Lambert SA* [1977] 1 Lloyd's Rep 487 the court held that the arranging bank's duties, rights and obligations under the loan agreement did not prevent a general duty of care arising in tort. The fact that the arranging bank owed a limited scope of duties as an agent under the terms of the contract governing the loan agreement did not prevent wider duties being imposed under tort.

Law and participations

In loan participation, the lead bank enters into a loan agreement with the borrower and then sells part of his interest in the loan to other banks (to participants). The methods for granting participation are:

◆ assignment;
◆ novation;
◆ sub-participation;
◆ risk participation

An **assignment** will involve the transfer of the lead bank's rights to all or part of its interests in the loan to the participants. The participant is given a proprietary interest in the loan that under s 136 of the Law of Property Act 1925 will be a legal interest. Alternatively, an equitable interest will be granted where the legal assignment does not fulfill the terms of s 136. A term in the loan agreement may prohibit the assignment of a loan by the lead bank. In such circumstances, any purported assignment will be void against the borrower (*Linden Gardens Trust Ltd v Lenesta Sludge Disposals Ltd* [1994] 1 AC 85). An assignment will only transfer the rights, and not the obligations of the lead bank to the participant (*Tolhurst v Associated Portland Cement Manufacturers Ltd* [1902] 2 KB 660).

Novation involves the substitution of a new contract for an existing contract. Novation actually involves a change of the parties in circumstances where it is agreed between the borrower and the lead bank that the lead bank will be released and the participant will take its place as the other party to the contract. The participant's agreement to provide further finance to the borrower generally constitutes consideration to support this new contract. Unlike an assignment, novation requires the consent of all the parties and may actually be provided for in the original contract.

Sub-participations and risk participations can be distinguished from assignment, and novation has no effect on the underlying loan agreement made between the lead bank and the borrower. Sub-participations and loan participations are no more than separate contracts made between the lead bank and the participant. In the case of a sub-participation, the participant places a deposit with the lead bank equal to the amount of its participation and the lead bank agrees to pay to the participant amounts equal to the participant's share of the receipts by the lead bank. The participant has no claim against the borrower and may save the risk of both defaults by the borrower and by the lead bank. In the case of risk participation, the participant, in return for payment of a fee, gives the lead bank a guarantee in relation to the failure of the borrower to pay under the terms of the loan agreement. The participant does not provide funding to the lead bank but takes the risk of default by the borrower.

In order to allow the transfer of relevant information between the lead bank and participants, the loan agreement usually contains a clause under which the borrower consents to disclosure of information about the loan that might otherwise be caught by the duty of confidentiality.

Lender liability

Lender liability can arise in a wide variety of circumstances, eg a bank is guilty of misrepresentation, gives negligent advice to the borrower, does not exercise reasonable skill and care, or knowingly receives trust property in breach of trust and is liable as a constructive trustee etc. These forms of claim are well recognized and are dealt with elsewhere. The basis of this section is to explore liability against commercial lenders in a number of distinct areas.

Pre-contractual negotiation

Where a bank gives investment advice, it owes a contractual duty, as well as a duty in tort under *Hedley Byrne & Co v Heller Partners Ltd* [1964] AC 465 and it must take reasonable care in order to avoid liability. Consequently, when acting as a financial adviser, the bank owes a duty to exercise reasonable skill and care in the execution of its functions. The question that has arisen is whether a bank or other commercial lender is under a duty to give investment advice to a prospective borrower. Normally, the bank does not assume a duty of care to advise its customer on the soundness or viability of the transaction for which the loan is required. In *Williams and Glyn's Bank Ltd v Barnes* [1981] Com LR 205 the defendant, an experienced businessman, was a customer of the bank, as was his company. In his personal capacity he borrowed in excess of £1 million to invest in the company, which was heavily indebted to the bank. When the company collapsed and the bank called in the personal loan, the defendant argued that the bank should have warned him, as its customer, that the transaction involved was unsound. The court rejected this argument and held that the bank was under no duty in law to consider the prudence of the lending from the customer's point of view, or to advise on its commercial soundness. Such a duty can only arise in contract (express or implied), on the assumption of responsibility under *Hedley Byrne,* or in a fiduciary situation. The position is the same even if the bank knows that the borrowing, as intended by the customer, is imprudent. Following the Barnes case, therefore, the mere grant of a loan does not in itself involve an assumption of a duty of care in tort under *Hedley Byrne* and nor does it impose a fiduciary relationship between the borrower and the lender. This reasoning was further followed in *Lloyd's Bank plc v Cobb* (18 December 1991, unreported) where the court held that the mere request for a loan coupled with the supply of information to the bank in respect of the project is not sufficient to make clear to the bank that its advice is being sought on the prudence of the transaction in respect of which the loan will be used. Moreover, where the bank examines a borrowing proposal or business plan it does so merely for its own purposes as a lender and not for the benefit of the borrower. A lender can become liable for failing to give proper advice when it has assumed responsibility and reliance can be shown on the part of the borrower. In *Verity and Spindler v Lloyd's Bank plc* [1995] CLC 1557 the claimants were looking for property to buy and renovate and approached the bank because it advertised a financial advisory service. They proposed to buy a particular property that had major structural defects but at the same time looked at another property. The bank manager encouraged them to buy the second property and agreed to a loan. The claimants purchased the property and lost money in the property slump that followed. When the bank sought repayment of the loan, the claimants resisted claiming that the bank had assumed a duty of care that it had breached in giving negligent advice. The court held, on the particular facts, the bank had assumed a duty to the claimant and should have given advice with due care. The court appears to have been influenced by the fact that the claimants were financially inexperienced; the manager had inspected the properties (not usual) and encouraged them to purchase the second property. The court also had regard to the wording of the bank's business literature advertising its services. In *Frost v James Finlay Bank Ltd* [2001] All ER (D) 261 the court held that the bank owed no duty of care to consider the matter from the borrower's point of view when it made it a condition of lending that the borrower changed her insurers, although the bank came under a duty of care when it acted as broker in effecting the new insurance.

The courts appear to a draw distinction between financially experienced and financially inexperienced customers when assessing the extent of a bank's duties. In the *Barnes* case [1981] Com LR 205, the court took into consideration that the borrower was a businessman 'of full age and competence' whereas in *Woods v Martins Bank Ltd* [1959] 1 QB 55, the claimant was seen as a gullible young man with no business experience.

Management and termination of the loan facility

The terms of the loan facility are generally considered to be paramount and the courts will construe these terms to give effect to the intention of the parties. Only in exceptional circumstances will the courts imply additional duties into such contracts, eg a duty to increase the facility or to give adequate notice of refusal to do so. There is no general power given to the courts to review the fairness of terms imposed on corporate borrowers, although relief may be given in certain areas, eg in relation to penalties. Nevertheless, there is no general doctrine of 'unconscionability' recognized as part of English law. In favour of consumer borrowers, the Unfair Terms in Consumer Contracts Regulations 1999, SI 1999/2083, allow the courts to set aside a term in consumer contracts that if it has not been individually negotiated, is contrary to the requirement of good faith and causes a significant imbalance in the parties rights and obligations. Thus in *Director General of Fair Trading v First National Bank plc* [2000] QB 672 the Court of Appeal held that a default provision in a loan agreement made between a lending bank and a consumer borrower was unfair under the 1999 Regulations and that a term had not been drawn to the consumer's attention and would operate to his detriment in a way he could not reasonably expect.

The courts take a strict approach to the lender's right to terminate a loan facility. Where the facility agreement gives the lender the right to terminate, the courts will not readily interfere with the exercise of that right. The rules of estoppel may prevent withdrawal of the facility without reasonable notice. Moreover, with regard to overdraft or on demand facilities, the courts are reluctant to imply a term to give reasonable notice before a bank refuses further finance (*Socomex Ltd v Banque Bruxelles Lampert SA* [1966] 1 Lloyd's Rep 156). Moreover, an express term, eg for repayment of an overdraft of loan on demand, will be upheld by the courts unless the agreement as a whole shows the term to be contrary to the main provisions of the contract (*Williams & Glyn's Bank v Barnes* [1981] Com LR 205). With an 'on demand' facility, the most the borrower can expect is reasonable time to repay, and not necessarily reasonable time to re-finance from another lender. In *Bank of Baroda v Panessar* [1987] Ch 335 the bank was entitled to appoint a receiver within one hour of demanding repayment of an unspecified sum. The court expressed the view that money payable 'on demand' is repayable immediately. It may be physically impossible for a person to keep the money required to discharge the debt about his person and therefore the debtor is not in default in making the payment demanded unless and until he has had a reasonable opportunity of implementing 'whatever reasonable mechanisms of payment he may need to employ to discharge the debt'. This is limited to the time necessary for the mechanics of payment and does not extend to time required to raise money. In *Sheppard & Cooper Ltd v TSB Bank plc* [1966] 2 All ER 654, the court held that the bank was entitled to send in the receivers within 30 minutes after demanding repayment of over £600,000 from the debtor. The court expressed the view that the time available to the debtor to implement the mechanics of payment depends on the circumstances of the case. If the sum demanded is an amount that the debtor is likely to have in a bank account, the time permitted must be reasonable in all the circumstances to ensure that the debtor has time to contact his bank and make the necessary arrangements for the sum to be transferred to the creditor. If, however, the demand is made out of banking hours, the time likely to be required by the debtor to implement the mechanics of payment is likely to be longer than if the demand is made during banking hours. Where a proper demand has been made and the debtor makes it clear to the creditor that the necessary money is not available, the creditor need not give the debtor any further time before treating him as in default as in the *Sheppard* case.

Unauthorized acts by agent banks

An agent bank may be liable to a borrower for breach of warranty of authority, eg if the agent bank incorrectly confirms that the banks have consented to a waiver. The rule is that a person, or institution, who expressly or impliedly warrants that he has the authority of another, is liable for breach of warranty of authority to any person to whom the warranty is made and who suffers damage by acting on the faith of the warranty, if in fact he has no such authority (*Collen v Wright* (1857) 8 E & B 647).

♦ The borrower must have relied on the agent's representation as a warranty. Therefore if the borrower has knowledge that the agent bank has no authority his action will not succeed. If the agent bank acts without actual authority, the remaining banks in the syndicate can ratify the agent bank's conduct (*Firth v Staines* [1897] 2 QB 70). Conversely, banks may be bound by the act of their agent bank if they have expressly or impliedly represented that the agent bank has ostensible or apparent authority, even if the agent bank is not actually authorized, eg why the banks privately place limits on the agent's discretions set out in the loan agreement without informing the borrower.

♦ Where an agent bank is given discretion by the participating bank, the agent bank must exercise reasonable skill, care and diligence in the performance of its duties as an agent. If the bank complies with this standard of care, it will not be liable for negligence even though the agent bank has made a mistake or error of judgment. In *Chown v Parrott* (1863) 14 CBNS 74 an attorney exercising reasonable skill and care was held not liable for having compromised his client's action without his consent. In *Re Kingston Cotton Mill Co* [1896] 2 Ch 279 the court held that what is a reasonable amount of care and skill depends on the circumstances of the case. A sophisticated agent bank will therefore be expected to exercise a higher standard of care in the due performance of its undertakings. An agent bank is not responsible for failure to go beyond its reasonable duty, even though the loss occasioned could have been awarded by exercising an extra level of care, skill or diligence (*Morten v Hilton Gibbes & Smith* (1908) [1937] 2 KB 176).

Whether an agent bank is under a positive duty to monitor the financial condition of the borrower and to ensure that the interests of the syndicate are protected will depend on the express or implied terms of the agency contract.

♦ Where an agent bank has expressed power, eg to call for financial information and compliance certificates from the borrower, the frequency with which and the circumstances in which such powers are exercised will be determined in the light of the contractual terms or in the absence of express provisions in accordance wit the agent's duty to exercise care and skill in the interests of the banks. Normally the agent bank will call for compliance certificates at fixed intervals depending on the complexity of the loan, and may do so additionally if it appears that an un-notified default has occurred. Accounts and other formal notices received from the borrower should be passed to the syndicate members without delay.

Loan agreements may provide that the agent is to act as the representative of the banks with the purpose of the receipt of formal notices from the borrower.

♦ A formal notification so provided is effective if the agent receives it within the scope of his actual or apparent authority, whether or not it is subsequently communicated to the principal. This would not, however be the case if the borrower knew that the agent bank intended to conceal the matter from the other syndicate banks (*Blackley v National Mutual Life Association of Australasia Ltd* [1971] NZLR 1038).

Whether an agent bank is under a duty to pass on information relating to the loan to the syndicate bank depends on the express and implied terms of the agency contract. In the absence of a specific clause, the agent bank is under a duty to keep the principal advised on matters material to the agency (*Keppel v Wheeler and Atkins* [1927] 1 KB 577).

Facility letters

In some cases, a bank may not be willing to give its customer an advance or extend to him loan facilities but may be willing to back his arrangements with another credit provider.

♦ The bank may therefore be willing to guarantee a loan obtained by the customer from another financial institution.

♦ Another method is to provide the customer with a line of credit or an acceptance credit.

In such circumstances, the letter of facility issued in respect of an acceptance credit will enable the customer to draw bills of exchange on the bank for an amount not exceeding an agreed ceiling. The bank's signature as acceptor enables the customer (drawer) to discount the instruments in the commercial bills market. When the bill becomes due, the discounter, who acquires the bill through a bill broker, presents it for payment to the bank that issued the acceptance (issuing bank). The customer will place the issuing bank in funds for meeting the acceptance or may require the bill to be 'rolled over'. Under the roll-over arrangement, the customer draws a fresh bill for the amount to require discharging the original bill, together with any fee charged for the grant of the facility plus an acceptance fee for each bill.

The customer must bear in mind that the amount paid to him when the bill is negotiated will be its face value less the discount charge and therefore must draw a bill for a total amount that will ensure he receives the required net. It therefore follows that whenever a rollover is required, the new instrument will be for an amount higher than that of the retired bill.

The effect of an acceptance credit is to enable the customer to raise funds on the issuing bank's credit. In this sense, the arrangement is similar to one in which the customer obtains a loan granted by a financial institution in reliance on the bank's guarantee. In the case of acceptance credits, the bank functions as a surety. It has the right to obtain reimbursement from the customer for any amount paid out on bills drawn under the facility. As against the discounters of the customer's bills, the bank that accepts the bills assumes primary liability. An advantage of an acceptance credit is that it leaves the customer with freedom in respect of the sources from which he obtains each advance and discounts the bills accepted by the bank with the credit proviso which offers him the most favourable terms.

Bills of exchange drawn under an acceptance credit give rise to special problems. They stem from the fact that, as between the bank that assumes the role of acceptor of the bills and the customer, the bank acts in a role similar to that of the surety. It accepts the bills in order to facilitate their discount. The object of the transaction is to enable the customer to obtain funds on the bank's credit. There are two questions, which must be asked in respect of these bills.

1. Are bills drawn under acceptance credits accommodation bills? Section 28(1) of the Bills of Exchange Act 1882 provides that 'an accommodation party to a bill is a person who has signed a bill as drawer, acceptor, or endorser, without receiving value therefore, and for the purpose of lending his name to some other person'. In practice, a bill is called an accommodation bill where it is accepted, drawn or endorsed for the accommodation of a party who furnishes no consideration for it. Special principles apply to such bills as follows.

   – An accommodation party is liable on the bill to hold of a value even if, at the time the holder took the bill, he knew that the party involved signed it for accommodation purposes (s 28(2)). Thus, the absence or failure of consideration cannot be pleaded as a defense to an action brought by a holder for value, although the accommodation party can raise, as a defense to the holder's action, any specific defect in the transferor's title of which the holder was aware when he took the bill.

   – The party accommodated is not always discharged from his liability if the holder fails to comply with one of the procedural steps described by the Bills of Exchange Act. Thus, presentment for payment is dispensed as against an endorser, for whose accommodation the bill has been drawn, if he has no reason to expect that payment will be made is presented (*Hormby v McLaren* (1908) 24 TLR 494). Notice of dishonour and protest are dispensed with in similar circumstances.

–   Where the party accommodated pays an accommodation bill in due course, the bill is discharged (s 59(3)). The bill ceases to be a negotiable instrument and the accommodated party, either the drawer or an endorser, cannot enforce it against the acceptor.

An accommodation bill is therefore governed by the general rules of negotiable instruments and is subject to some modifications.

2.   It is important to consider whether a bill, drawn under an acceptance credit, is an accommodation bill.

–   Although the answer is not entirely clear, it must be remembered that a person is an accommodating party if he draws, accepts, or endorses the bill for another person's accommodation and he acts without receiving value.

3.   A bank that accepts a bill drawn under an acceptance credit will act for the drawer's accommodation but will invariably receive a fee and the question, therefore, is whether or not it receives consideration for acceptance. In *Oriental Financial Corpn v Overend, Gurney & Co* (1871) LR 7 Ch App 142 (a case decided before the Bills of Exchange Act 1882 was enacted) the court took the view that bills drawn under an acceptance credit were not accommodation bills, as the acceptor had received a fee. More recent authorities are equally inconclusive: in *Re Securitibank Ltd* [1978] 1 NZLR 97 the New Zealand Supreme Court expressed the view that bills drawn under an acceptance credit were not accommodation bills. The fee paid by the customer was not a mere acceptance fee, the amount of which was to escalate if the customer failed to remit to the bank on time the amounts required for meeting the acceptances. The bank therefore received a valuable consideration beyond a mere acceptance fee. In *KD Morris & Sons Property Ltd (In Liquidation) v Bank of Queensland Ltd* [1980] 50 ALJR 424 those issued under a facility were referred to as accommodation bills although the issuing bank that received an acceptance fee.

The legal authorities, such as they are, do not provide a solution and the question which must be asked is whether a consideration, received by the accommodation party, is furnished for his becoming a party to the bill. The question is whether the fee is received by the bank for its acceptance of the bill or for the issuing of the facility.

Bankruptcy problems

An issuing bank that provides an acceptance credit may require the customer to furnish security, eg the customer may be asked to deposit commercial paper with the bank or may be asked to give a charge over assets. Problems may arise where the bank fails after receiving the securities but before it meets bills drawn under the acceptance credit.

In such circumstances, the customer, acting as drawer and possibly also as first endorser, is liable jointly and severally with the bank to pay the bills. If the bank dishonors the bills, the customer is obliged to pay them. The position must be treated as similar to that relating to commercial documentary credits, where the customer's obligation to pay for the goods will revive if the issuing bank becomes insolvent (*ED and F Man Ltd v Nigerian Sweets & Confectionery Co Ltd* [1977] 2 Lloyd's Rep 50). A customer who has remitted the funds needed for meeting the bills to the issuing bank before its insolvency has no option but to pay the amount involved over again to the holder. The customer's remedy then will be to prove for the debt as a general creditor.

When the customer pays the bills drawn under the acceptance credit, he is entitled to reclaim any securities deposited with the bank. Where an endorser pays the bill then he has a right to be subrograted to the holder's rights.

Seven

Insolvency, bankruptcy and liquidation

7.1 Corporate insolvency and the position of the lending bank

The realization of the security

Only as a last resort, and after the possibility of obtaining payment through other methods have failed, will the bank rely on its right to realize any security it holds for a loan or advance made to the borrowing customer. If the borrowing customer is a company and clearly insolvent, so that full recovery of the company's indebtedness is not possible, a bank will rely on its security. For this reason it is important for a bank to ensure that the value of the security is sufficient to cover the amount advanced when it makes its initial advance, and to check periodically to ensure that the advance and any further sums are covered by the security.

Insolvency practitioners

Only an authorized insolvency practitioner may act as a liquidator (or as a receiver, administrator, supervisor of a voluntary arrangement, etc). He must be an individual. Companies and partnerships cannot act as insolvency practitioners. If he is an undischarged bankrupt he may not act in this capacity except by leave of the court (Insolvency Act 1986, s 390). To obtain authorization the applicant must satisfy either a professional body to which the DTI has delegated its powers of authorization in respect of its own members, or a competent authority (tribunal) appointed by the DTI that he is:

(a) a fit and proper person;

(b) satisfies prescribed requirements in respect of education, practical training and experience.

The intention and effect of this system is to confine the functions of insolvency practitioners to members of certain prominent professional bodies, mainly accountants, and among members of those bodies whose members have specialized in insolvency work. An authorized insolvency practitioner is required to obtain renewed authorization at intervals, when his record will be taken into account.

The Company Directors Disqualification Act 1986, s 7 contains 'reporting provisions' by which an insolvency practitioner who is acting in any of the capacities mentioned above in connection with a company will report to the DTI on certain aspects of the past performance of the directors. Indirectly, therefore, the restriction of insolvency work to authorized practitioners is a means of introducing much closer examination of the record of directors of companies which have become insolvent, possibly owing to the neglect of those directors.

The system of authorized insolvency practitioners is intended to go much further than restraining malpractice. Its purpose is to promote a stringent review by competent experts of the management of companies that have become insolvent, with some pressure on them to be thorough in their investigations.

Voluntary arrangements

The Insolvency Act 1986 (ss 1–7) introduced the voluntary arrangement scheme. The scheme allows a three-quarters majority of the company's unsecured creditors, voting at a meeting of the creditors, to impose on all unsecured creditors a scheme of arrangement or composition of arrangement that has been proposed by the company's directors. A voluntary arrangement is an insolvency procedure and is usually invoked in relation to insolvent companies and not solvent companies. A proposal for a voluntary arrangement must be reported to the court but does not require the court's approval.

Proposal for a voluntary arrangement

Where the company is a going concern, the proposal will be made by the company's directors acting collectively (Insolvency Act 1986, s 1(1)). In such circumstances the directors retain their powers of management and although the company does not benefit from a general moratorium under which creditors are prevented from enforcing their debts, the creditors who agree to be bound by it once it has been approved will be prevented from taking independent action for recovery of their debts.

The scheme is prepared under the supervision of a qualified insolvency practitioner, known as 'the nominee'. If the person nominated to act as nominee is already the liquidator or administrator of the company he can submit the proposals to the creditors as part of the normal liquidation, or administration process. If the nominee is not the liquidator or administrator of the company he must submit a report to the court stating whether or not, in his opinion, the scheme is viable and whether a meeting of the creditors should be called.

The purpose of the creditors' meeting is to decide whether or not to approve the proposal. The creditors have considerable discretion in dealing with proposals before them; they are not restricted to simply approving or rejecting the scheme as presented but they may modify the arrangements provided that the fundamental characteristics of the scheme remain unaltered and provided that the debtor company agrees (Insolvency Act 1986, s 4(1)). The meeting cannot approve any proposal or modification that adversely prejudices the rights of any secured or preferential creditors to be paid in priority or to be paid pari passu with each other, unless those likely to be affected approve the arrangement (s 4(3)). This means that no proposal can go forward without the consent of the holders of the floating charges over the company's property. The outcome of each meeting must be reported to the court. Once the proposals have been approved at the creditors' meeting, they become binding on every person who had notice and who was entitled to vote at the meeting, whether or not such persons actually attended.

If at the time the creditors consent to a voluntary arrangement there is an administration or a winding-up order in force, the court may decide to stay all proceedings in the administration or liquidation, or may give directions in respect of the order modifying the normal course of the administration or liquidation (s 5(3) and (4) of the Insolvency Act 1986).

The voluntary arrangement involves the minimal degree of court involvement and formal approval of the scheme by the court is unnecessary. If, however, the scheme is challenged within 28 days of the court receiving the chairman's report of the creditors' meeting, it will be subject to a full scrutiny. A creditor of the company, its liquidator or administrator, or any insolvency practitioner may challenge the scheme on the grounds that it unfairly prejudices the interests of the creditors, member or contributory of the company, or that there was some material irregularity at, or in relation to, the meeting (Insolvency Act 1986, s 6).

If a proposed scheme is approved or is not subject to challenge, the nominee then becomes the supervisor of the composition or scheme and assumes full responsibility for its implementation. The terms of the scheme must follow the requirements of s 1 of the Insolvency Act 1986. The position of the secured and preferential creditors is protected by s 1(3) and (4), but such creditors could choose to modify their rights under the arrangement.

Alternative procedure for small companies

One of the difficulties for a company in preparing a proposal for a voluntary arrangement is that, when the proposal is circulated to creditors before their meeting, any creditor may take individual action to defeat the proposal, eg by appointing a receiver, repossessing hire-purchase goods or presenting a winding up petition. This can be prevented where the company goes into administration, although that process in itself may prove expensive. To solve this problem the Insolvency Act 1986, s 1A and Sch A1 (which came into force on January 2003), enables an 'eligible company' (a small company) to obtain a moratorium on creditor action while a proposal for a voluntary action is considered, without having to go into administration. A moratorium cannot be obtained until there is a viable proposal for an arrangement and a nominee has agreed to act.

The principle condition for being eligible for a moratorium is in Sch. A1, Para 3, and is that, in the year ending with date of filing, or in the company's financial year that ended last before that date, the company has satisfied two or more of the requirements for being a small company (turnover does not exceed £11.2m; its balance sheet total (total assets) does not exceed £1.4m; its weekly average number of employees during the financial year does not exceed 50). A company will not be eligible for a moratorium if it is a holding company of a group that did not qualify as a small or medium-sized group. The moratorium procedure is not available to insurance, banking or various financial group companies.

The directors must notify the nominee that the moratorium has begun (Insolvency Act 1986, Sch A1, para 10). The effect of the moratorium is that the company must state that such an order is in force and identify the nominee in every invoice, order for goods or business correspondence issued by or its behalf, or in which its name appears. It must not obtain credit, including advance payments from customers of or more than £250, from anyone informed of the moratorium (Insolvency Act 1986, Sch A1, para 17). Further, it is not possible for a floating charge to specify that obtaining or preparing for a moratorium crystallizes the charge (Insolvency Act 1986, Sch A1, para 43).

Administration orders

'Administration orders' were introduced by the Insolvency Act 1986, and the Enterprise Act 2002, s 248, has introduced improvements. This replaces IA 1986, Pt II, with a single new s 8, which introduces new Sch B1 that now contains the statutory regime relating to administration. The administration procedure requires greater judicial involvement and affords protection to the company's assets during the period of administration. The function of the administrator is to devise and implement a satisfactory rescue plan. An administrator may be appointed in the following ways.

(a) By the court making an administration order, on the application of the company itself, its directors, one of more creditors, the supervisor of a voluntary arrangement, or a justices' chief executive following non-payment of a fine imposed on a company (Insolvency Act 1986, s 7(4)(b) and Sch B1, paras 10 and 12).

(b) By the holder of a floating charge over the whole or substantially the whole of the company's property (para 14).

(c) By the company itself or its directors (para 22).

An appointment by the court or the company or its directors cannot be made unless the company is, or is likely to become, unable to pay its debts (para 11(b) and 27(2)(a)), and an appointment by the floating charge cannot be made unless the floating charge is enforceable (ie the company is unable to pay the debt secured the charge (para 16).

Prior to the Enterprise Act 2002 only the court could appoint an administrator. Companies and creditors now also have this power to make an appointment out of court. An application to the court will be required under the following circumstaces.

(1) The company is being wound up voluntarily or by the court, in which case an administration application may be made only by the liquidator (Insolvency Act 1986, Sch B1, paras 8 and 37).

(2) An administrative receiver of the company has been appointed, in which case the court will make an appointment only if the chargee who appointed the receiver consents or the court is satisfied that, if an order were made, the floating charge under which the receiver was appointed would be discharged or avoided or declared invalid by the court under ss 238–240 or 245 (Sch B1, paras 17(b), 25(c), and 39).

The administrative receiver must vacate office if an administrator is appointed (para 41(1)).

Appointment by the company or its directors

Either the company or its directors may appoint an administrator (Insolvency Act 1986, Sch B1, para 22) but no such appointment can be made if any insolvency or liquidation procedure is already in progress or there is pending an application for the appointment of an administrator or winding-up order. A qualified insolvency practitioner willing to act as an administrator must be found and notice giving the name of the proposed administrator must be given to the holders of floating charges entitled to appoint an administrative receiver or administrator. If the notice period (five business days) has lapsed and no floating charge holder has appointed an administrative holder or applied to the court for a winding-up order, then the directors may appoint the person named as administrator. A notice of appointment must be filed with the court.

Appointment by holder of floating charge

The holder of a 'qualifying floating charge' over a company's property may appoint an administrator under the Insolvency Act 1986, Sch B1, para 14. No appointment may be made under para 14 if any insolvency or liquidation procedure (apart from a voluntary arrangement) is already in process.

Administrator's proposals

The administrator's initial task will be to prepare proposals to achieve the purpose of administration (Insolvency Act 1986, Sch B1, para 49(1)). A statement of proposals must be sent to the Registrar and to creditors and members of the company within eight weeks of the company entering administration, although that time limit may be extended, on an application to the court (paras 49 and 107).

The proposals must be put to a creditors' meeting within ten weeks of the company entering administration, but this is again subject to an extension permitted by the court. A creditor's meeting is not required if the administrator advises that the company can pay all creditors in full, or that it cannot pay unsecured creditors anything other than their statutory share of assets covered by a floating charge (s 176(a) of the Insolvency Act 1986, will provide that an administrative receiver must set aside 10% of the property covered by a floating charge for the satisfaction of unsecured debts) or that objectives (1) and (2) cannot be achieved (para 52(1)). Even then, a meeting can be requisitioned by 10% (in value) of the creditors.

The creditor's meeting may approve the administrator's proposals, approve the proposals with modification provided the administrator accepts any modifications or further gives any approval. The administrator must then report the meeting's decision to the court and the registrar of a company. An administrator may propose a composition or arrangement (para 49(3)) but the creditor's meeting in administration cannot impose a composition or an arrangement.

Decisions to adopt resolutions at the meeting of creditors are taken, by a simple majority in value, of the creditors who are present and vote. Only unsecured creditors can vote.

If creditors approve the proposals, the administrator must manage the company's affairs and property in accordance with the proposals (Insolvency Act 1986, Sch B1, para 68).

Powers of an administrator

An administrator has wide powers that are set out in the Insolvency Act 1986, Sch B1 para 59(1).

> 'The administrator of a company may do anything necessary or expedient for the management of the affairs, business and property of the company.'

The administrator has all the powers listed in Sch 1. In the discharge of his powers the administrator will act as an agent of the company, like an administrative receiver. An administrator is not burdened with a statutory liability on contracts. A person dealing with an administrator in good faith and for value is entitled to assume that the administrator is acting within his powers. The administrator may therefore dispose of any of the company's property that is subject to a charge, which as originally created was a floating charge, as if the property was not subject to the charge. The chargee will then have the same priority in respect of any property of the company directly or indirectly representing the property disposed of as he would have had in respect of the property disposed of.

The administrator may apply to the court for authority to dispose of property subject to any charge other than a floating charge as if it were free from the charge, provided the proceeds of the sale go first towards paying the chargee.

Purpose of administration

An administrator must perform his functions with the objectives of para 3(1):

(1)   rescuing the company as a going concern;

(2)   achieving a better result for the company's creditors as a whole than would be likely if the company were wound up (without first being in administration); or

(3)   realising property in order to make a distribution to one or more secured or preferential creditors.

The first objective must be given priority unless the administrator believes it is not reasonably practicable or that objective (2) would achieve a better result for the company's creditors as a whole. Objective (3) should only be pursued if the liquidator believes that the other two objectives cannot be achieved or are likely to harm the interests of the creditors.

Once an administration order is made the administrator must send to the company and publish in the prescribed manner a notice of the order. He must notify the company's registry within 14 days and the company's creditors within 28 days of the making of the order.

The company's business correspondence, including invoices and orders issued during the period of administration must indicate that an administration has been made against the company.

On appointment, the administrator must take control of the company's assets. If the administrator is to carry out his functions and devise a rescue plan there must be an exchange of information between him and the company directors who must prepare a statement of the company's affairs. The statement of affairs must be verified by affidavit and should include details of the company's assets, debts and liabilities, details of the creditors and the nature of securities held by them, together with any other necessary information.

The administrator has considerable powers to do such acts and enter into such transactions as are necessary for the management of the company's affairs and business and the achievement of the purpose for which the administration order was made. He has specific powers to carry on the business of the company, to raise or borrow money and to grant security over the company's property, to refer disputes to arbitration, to appoint a solicitor, accountant or other professionally qualified person to assist him in the performance of his functions, to present or defend a petition for the winding up of the company, to employ and dismiss employees and to do all things incidental to the exercise of these and other specific powers conferred on him. Additionally, the administrator has authority to remove and appoint directors and unless the administrator consents, neither the company nor its officers can exercise any power so as to interfere with the administrator's functions.

In exercising his powers, the administrator is deemed to be acting as the company's agent and a person dealing with him in good faith and for value is protected if the administrator exceeds his authority.

An administrator may be personally liable on any contracts made by him and any contracts of employment adopted by him. On vacating his office an administrator will normally be released from all liability for any acts or omissions unless he has misapplied company assets or acted in breach of duty.

Moratorium

When a company is in administration the Insolvency Act 1986 (Sch B1, para 43) prevents creditors, unless they act with the consent of the administrator or the permission of the court, from enforcing security, entering in execution or distraining on the company's goods. Further, no steps may be taken to repossess goods in the company's possession under any hire purchase agreement except with consent or permission. The company cannot adopt a resolution to wind up and the court cannot make a winding-up order, except on grounds of public interest. The moratorium also applies during the period when an application is made to the court for an administration order until the administration order takes effect or the application is dismissed, when the holder of a floating charge files with the court a notice of intention to appoint an administrator until the appointment takes effect (provided this is within five business days) or from when a notice of intention to appoint an administrator if filed with the court by the company or its directors until the appointment takes effect (provided this is within ten days business days).

An interim moratorium order may be made under para 44. It does not prevent or require the court's permission for:

(i)   presentation of a public-interest winding-up petition by the Secretary of State or the Financial Services Authority;

(ii)   the appointment of an administrator by the holder of a floating charge;

(iii)   the appointment of an administrative receiver;

(iv)   the carrying out of an administrative receiver of his functions.

Administration automatically ends after one year unless the administrator's term is extended by consent of the creditors or by court order. There can only be one extension by consent for a period no longer than six months. The court can give any number of extensions it thinks fit.

An administrator may terminate the administration, by application to the court if he was appointed by the court, if he thinks that its purpose has been sufficiently achieve or by notice to the court and the registrar.

Administrative receivers

An administrative receiver is a receiver or manager of the whole, or substantially the whole, of a company's property appointed by the holders of a debenture secured by a floating charge. Administrative receiverships arise because of the security contract made between a company and when one or more of its creditors under the company agrees to confer a certain type of contractual advantage on that creditor over the others.

Administrative receiverships are being restricted. Under the Insolvency Act 1986 (Sch B1 para 14) the holder of an existing floating charge that confers a right to appoint an administrative receiver will instead be entitled to appoint an administrator, who will be an officer of the court and who must perform his functions in the interests of the company's creditors as a whole (Sch B1, para 3(2)). For floating charges created, the provision becomes ineffective, and it will not be possible to appoint an administrative receiver at all (s 72A(1)) except for: a debt of £50million or more financed by a marketable loan (s 72B); where a person has step-in rights in relation to a project company (ie rights to take over responsibility for carrying out the project or arranging for it to be carried out and where the project is a public-private partnership project, a utility project or will involve £50milion or more of financing (Sch A, para 6 and ss 72C-E); to enforce charges that secure payment for purchases on recognized investment exchanges (s 72F); where the company is a registered social landlord (s 72G).

An administrative receiver is a receiver or manager of the whole (or substantially the whole) of a company's property, appointed by or on behalf of the holders of any debentures of the company secured by a charge which was created as a floating charge, or a person who would be such a receiver or manager but for the appointment of some other person as the receiver of part of the company's property (Insolvency Act 1986, s 29(2).

A receiver is, therefore, a person appointed to take control of certain property. The power to appoint a receiver will be exercisable on the occurrence of one of several specified event provided for in the debenture. The occurrence of these specified events usually indicates that the company is in financial difficulties. The most common event of non-compliance is a failure to make a demand for payment, although the demand need not specify the exact amount being claimed (*Banbury Foods Pty Ltd v National Bank of Australasia* (1984) 51 ALR 509).

From the time of appointment an administrative receiver of a company has sole authority to deal with the charged property. The directors of the company no longer have any authority to deal with the charged property, although they continue in office and are still liable, eg to submit returns and documents to the registrar (*Newhart Developments Ltd v Co-operative Commercial Bank Ltd* [1978] QB 814, although doubt was cast on the *Newhart* case in *Tudor Grange Holdings Ltd v Citibank NA* [1992] Ch 53).

The administrative receiver of a company is deemed to be an agent of the company unless and until the company goes into liquidation (Insolvency Act 1986, s 44(1)(a)). Because an administrative receiver is an agent of the company and not an agent for the chargee by whom he was appointed, the chargee avoids incurring the onerous duties of a mortgagee in possession. The debenture-holders who appoint a receiver cannot, therefore, be made liable for a wrong committed by him during the course of his appointment (*Re Simms* [1934] Ch 1), neither will he be liable for debts incurred by the receiver (*Cully v Parsons* [1923] 2 Ch 512), nor will the receiver's remuneration be a liability of the debenture-holder (Insolvency Act 1986, s 60(1)). Indeed, the chargee escapes all liability unless he meddles in the receivership, in which case the chargee will become liable for the consequences of that meddling (*Standard Chartered Bank Ltd v Walker* [1982] 3 All ER 938).

If an administrative receiver of a company carries on its business then the business is nonetheless that of the company and not the receiver (*Gosling v Gaskell & Grocott* [1897] AC 575). The actions and conduct of the administrative receiver of a company are 'affairs' of the company that may be investigated by inspectors appointed by the Secretary of State for Trade and Industry under the Companies Act 1985 (*R v Board of Trade, ex parte St Martins Preserving Co Ltd* [1965] 1 QB 603).

When an administrative receiver is appointed to a company, the property coming into the hands of the receiver has to be devoted first to paying the company's preferential debts and then to meeting the obligation owed to the chargee (Insolvency Act 1986, s 40). The rights of any other persons to the company's property must be protected if they were acquired before crystallization (*Re Morrison, Jones & Taylor Ltd* [1914] 1 Ch 50), eg if any property of the company is subject to a fixed charge ranking before the charge or charges in respect of which the administrative receiver has been appointed, then the administrative receiver cannot utilize that property either to pay the debt secured by the floating charge or to pay preferential debts. Any property subject to a prior floating charge can be used because its priority was lost when the appointment of a receiver crystallized the floating charge under which he was appointed and turned it into a fixed charge (*Griffiths v Yorkshire Bank plc* [1994] 1 WLR 1427).

Reports to creditors

Within three months of his appointment an administrative receiver of a company must prepare a report for the company's creditors (Insolvency Act 1986, s 48(1)). The report must cover certain principal matters, eg the events leading up to the appointment of the receiver; the disposal or proposed disposal by the receiver of any company property or any business transactions entered into by the receiver; the amounts payable to the chargee and the amounts of any preferential debts; the amounts payable to other creditors.

An administrative receiver not in liquidation must, having prepared the report, either summon a meeting of the company's unsecured creditors or state in the report of his intention to apply to the court for a direction that no meeting be held (Insolvency Act 1986, s 48).

Preferential creditors

A disadvantage of a floating charge is that if an administrative receiver is appointed, or if the company is wound up before an administrative receiver is appointed, then certain debts of the company called preferential debts will be paid out of the assets subject to the floating charge in priority to the chargee's debts (Insolvency Act 1986, ss 40 and 175(b)). The preferential debts are defined in s 386 and Sch 6 and are, eg money owed to the Inland Revenue for PAYE deductions in respect of employees' wages and salaries, VAT, vehicle license duty, betting and gaming duties, etc. The preferential status of debts due to the Inland Revenue and Customs and Excise which have always been the most significant preferential debts are abolished by the Enterprise Act 2002.

A further disadvantage of a floating charge is that any assets of a company in liquidation that are subject to a floating charge are assets from which the expenses of the liquidation (including the liquidator's remuneration) are payable in priority to any other claim (*Re Barleycorn Enterprises Ltd* [1970] Ch 465).

Duty of care

A mortgagee exercising a power of sale owes the mortgagor a duty of care to take reasonable care to obtain the 'true market value' or 'the proper price' of the property (*Cuckmere Brick v Mutual Finance* [1971] Ch 949; *Tse Kwong Lam v Wong Chit Sen* [1983] 1 WLR 1349). A receiver who exercises a power of sale owes a similar duty (*Standard Chartered Bank v Walker* [1982] 1 WLR 1410).

If the mortgagee or receiver is to discharge his duty, he must ensure that the sale of the company's assets are fully advertised and he obtains professional advice as to the best method of sale. If the sale is by auction then the appropriate reserve price must be fixed and matters such as the desirability of seeking planning permission etc must be attended to (*American Express International Banking Corpn v Hurley* [1985] 3 All ER 564). A bank is allowed to sell promptly and does not have to delay the sale in the hope that a better price may be obtained at a later date (*Reliance PBS v Harwood-Stamper* [1944] Ch 362; *Bank of Cyprus (London) Ltd v Gill* [1980] 2 Lloyd's Rep 51). The duty of care obliges the mortgagee not to fix a date for the sale so early that there is no time to advertise it properly. The duty requires that features that may tend to increase the value of the property be properly advertised. If the duty of care is satisfied, the receiver will be entitled to sell or otherwise enforce the security even thought this is not in the interests of the mortgagor (*Shamji v Johnson Matthey Bankers Ltd* [1991] BCLC 36).

The duty of care is owed to the mortgagee, and also to any third party who has guaranteed the mortgage debt and will therefore have to pay more if the primary security realizes less than it should (*Standard Chartered Bank v Walker*). In *Downsview Nominees Ltd v First City Corpn Ltd* [1993] AC 259 the Privy Council held that an administrative receiver of a company does not owe any duty of care to the company or to persons who have a charge over the company's property ranking after the one under which the administrative receiver was appointed.

7.2 The process of liquidation

Liquidation or dissolution of companies

A company as an artificial person comes into existence when the Registrar enters its name on the Register of Companies and issues a certificate of incorporation. Its existence ends three months after the Registrar removes its name from the Register of Active Companies (Insolvency Act 1986, s 205). This is called 'dissolution'. Before a company can be dissolved it must usually be wound up or 'liquidated'. Liquidation entails collecting the company's assets and converting them into money, using the money to pay its debts, and if anything then remains, distributing the surplus to the members in accordance with their entitlement.

The first step is therefore to put the company into liquidation and appoint a liquidator or joint liquidators. When the liquidation is completed the liquidator gives notice of it to the Registrar. There are now three types of liquidation.

(i)   Compulsory liquidation by order of the court. The High Court, or if the company's paid up share capital does not exceed £120,000, the local county court, has jurisdiction to order that the company shall be wound up by the court.

(ii)   Voluntary liquidation which may be either a:

    (a)   members' voluntary liquidation;

    (b)   creditors' voluntary liquidation.

Compulsory liquidation

The majority of company liquidations is voluntary, and is therefore initiated by a resolution passed in general meeting. Compulsory liquidation is the remedy of last resort for the creditor or member if a company refuses to satisfy its legitimate demands or is simply unresponsive, usually because the directors have abandoned it. In every case a petition to the court for compulsory liquidation must state, and be supported by evidence of, certain specified grounds upon which the court may order compulsory liquidation at its discretion.

Grounds for a winding-up order

A company may be wound up by the court on the following grounds specified in s 122 of the Insolvency Act 1986:

(i)   the company has so resolved by special resolution;

(ii)   default is made in delivering the statutory declaration of capital etc. in order to obtain the Registrar's certificate that a public company may commence business;

(iii)   the company does not commence its business within a year from its incorporation or suspends its business for a whole year;

(iv)   the number of members is reduced below the statutory minimum (two, for private and public companies);

(v)   the company is unable to pay its debts;

(vi)   the court is of the opinion that it is just and equitable that the company should be wound up.

Company's inability to pay debts

A company is deemed to be unable to pay its debts if it defaults for three weeks or more in meeting a demand for a debt exceeding £750 (or such other limit as the Secretary of State may fix under the Insolvency Act 1986), if it fails to satisfy a judgment debt, or the court is satisfied that it is unable to pay its debts (in which case it can take account of the company's contingent and prospective liabilities). The demands of two or more creditors may be aggregated. The fact that, for the time being, the company has insufficient liquid assets to pay its present debts where payment of those debts has not been demanded is insufficient (*Re Capital Annuities Ltd* [1978] 3 All ER 704).

Who may petition

Most petitions are presented either by one or more creditors on the ground that the company is unable to pay its debts in excess of £750, or by one or more contributories on the basis that deadlock or oppressive conduct in the management, or other grounds, make it just and equitable to wind up the company. The full list of those who may present a petition is longer. Thus, the petition may be presented by:

(a)   the company;

(b)   any creditor or creditors who establish a prima facie case.

Generally the court ought not to deprive a petitioning creditor of his prima facie right to a winding-up order unless his petition is opposed by the majority of the creditors in the value of their debts. Where the petitioning and supporting creditors belong to the same group of companies as the company in liquidation, the court should have regard to the nature of their debts (eg that they were 'domestic' (intra-group) debts owed to a member company). Furthermore, where the petitioning creditor was the parent company, it could control the activities of the company in liquidation (*Re Southard & Co Ltd* [1979] 1 All ER 582).

The court can and will restrain a petition which s an abuse of process. In *Re a Company (No 001573 of 1983)* (1983) Times 12 May it was held an abuse to petition for winding up on the same day that an order for costs was made against the company and the petitioner doubted its ability to pay. If a debt is genuinely disputed, the court may restrain a winding-up petition but the court will take due heed of potential difficulties in establishing a debt against, for example, a foreign company (in *Re Russian and English Bank* [1932] 1 Ch 663). This is a rule of practice and the court will always consider whether there appears to be a substantial dispute (*Re Claybridge Shipping Co SA* [1981] Com LR 107). In *Re a Company (No 0012209 of 1991)* [1992] 2 All ER 797 Hoffmann J granted an injunction to restrain the presentation of a winding-up petition by a creditor as the company was solvent and it appeared that its defence to the creditor's claim had a prospect of success. The creditor was ordered to pay the company's costs on an indemnity basis:

(c) contributory or contributories, when the number of members has fallen below the statutory minimum or if the contributory is an original allottee or has held shares for six months in the 18 months preceding the winding up or received them through devolution from a former member;

(d) the DTI after an investigation (Insolvency Act 1986, ss 440 and 124(4)) and on certain other grounds. The court may use a report of the inspectors as prima facie grounds for ordering a winding up (*Re Armvent Ltd* [1975] 3 All ER 441);

(e) the Official Receiver, where a voluntary winding up cannot be continued with due regard to the interests of creditors or contributories. The power of the Secretary of State is not so limited (*Re Lubin, Rosen and Associates Ltd* [1975] 1 All ER 577).

Procedure

The petitioner will present a petition supported by affidavit verifying the facts stated therein. Unless the petition is presented by the company a copy is supplied for service on the company, which is entitled to appear and oppose the petition at the hearing. The petition is advertised in the *London Gazette* at least seven business days in advance of the date fixed for the hearing. This is to enable creditors of the company, and other interested parties, to have notice in time to be represented at the hearing if they wish. The petition is heard in open court. On hearing the petition the court may:

(i) dismiss it;

(ii) adjourn the hearing;

(iii) make an interim order;

(iv) make any other order it thinks fit;

(v) make an order for compulsory winding up.

At any time after the presentation of the petition the court may appoint a provisional liquidator, usually to safeguard the assets of the company pending the outcome of the hearing of the petition (Insolvency Act 1986, s 135). It is not normally necessary to take this precaution but may be desirable since the petition, if granted, is retrospective to the date of presentation of the petition.

The order when made leads to an investigation by the Official Receiver as provisional liquidator into the causes of the company's failure and the general record of its management. The Official Receiver, like an administrative receiver may call for a statement of affairs from company officers. He will report to the court and he may also apply to the court for the public examination of officers in open court. Such an examination of a director of a company in compulsory liquidation may be ordered irrespective of the nationality of the director and notwithstanding that he is resident abroad (*Re Seagull Manufacturing Co Ltd* (1993) Times, 8 February).

The conduct of the liquidation

The Official Receiver is automatically appointed provisional liquidator on the making of the order (Insolvency Act 1986, s 136(2)) so that there is from the outset a liquidator in office. The Official Receiver resumes the office of liquidator if it later falls vacant. The liquidator has 12 weeks in which to decide whether to convene meetings of creditors and contributories with a view to appointing someone else. If meetings are held, each meeting may nominate a liquidator but the nominee of the creditors automatically takes office, subject to a right of objection to the court. The same meetings, or subsequent meetings, may resolve to establish a liquidation committee, including representatives of creditors and of contributories, to work with the liquidator. As the liquidation progresses, the liquidator calls meetings as necessary, and in the end he will call a final meeting of creditors and of contributories.

The effect of the winding-up order

The winding up is deemed to have begun at the time of presenting the petition (or the commencement of voluntary liquidation if that preceded compulsory liquidation) and the Official Receiver becomes provisional liquidator, unless already appointed as such at an earlier stage. In addition a standstill is imposed on the company's transactions with retrospective effect to the commencement of the winding up as follows:

(a) any disposition of property of the company is void unless sanctioned by the court;

(b) any transfer of shares or alteration of status of members is similarly void;

(c) any attachment etc of assets of the company is void;

(d) no legal proceedings against the company may be commenced or continued except by leave of the court;

(e) the employees of the company are dismissed but the liquidator may by mutual agreement retain them in the service of the company;

(f) the management of the company and the control of its business and property are in the hands of the liquidator, who has wide statutory powers. He may also apply to the court for an order vesting assets in him;

(g)   charges on company property and dispositions of that property may become void.

Voluntary winding up

Passing a resolution in general meeting commences a voluntary winding up. The type of resolution required varies according to the circumstances.

(i)   If the articles fix the period of duration of the company or provide that upon the happening of an event it shall be dissolved, and the period has expired or the event has occurred, it suffices to pass an ordinary resolution referring to the articles and resolving that the company be wound up accordingly. In practice articles rarely include any such automatic winding up provisions.

(ii) The company may resolve to wind up by special resolution (which states no reasons). This is the normal method of winding up a solvent company.

(iii) The company may by extraordinary resolution resolve that, by reason of its liabilities, the company is unable to continue its business and that it is advisable to wind up.

Any such resolution must be advertised in the *London Gazette* within 14 days of the meeting. A copy of it must also be delivered to the registrar within 14 days.

Members' voluntary winding up

Any voluntary winding up is a creditors' voluntary winding up unless the directors have made and delivered to the Registrar a declaration of solvency. The company must be assumed to be insolvent unless the directors accept personal responsibility for stating that they believe the company is solvent. The declaration, if made, is on a form that incorporates a statement of estimated assets and liabilities up to the latest practicable date. The directors must state that after making full inquiry they are of the opinion that the company will be able to pay its debts in full within a specified period, which may not exceed 12 months. If in the event the company is unable to pay its debts in full within the 12-month period, the directors are presumed to have made their declaration without having reasonable grounds for it, which is a criminal offence. The burden of showing that they did have reasonable grounds rests on them.

The creditors have no part in the liquidation because it is expected that they will be paid in full and they have no right to interfere with the company's conduct of its affairs.

If, in the course of the liquidation, the liquidator concludes that the company will after all be unable to pay its debts in full within the specified period, he must call a meeting of the creditors that is advertised in the *London Gazette* and in two local newspapers. The creditors may, before the meeting, demand information about the company's affairs. At the meeting, the liquidator will lay before the creditors a statement of affairs. Thereafter the liquidation proceeds as a creditors' voluntary winding up, as if the declaration of solvency had not been made.

At the end of each year of the liquidation, and within three months of the anniversary date, the liquidator is required to hold a general meeting of the company and lay before it a statement of his acts and dealings. When the liquidation has been completed, the liquidator will call a final meeting by advertisement in the *London Gazette*. He is required to lay before the meeting accounts of his dealings with the company's property. Within the week after the meeting the liquidator must send to the Registrar a copy of his accounts and a return that the meeting has been held (or if there was no meeting due to lack of a quorum, a return that it was duly summoned). This leads on to the dissolution of the company.

Creditors' voluntary winding up

There is no declaration of solvency and consequently the company is required to call a meeting of its creditors not later than the fourteenth day after it holds its own meeting to resolve to wind up. The meeting of creditors is called on seven days' notice and this is advertised in the *London Gazette*. The notice must either give the name and address of an insolvency practitioner from whom creditors may obtain information in advance or it must specify a place where, in the final two business days before the meeting any creditor may obtain a list of all the creditors. No charge is to be made for these services.

At the creditors' meeting one of the directors will preside and lay before the meeting a statement of the company's financial affairs. The members and the creditors at their respective meetings may nominate an insolvency practitioner to be appointed liquidator. If different persons are nominated, the creditors' nominee takes office, subject to a right of appeal to the court given to directors, members and creditors to be exercised within seven days.

As there may be an interval between the meeting of members and the meeting of creditors, any liquidator appointed by the members will take office until, if ever, the creditors appoint a different person. A liquidator appointed by the members has no power to dispose of the company's assets, except those that are perishable, etc. and such as the court may sanction, until the meeting of creditors is held. Then, if the creditors do not appoint a different liquidator, the members' nominee has the usual powers conferred on a liquidator.

The creditors may resolve at their meeting to establish a liquidation committee with up to five representatives of each of the creditors and members. The function of such a committee, if established, is to work with the liquidator who may seek its sanction for the exercise of his statutory powers.

The effect of going into voluntary liquidation

The decision to go into liquidation is effective from the day on which the resolution is passed in general meeting. The directors remain in office but their powers cease except insofar as they may be authorized by the competent authority to continue. The company's property must be applied in payment of its debts and any surplus may then be distributed to its members. The company, through the liquidator, may carry on its business but only for purposes of the beneficial winding up of the company, ie ultimate sale or closure. No transfer of shares or alteration of members' status may be made unless the liquidator sanctions it. There is no automatic restraint on legal action against the company or its property. The liquidator may apply to the court for an order to halt any action of that kind by a creditor.

7.3 Distribution of company assets

Assets and liabilities in a compulsory or voluntary liquidation

The liquidator's duty is to convert the company's assets into money and apply it in payment of the company's debts before distributing what remains, if anything, to the shareholders. The liquidator may take action to set aside recent company transactions or to recover contributions or compensation from company officers.

In the distribution of surplus assets to shareholders, the liquidator must conform to their respective rights. In principle they all participate equally, but if the company has issued preference shares, the holders of those shares usually:

(a)   have a priority entitlement to repayment of capital; but

(b)   have no right to participate in distribution of any surplus assets remaining after the repayment of capital on ordinary shares.

If there are arrears of unpaid preference dividends, they lapse, unless it is expressly provided that they shall be paid off (as capital) in liquidation.

Apart from considering the order of priority of debts of different kinds, the liquidator must ensure that only legally enforceable claims are recognized. If, for example, a debt is statute-barred, he must refuse to pay it (*Re Art Production Co Ltd* [1952] Ch 89). It is the liquidator's duty to satisfy himself that a creditor has a valid claim and that the amount demanded is correct. There is a formal procedure for 'proof of debts' in compulsory liquidation. The liquidator would, as a matter of course, write to every creditor of whom there is a record in the books and invite him to give notice of the amount due to him, with supporting papers.

The liquidator has statutory power to pay any class of creditors in full and also to negotiate a compromise or arrangement, eg with debenture holders. These are powers that he may only exercise with the prescribed sanction, eg of the liquidation committee.

Assets in the hands of creditors

A creditor who has obtained judgment against the company for a debt that the company fails to satisfy may then issue execution to attach property of the company. Unless he has completed this process before the liquidation commences, he must hand back to the liquidator the property that he has attached. Execution is completed by seizure and sale of the attached property, or the appointment of a receiver or obtaining a charging order under the Charging Orders Act 1979. The method varies according to the type of property, which is affected.

In the course of the execution, the sheriff (a county court officer) may have seized goods of the company with a view to sale. If, before he has sold them, the sheriff has notice of an order for compulsory liquidation or of the passing of a resolution for winding up, he must return the goods to the liquidator. Moreover, if the judgment debt exceeds £500, he must after sale retain the proceeds (less any expenses) within 14 days and account for the money to the liquidator, if within that period he has notice of an order for compulsory liquidation or of the issue of a notice to convene a meeting to wind up voluntarily.

If, however, the company pays its debt to the sheriff after he has seized its goods, to avoid sale of the goods this is not money paid in the course of execution and the creditor is entitled to retain it (*Re Walkden Sheet Metal Co Ltd* [1960] Ch 170).

In a compulsory liquidation, execution or distress by a creditor or landlord after the presentation of the petition is void. In voluntary liquidation the liquidator may apply to the court for an order to avoid execution or distress affected after the passing of the resolution to wind up. The order would be made unless the company had deceived the creditor in order to delay his action against its goods.

Disclaimer of assets

The liquidator has a statutory power to disclaim 'onerous property' of the company. He is no longer required to obtain leave of the court for a disclaimer. Onerous property is defined to include unprofitable contracts and other property, which it would be difficult to sell (Insolvency Act 1986, s 178(3)).

The effect of the disclaimer is that the company's entire interest in the property ceases, but any person who thereby suffers a loss becomes a creditor of the company for the amount of his loss.

A liquidator may disclaim property although he has taken possession, exercised rights of ownership over it or tried to sell it. The other party who would be affected by a disclaimer may bring the liquidator to an immediate decision by serving on him a notice, requiring the liquidator to state whether or not he intends to disclaim. Unless he then within 28 days gives notice of disclaimer, he loses the right to do so.

Secured creditors

A secured creditor has a dual relationship with the company. Like any other creditor he may claim from the company, as its debtor, payment of the amount due to him. In addition he is in the position of, or analogous to, a mortgagee with a limited interest in the property of the company over which he has security. He may enforce those proprietary rights, usually by appointing a receiver.

Against a company in liquidation the secured creditor must opt for one remedy or the other. If he elects to prove his debt by notice to the liquidator, he is deemed to have surrendered his security. He is more likely to enforce the security and recover the debt by that means without making a claim against the liquidator. If the property that is the security has a realizable value that is less than the secured debt, then the creditor may sell the property charged to him and claim as an unsecured creditor for the amount by which the proceeds of realization fall short of the debt. If the creditor merely values his security, ie puts an estimated value on it, and claims the balance as an unsecured debt, the liquidator may redeem it at that value or have it sold.

If the security yields a surplus over the debt and expenses, the creditor accounts for the surplus to the liquidator.

Preferential unsecured debts

It is often convenient to refer to 'preferential creditors' but strictly it is only the debt that can be preferential. It may happen, for example, that part of the same debt is preferential and the rest is not. The Enterprise Act 2002 reduced the categories of preferential debts again. The categories of preferential debts are defined as:

(a)   salaries or wages of company employees in respect of the period of 4 months ended on that date, subject to a maximum of £800 for each employee;

(b)   holiday pay and employer's contributions to occupational pension schemes.

In addition some other unpaid taxes such as vehicle license duty, taxes on gaming and betting, and social security contributions in respect of the 12 months before the relevant date are preferential.

Employees' pay is often the largest item amongst the list of preferential debts to be met. Loans to pay wages are preferential debts to the extent that the loan money, often lent by a bank, has been used to pay wages etc that, if unpaid, would have been preferential. Alternatively, the Department of Employment has statutory power, within certain limits, to pay the wages of employees (otherwise unpaid) of an insolvent employer. If it does so, it becomes a creditor of the company for the amount it has paid out and has the same preferential claims as the employees would have had.

Where the bank has provided a loan, it is a question of fact whether the loan creditor has provided money used to pay wages that would otherwise be preferential debts. The banks usually insist that money advanced for this purpose shall be paid from a separate wages account. Where the company has borrowed from the bank through its main account and has made transfers from that account to a specially designed wages account that was not overdrawn at the commencement of liquidation, the bank was treated as a preferential creditor (through the overdraft on the main company account) of money paid out by the company in wages (*Re James R Rutherford & Sons Ltd* [1964] 3 All ER 137).

A director of a company is not as such an employee, so that his fees due under the articles cannot be a preferential debt. If he is also a working director, his arrears of unpaid salary as a manager are preferential within the usual limits indicated above.

The priority of preferential debts

A liquidator (and also a receiver or an administrator) is required to pay preferential debts, rateably between all debts in that category, in priority to either debt secured by a floating charge on the company's assets and unsecured non-preferential debts. If a secured creditor has more than one debt owing to him by the company and covered by his security, and some are preferential and others are not, he is not required, on realizing his security, to apply the money evenly in part payment of all the debts. Instead he may, since it improves his position, apply the money first to repayment of his non-preferential debts, so that he preserves the maximum entitlement as a creditor for preferential debts (*Re William Hall (Contractors) Ltd* [1967] 2 All ER 1150).

Ordinary and deferred debts

After the preferential debts have been paid in full, the non-preferential, ordinary unsecured debts come next to be paid. These are usually sums owed to trade creditors for goods or services supplied to the company. A secured creditor whose security has proved to be insufficient to discharge his debt in full and a creditor for a preferential debt in excess of the limits may claim the balance as an ordinary debt.

Voluntary payments to employees

As the word 'voluntary' indicates these are not debts at all, but it is convenient to deal with them here since they are payments that the liquidator may be authorized and bound to make, after payment of all debts, before distributing what remains to shareholders.

These are payments to employees of the company who have been made redundant by reason of the closure or sale of the company's business. A company has statutory power (Insolvency Act 1986, s 719) to make such gifts subject to compliance with the proper internal procedure for authorization. From the liquidator's stand-point, he must ensure that he has paid all debts of the company and that he has authority to make such payments.

Order of application of assets

Secured creditors normally recover their debts from the realization of their security. Only if there is a surplus resulting from the security will any part of its value go to the fund from which unsecured creditors are paid. To that extent, the secured creditors have an automatic priority over unsecured creditors, except that preferential unsecured debts are paid out of property subject to a floating charge. The order of application of assets in the hands of the liquidator is (in order or priority):

(i) **liquidation expenses** including the cost of selling, preserving, collecting in assets etc, the liquidator's remuneration and the incidental expenses of the liquidation, such as the costs of a petition for compulsory liquidation if the court awards costs to the petitioner;

(ii) **preferential unsecured debts** (and the balance remaining is then used to pay the debt owing to the holder of a floating charge);

(iii) **ordinary unsecured debts** (including the claims of secured and preferential creditors for deficiencies remaining after they have taken their priority entitlement higher up the scale);

(iv) **deferred debts**;

(v) **repayment of members' capital**, ie first, capital paid up on their shares and then any surplus remaining to members according to their entitlement (usually it goes to the ordinary shareholders alone).

Voidable transactions and compensation

Avoidance of floating charges

The basic rule is that the commencement of liquidation or the making of an administration order will automatically render void a floating charge on the company's property if created within the previous 12 months (Insolvency Act 1986, s 245). Unless the charge was created in favour of a person connected with the company, the charge is not void if:

(i)   the company was solvent at the time of creation of the charge;

(ii) the charge was created more than 12 months before the liquidation or the presentation of the petition for the administration order.

If, however, the charge was created in favour of a connected person, the solvency of the company at the time is immaterial and the period over which s 245 has retrospective effect is extended from 12 months to two years.

Further, the charge is still valid insofar as it is security for consideration given at the time or after the creation of the charge. The charge is therefore void only to the extent that it is to secure liabilities that existed before the charge was created. The subsequent consideration, for which the charge would be valid, may be money, goods or services supplied to the company or a reduction of its indebtedness, plus interest at the agreed rate (if any) on that consideration.

The term connected person is elaborately defined by the insolvency legislation (ss 249 and 435). In a typical, but by no means the only, case, a connected person is a director or a shareholder who has control (alone or jointly with others). The period of 12 months, or two years, prior to the petition for an administration order is also extended forward to cover the period between the petition and the making of the order, so that a charge created after the petition has been presented becomes void if an administration order is later made on it.

Although there are differences of detail, s 245 is a reformulation of provisions found in the Companies Act 1986, s 617 and some of the earlier cases continue to afford guidance. A loan to the company made after it had created a floating charge, but for the purpose of enabling the company to repay an existing loan from the same lender obtained before the charge, is a transparent evasion of the requirement that, to be valid, the loan must follow the charge and so the charge is not a valid security for the second (or the first) loan (*Re Destone Fabrics Ltd* [1941] Ch 319). On the other hand if the loan is granted on the understanding that a floating charge will be created as security for it, the charge may be security for the loan even though it follows the loan in strict time sequence (*Re F and F Stanton* [1929] 1 Ch 180).

The banks rely on the decision in *Re Yeovil Glove Co Ltd* [1965] Ch 148 in taking a floating charge as security for a current or running account. In the *Yeovil Glove* case the essential facts were that the company had a bank overdraft at the time when the charge was created and an overdraft of approximately the same amount at the commencement of liquidation. In the interval, credits to the account exceeded the amount of the overdraft at the time of the charge. It was held that these credits (under the rule in *Clayton's Case, Devaynes v Noble* (1816) 1 Mer 572) should be treated as repayment of the earlier debt and the subsequent drawings on the account were new loans subsequent to the charge, which was therefore a valid security for the overdraft resulting from them.

Voidable preferences

The current rules on voidable preferences (Insolvency Act 1986, s 239) are a revised version of the earlier law (Companies Act 1985, s 615) on what was then called 'fraudulent preference'. The basic rule is that the court, on the application of a liquidator or administrator of a company, may make an order to set aside a preference given by a company to one of its creditors, or to a guarantor of its debts, at a time when the company is already (or becomes by reason of the preference) unable to pay its debts. An obvious case is where the company reduces its bank overdraft, by suspending drawings to make payment of its debts to trade creditors, in order to reduce the liability of one of its directors as guarantor of the overdraft (*Re M Kushler Ltd* [1943] 2 All ER 22). New credit advanced to the company in exchange for security, or terms that put the creditor in a better position than the other creditors, does not amount to a preference to the extent that it is represented by new value provided by him. It is the putting in a better position of an existing creditor for existing debts that can amount to a preference.

In addition to demonstrating the advantage that the preference yields, it must be shown either that the person preferred was a 'connected person' or that in granting the preference the company was 'influenced ... by a desire to produce' such a preference, ie it must be intentional. This is in accord with case law on the previous statutory provision (on 'fraudulent preference'), where the act was valid if it appeared that it was done for good commercial reasons and not in order to grant preference (*Re Paraguassu Steam Tramway Co, Adamson's Case* (1874) LR 18 Eq 670; see also *Re Beacon Leisure Ltd* [1990] BCC 213).

If the person preferred is a connected person, he may still be able to resist an order to reverse the preference shown to him if he is a connected person solely by reason of being an employee of the company, or if he can show, ie the burden of proof is on him, that the company was not 'influenced by a desire' to prefer him. The statutory formula (in s 239) 'influenced by desire' is new and the test was applied in *Re DKG Contractors Ltd* [1990] BCC 903.

The other major limitation is that the preference must have occurred within 'the relevant time' (see, eg *Re DKG Contractors Ltd*). The standard period is six months before the commencement of liquidation or the date of the petition for an administration order (plus the subsequent interval between petition and making

261

the order). But the period is two years if the person preferred is connected with the company otherwise than merely as an employee.

If s 239 is complied with and a fraudulent preference found to have occurred, the court is required to make whatever order it thinks fit to restore the position to what it would have been had there been no preference.

Transactions at an undervalue

The court has a similar power under s 238 of the Insolvency Act 1986, to make an order to neutralize a transaction at an undervalue into which the company entered at a time when it was unable to pay its debts. A liquidator may only make the application to the court or an administrator, and certain limiting conditions restrict the court's powers. A transaction is at an undervalue if it is an outright gift or is for significantly less in consideration received by the company than the value of the consideration that it gave. Such a transaction may not be set aside if either the company entered into it in good faith and for the purpose of carrying on its business (*Re Welfab Engineers* [1990] BCC 600) and company. The effect of these requirements is substantially to confine the scope of the avoidance power to artificial transactions. These criteria have something in common with those that are applied in determining what powers, if not expressed in the objects clause, may be implied.

A transaction at an undervalue may only be set aside under s 238 if it occurred within the period of two years before the commencement of liquidation or of the petition for an administration order (with an extension forward to take in the interval between the petition and the making of the order). While s 238 has unrestricted extra-territorial effect and allows service of process on a foreign bank not carrying on business in England, the court has an overall discretion not to make an order under the section, in particular if it is not satisfied that the foreign defendant is sufficiently connected with England for it to be just and proper to grant the relief sought (*Re Paramount Airways Ltd* [1992] 3 All ER 1).

Fraudulent trading

If, in the course of the liquidation of a company, it appears to the court that its business has been carried on with intent to defraud its creditors or the creditors of any other person for a fraudulent purpose, the court may, on the application of the liquidator, declare that any persons who were knowingly parties to carrying on the business in this way shall make such contribution to the company's assets as the court may determine (Insolvency Act 1986, s 213). Liability may be imposed on any person and in *White & Osmond (Parkstone) Ltd* the court took the view that a director who continued trading during difficult times in the hope that 'there was light at the end of the tunnel' could not be made liable under s 213. This approach was disapproved in *R v Grantham* [1942] 2 All ER 166 where it was said that directors may be exposed to liability for fraudulent trading simply because they continued trading where the company could not pay its debts as and when they fell due or shortly thereafter. A single transaction will suffice to impose liability, although it is more likely that a series of transactions will together indicate fraud.

Only the liquidator can seek this remedy. Further, the court has a discretion as to the amount of the contribution that it may order. It is not a question of ordering payment of specific debts, eg *Re a Company (No 001418 of 1988)* [1990] BCC 526, where it was decided that the amount ordered to be paid would include a punitive element.

Fraudulent trading is also a criminal offence and in this instance it is not required that the company shall have gone into liquidation (Insolvency Act, 1986, s 458).

The normal grounds for invoking the sanctions against fraudulent trading are that the directors have failed to take proper steps to avoid or to minimize the consequences of impending insolvency. Normally, this will involve them in continuing to trade at a time when there was no prospect that the company would be able to pay the debts incurred in the course of this trading. A single transaction can constitute carrying on the business (*Re Gerald Cooper Chemicals Ltd* [1978] 2 All ER 49). Payment of some debts but not all may also amount to carrying on business (*Re Sarflax Ltd* [1979] 1 All ER 49).

Proceedings against directors under what is now s 213 of the Insolvency Act 1986 have rarely been successful because it is necessary to prove fraud on their part. As fraudulent trading is also a criminal offence, the standard of proof required, even in civil actions, is demanding. Yet it is rarely possible to prove actual dishonest intent. It was once held that this intent would be inferred from the directors' decision to incur debts without any reasonable prospect that the company would be able to pay them (*Re William C Leitch Bros (No 1)* [1932] 2 Ch 71). The same judge in another case said that it was necessary to show 'real dishonesty ... involving moral blame' (*Re Patrick & Lyon Ltd* [1933] All ER 590). Evidence of that is not easy to get.

Wrongful trading

The Cork Committee's proposal for civil liability for wrongful trading, with a lower standard of proof, has been adopted (Insolvency Act 1986, s 214), but the Cork Committee defines the basis of liability in a different manner from that proposed. In framing what is now s 214, the DTI decided that a wider test was desirable. It provides that liability for wrongful trading will be imposed if the following conditions are satisfied, namely:

(a) the person to be made liable must be or have been a director of a company that has gone into insolvent liquidation (*Re DKG Contractors Ltd* [1990] BCC 903);

(b) at some time before the commencement of liquidation, he actually knew or 'ought to have concluded' that there was no reasonable prospect that the company would avoid going into insolvent liquidation (*Re Purpoint Ltd* [1991] BCC 121);

(c)   on reaching stage (b) he did not, in the court's view, 'take every step' that he ought to have taken 'with a view to minimizing the potential loss to the company's creditors'. That he did take such steps is the defence open to him in any proceedings against him under s 214.

In considering the conduct of a defendant director, he is to be judged by the standard of 'general knowledge, skill and experience' that might reasonably be expected of (i) any person in his position and (ii) of this individual in particular. The latter point means that the director's personal qualifications and experience, eg as an accountant, are to be taken into consideration, as well as more general criteria, in deciding whether he acted correctly (*Norman v Theodore Goddard* [1992] BCC 14 in which the director was involved (director was absolved as he had taken expert professional advice).

Much of the argument about this involved formula relates to the words 'ought to have concluded'. The critics object that it tests the actual performance of an individual by reference to matters of which he may have been ignorant. The DTI argued that it imposes on directors, at all times, a duty to keep themselves informed of the financial position of the company, eg by insisting that management accounts of some sort should be laid before each board meeting.

A particular criticism is that these wide and uncertain provisions may make it difficult for major creditors of companies, such as banks, to arrange with a company that some experienced 'company doctor' shall join the board to improve its financial expertise in time of need.

In *Re Purpoint Ltd* [1991] BCC 121 Vinelott J explained that the purpose of a court order under s 214 is to recoup the loss to the company so as to benefit the creditors as a whole. The court has no jurisdiction to direct payment to creditors or to direct that money paid to the company should be applied in payment of one class of creditors in preference to another.

Directors who seek to justify themselves must relate their defence to s 214. Their defence will not succeed merely on the general grounds that they claim to have acted reasonably and ought fairly to be excused (*Re Produce Marketing Consortium Ltd* [1989] 1 WLR 745; see also *Re DKG Contractors Ltd*).

Index